JAMES A. MURRAY

Butte's Radical Irish Millionaire

James A. Murray

Butte's Radical Irish Millionaire

BILL FARLEY

Foreword by David M. Emmons

2018
Mountain Press Publishing Company
Missoula, Montana

First Printing, January 2018

Cover photo of James A. Murray taken around 1900.

Library of Congress Cataloging-in-Publication Data

Names: Farley, Bill, 1959- author.
Title: James A. Murray : Butte's radical Irish millionaire / Bill Farley ; foreword by David M. Emmons.
Other titles: Butte's radical Irish millionaire
Description: Missoula, Montana : Mountain Press Publishing Company, [2018] | Includes bibliographical references and index.
Identifiers: LCCN 2017057749 | ISBN 9780878426829 (pbk. : alk. paper)
Subjects: LCSH: Murray, James A., approximately 1840-1921. | Butte (Mont.)—Biography. | Butte (Mont.)—History. | Mineral industries—Montana—Biography. | Millionaires—Montana—Biography. | Millionaires—Californa—Monterey—Biography. | Businessmen—West (U.S.)—Biography. | Irish Americans—Politics and government. | Murray, James E. (James Edward), 1876-1961—Family. | Irish Americans—Montana—Butte—Biography
Classification: LCC F739.B8 F37 2018 | DDC 978.6/6802092 [B] —dc23
LC record available at https://lccn.loc.gov/2017057749

PRINTED IN THE USA

P.O. Box 2399 • Missoula, MT 59806 • 406-728-1900
800-234-5308 • info@mtnpress.com
www.mountain-press.com

To the archivists and librarians who preserve and lay bare the complexities of our untidy past.

Contents

Foreword

Montanans not from Butte have always had a hard time making sense of the place. Buttians, however, being the resourceful lot they are, delight in explaining themselves to those in the state not lucky enough to live there. Some of the aphorisms about the place make jangling noises in our heads. They sound a lot like Irish Bulls, one of those counterintuitive bits of contrarianism wisdom for which the Irish are known. Given the number of Irish in Butte, that's to be expected. Here, in no particular order, are three of my favorite "Butte Bulls."

This one is proudly displayed on the front of the Butte–Silver Bow Archives building on West Quartz Street. An immigrant Irishwoman wrote back to relatives in Ireland urging them to join her. She gave them some traveling advice: "Don't stop in America," she said, "come straight to Butte." I grant that that seems to contradict the well-known "Butte, America" reference, but join it to this next one and sense begins to emerge: "The best thing about living in Butte," an old-timer was supposed to have said, "is that you're so close to Montana."

Adding Bull No. 1 to Bull No. 2 provides you with a central truth: Butte is sui generis. It doesn't really belong anywhere or to anybody other than itself. And that makes Bull No. 3 especially important: It comes from a Butte state legislator who was explaining to his barely comprehending colleagues in Helena why a certain Butte commemorative holiday—the place has a multitude of them—was worth their time and some of the state's money. After all, he said, "if it weren't for Butte, Montana would be indistinguishable from North Dakota."

Butte has a lot to commemorate and celebrate because, as one of its affectionate interpreters put it to me, "the place produces far more history than the domestic market can absorb." It assuredly does. Strong characters make history and that history, in its turn, gives a place its character.

If Butte is a one-of-a-kind town, so was the subject of Bill Farley's book. James A. Murray was one of Butte's truly oversized characters. He's also one of its most underreported ones. Mike Malone in *The Battle for Butte* has only two (very useful) references to him. Some years ago, I wrote a book on Butte's Irish. Murray was born in Ireland, but I mentioned him only once. Adding error to oversight, I also said that he was not Irish-born. James A.'s nephew James E. Murray became a United States senator. A staunch New Deal Democrat, historians, most notably Don Spritzer, have paid attention to James E. It's uncle Jim who, until now, has been neglected.

And that is hard to explain. If character—and being one—are the criteria, he qualifies for the Butte Hall of Fame. Murray was born in County Clare, Ireland, in 1840. He survived the Great Hunger and immigrated, probably in 1848. If it was 1848, the then eight-year-old Jim Murray jumped ship while it was just off its docking site in Nova Scotia. He swam ashore. In the 1850s, he took a steamer to California. He mined there for a time, but in the early 1860s made his way to Montana, eventually to Butte City.

When he died in 1921 he was worth over three billion of today's dollars, enough to buy the current occupant of the White House out of his chump change drawer. But it's how he became so rich that is of greatest interest. He owned mines in Butte, of course. But he also owned the water companies in Pocatello and San Diego and a hotel in Livingston—the only thing named after him other than a dam in California. He owned resorts and racehorses, banks and bars. Many of them were in Butte. And everything he owned turned to gold.

That's the easy part, Murray the swashbuckling capitalist. Here's where he gets harder to explain. In 1917 there was a major strike of the copper mines of Butte. The United States had entered the Great War by then and its military needed copper. The 1917 Butte strike all by itself oversupplied the history market. But add this: The publisher of the *Butte Strike Bulletin*, the most radical labor newspaper in western America and the voice of the striking miners, was edited by an Irish American named William Francis Dunne. After the Bolshevik Revolution in the fall of 1917, Dunne became a communist. In the mid-1920s, he was elected to the executive committee of the Comintern, the Communists International. Bill Dunne made a lot of Butte history, too. Here's some more of it. In 1918 James A. Murray, by then a multimillionaire, gave Dunne the money necessary to buy the new printing press that allowed Dunne to turn the *Bulletin* into a daily (*Butte Daily Bulletin*). Farley's subtitle is "Butte's Radical Irish Millionaire." Murray was every one of those things.

Murray was also a consummate cheater. And as this terrific book makes clear he cheated at everything—random bets, cards, banking, and the buying and selling of mines and every other kind of property that he added to his remarkable portfolio. He cheated strangers, cheated his friends, cheated his family. Given the time and place, Jim Murray must have been either the luckiest or the toughest or the most disarmingly charming man in the room. As Farley's biography makes clear, he was a lot of all three. He stiffed people; he simply refused to pay some of his debts. But he also forgave more than a million dollars in debts owed him. He *was* lucky. He *was* tough and uncommonly smart. But mostly, he was great company, funny, generous, and fair. Granted, fairness was determined by what he thought it should be. But he lived to be eighty-one and he died a peaceful death.

Jim Murray deserved a biography. I think he would have loved this one. It's honest and it's thorough, just as—in his own strange way—Jim Murray was. I've been at this business for more than fifty years. I have never met a more enterprising and a more tireless researcher than Bill Farley. He went everywhere, from the Maritime Provinces of Canada to San Diego looking for—and finding—material. He read every book, article, and newspaper story, every letter and snippet of information about Murray. He interviewed everybody who knew Murray or knew anything about him. This is historical detective work of the first order. And it tells a fascinating story about Butte and about the characters who made it: Jim Murray and his friends, Fat Jack Jones, John Maguire, and hundreds more. If Butte made more history than the domestic market could absorb, so did James A. Murray. Bill Farley has squared supply and demand.

—David M. Emmons, author of
The Butte Irish: Class and Ethnicity in an American Mining Town

Preface

I discovered James A. Murray shortly after my father passed away in 2012. As I sorted through his family history papers, one newspaper article caught my attention. It was an obituary for Murray that described the breadth of his holdings under the title, "Prominent in Development of the Entire West." The article also mentioned he was fond of practical jokes. He sounded like someone I'd like to know a little better—first, because my career involved similar businesses; second, because I also like practical jokes; and finally, because we are related. Jim Murray was my third great-uncle.

My early research in historical newspapers uncovered several colorful stories about Murray involving an eclectic group of friends. Threads of secrecy and troublemaking weaved through many of the stories, inspiring me to dig deeper. I combed through records in libraries and archives throughout the West. Over a four-year period, I traveled three thousand miles retracing Jim Murray's steps. I visited the archives at the University of California, San Diego, and the University of Montana to read business letters left behind by his partners. I spent ten days in Monterey, California, reviewing three thousand pages of court documents from probate proceedings for Murray, his second wife, and stepson. I toured Mission Carmel to see remnants of the renovation work he sponsored in the early 1900s. I visited archives in Butte, Deer Lodge, Philipsburg, Helena, and Livingston, Montana. I spent a night at Murray's Boulder Hot Springs resort and toured sections of the hotel that remained just as they were in the Gilded Age. Across the country, I spent a day at the National Archives in Maryland reviewing military intelligence files focused on one of his most peculiar investments. Together, these sources revealed the story of an iconoclastic millionaire.

In the pages ahead, I present Murray's radical life and my views on why he chose to be a rebel, when all others of his station were simply content with piling up cash. In brief, the answer comes in part from what he considered to be his sacred duty to Ireland, in part from the connections he made with fellow pioneers in early mining camps, and in part from his disdain for corporate capitalism. These three elements combined to produce a unique and fascinating Western pioneer who built an impressive financial empire while fighting the concentration of power in business, politics, and institutions.

Murray's story is organized here in three parts: The Making of a Bonanza King (chapters 1–6), Wealth and Leisure (chapters 7–11), and End Games (chapters 12–16). Chapters 1 and 2 cover a period of time in which little is known of Murray or his family's life: his childhood in Ireland, his migration to Canada, and his early days scratching gravel in the California goldfields.

For his life in Ireland and immigration to Canada, I share a family tale—a very tall tale—which has been passed down through four generations. I take the basic premises of this family story—why the Murray boys left Ireland, how they traveled, where they landed—and dramatized them to retell the story as I would to my own family. I elaborate the family tale with scenery and events drawn from firsthand accounts of others who witnessed conditions in Ireland during the Great Hunger (County Clare, the Murrays' home, was among the hardest-hit regions during these years). My descriptions of the suffering the Murray boys may have encountered on their voyage to Canada are based on the eyewitness account of Robert Whyte, who sailed aboard a similar ship packed with Irish peasants seeking refuge in North America. The description of Murray's trip to California by steamship and his journey to the Montana wilderness is based on sparse, secondhand accounts from Murray's friends and family, many recounted at the time of his death, sixty to eighty years after the actual events. To provide additional detail, I use the firsthand accounts of sailors and pioneers who followed similar paths during the late 1850s and early 1860s.

The third chapter of the book starts when contemporary news reports, specific to Murray, emerge after he is firmly settled in the Pioneer mining district, forty-two miles west of Helena, Montana. This chapter introduces his first wife and the group of characters that will follow him through his ascent to abundant riches. The remaining chapters follow his rise to great wealth in Butte, Montana, known scornfully as the "Perch of the Devil." It is here that Murray's cold-blooded business model is revealed.

Part II details Murray's spending of his mostly ill-gotten gains. Part III covers the last eleven years of Murray's life and the fight over his estate. The epilogue provides brief summaries of the lives of those who survived Murray's death and the legacies of those who did not.

Acknowledgments

My father, James O. Farley, inspired my interest in family history, and my mother, Marlyn A. (Barnett) Farley, inspired my interest in writing. After they passed away in 2012, just two weeks apart, I started this passion project with the support of my wife, Nanette, and daughters, Lauren (my research assistant) and Catherine.

Writing a historical biography, with a subject that covered so much time and space, was a challenge. I relied on many people for encouragement, advice, and research assistance. Dr. William Deverell, professor and chair of the history department at the University of Southern California, provided valuable advice at the start of this project from his home base at the Huntington Library. Dave Emmons, professor emeritus at the University of Montana and an expert on the Butte Irish, was extremely gracious with his time. He reviewed iterations of my scholarly research, which eventually was presented at several sessions of the American Conference for Irish Studies and published in *Montana: The Magazine of Western History* and the *Journal of San Diego History*. The editors of both of these journals, Molly Holz and Molly McLain, were very patient and insightful and helped me shape the arc of Jim Murray's life. Finally, authors Irv Geller, Charles Salzberg, and Sally Koslow and editor Arnold Dolin gave encouragement and invaluable advice on getting published.

Throughout my travels, my research was supported by a number of librarians and archivists at libraries and archives across the West. In Monterey, California, where I spent most of my time, city historian Dennis Copeland, county archivist James Perry, and Carmel Mission archivist Jewel Gentry guided my research and provided invaluable suggestions and comments. On my trip to Montana, local historians Ted Antonioli and Richard Gibson took time out of their schedules to meet with a stranger and discuss a little known subject. After I left the Treasure State, both continued to respond to my emails seeking clarifications and suggestions. There are many others who helped me along the way. I owe my gratitude to the librarians and archivists at the Huntington Library, the W. A. Clark Library, the Autry Museum, the California History Room at the Monterey Public Library, the Monterey County Historical Society, the Butte–Silver Bow Public Archives, the Mohave Museum in Kingman, Arizona, the University of Montana, the University of California San Diego, the Deer Creek Library, and the Livingston Historical Society. Nikole Evankovich at the Butte–Silver Bow Archives was especially helpful tracking down pictures and proper citations as the book neared publication.

I also received great support from my immediate and extended family. Tom Farley, my brother, helped edit the manuscript. David Farley, another brother, helped develop a number of unrealized projects. Myrna Aldrich helped me understand the story of Sally Burchett, Murray's first wife. Letters from my great-aunt Margaret (Murray) Harvey provided the tall tale of the fabulous Murray boys, and cousins James and Erin Murray confirmed details of Senator James E. Murray's life. Offering encouragement along the way were uncle Joe and aunt Darlene (Murray) Farls, Dick Harvey, and Peggy Haddad.

I've enjoyed my time getting to know Jim Murray over these past several years. His life story has helped me understand the roots of capitalism in the United States and the depth of pain inflicted by the British Empire. Although neither history is pleasant, we cannot hope to change the future if we do not understand the past. Murray's life provides intimate details about the brutality of wealth creation and the measure of radicalism necessary to effect change in authoritarian regimes. It is in this latter effort, his life's work, where Murray finds a measure of redemption. Thank you to everyone who helped get his story published.

Part I

The Making of a Bonanza King

1840–1909

1

The Remarkable Murray Boys—A Tall Tale

Striding nearer every day, Like a wolf in search of prey, Comes the Famine on his way.

—*The Nation*, March 7, 1846

Milltown Malbay, County Clare, Ireland (Late 1840s)

Jimmy Murray was both a troublemaker and a saint as a young boy. He spoke his mind when he shouldn't, never missed an opportunity to steal food, and did everything he could to ease the suffering of his family. His parents, Michael and Ellen Murray, were pleased when he brought home a partial loaf of stale bread or scraps of food from a refuse pile. The means didn't matter to the Murrays or to other Irish peasants living under the merciless rule of the British Crown and struggling to survive An Gorta Mór. Weather and disease had decimated Michael's potato crops. Ellen could spend a week begging in town and have nothing to show for it. Life was a struggle every single hour, every single day during the Great Hunger.

Jimmy had three little brothers and a little sister. The oldest of his brothers, Danny, wanted to be just like him, as did Timmy and Andy. Baby Ellie was too young to appreciate the small measure of comfort Jimmy provided to the family.

The family home was a small, one-room mud hut built into the side of a small mound. It looked like a giant rabbit hole from the outside, and one for a very poor rabbit at that. On the inside, it was not much better. The dirt floor was covered with hay, except for a small clearing next to the fireplace. There was one pot and one stool, for which the family was grateful.

Jimmy was seldom in the rabbit hole with his mother and siblings except to eat and sleep. He stayed out all hours looking for work or scraps of food. Food was hidden everywhere; he just had to find it. It might be a tree root today, a discarded animal carcass the next. Danny wanted to help as well, but one of his attempts went terribly wrong.

It was a day like all the rest. Michael worked the family's small plot of leased land, growing wheat to pay the rent, every grain of his crop bound for England. Ellen took the young children—Danny, Timmy, Andy, and baby Ellie—to town to beg for food. Jimmy was already out hunting for scraps. With Ellen's focus on each passerby, desperately trying to make eye contact, Danny slipped away.

Ellen heard a whistle in the distance, and she could see a constable with his hand on the scruff of a young boy. So sad. She thought of her own children and turned her eyes to where they were sitting, all huddled together.

Danny was gone.

Despite Ellen's desperate efforts to gather her children and make a dash to the officer, it was too late. In an instant, Danny was taken off to jail. His crime: stealing a loaf of bread.

Ellen, grief-stricken and still starving, returned home to tell her husband. Michael was saddened by the news, partly for the loss of his son, and partly because he had lost a helping hand. Both knew Danny's fate was sealed. He would be sent abroad to a convict camp with all the other criminals. His time on the battered Emerald Isle was very short.

Jimmy returned home after dark. He had had a good day—several scraps of food and a handful of berries. He traveled more than ten miles to find these few morsels. He knew right away when he entered the hut that Danny was missing. But as soon as he learned about his brother's fate, he knew what he would do next.

It was a long and lonely night in the family's mud hut. Their hunger was stalled for a few hours by Jimmy's small bounty, but there was no cure for their broken hearts. During the night, as the children huddled together, Jimmy whispered instructions to Timmy and Andy.

As morning broke, everyone started their normal routine except for Michael, who headed into town to see if there was any chance to win Danny's release, although Ellen and he knew this was futile. Jimmy left to hunt for food, and Ellen gathered the rest of her children to walk to their spot in town, where she would beg until sunset. At midmorning, Michael found Ellen and told her what he had learned. Danny had been convicted and sentenced to five years in the Australian salt mines. They both knew this might as well be a death sentence for their young son, as he was unlikely to survive the brutal conditions in prison. Michael returned to his crops and Ellen to her corner.

Timmy and Andy knew what was coming next. Jimmy had been very clear. They looked for him in the crowd, and when they finally found him, he was crouched behind the wheel of a carriage, thirty feet away. With a burst, Jimmy sprinted toward the boys. Timmy and Andy rolled from a sitting to a crouching position, and then sprang up to join Jimmy as they ran toward the market. They heard their mother's screams but remained focused on following Jimmy as they darted among the shoppers. After fifty yards, Jimmy came to a halt as they reached the bakery. On display were several loaves of fresh bread. Jimmy looked at Timmy and Andy. All at once, just as planned, they each grabbed a loaf of bread and ran. The shopkeeper screamed at the boys and then for the police. The boys slowed to a walk and waited. A large, forceful hand grabbed each of them by the back of the neck. Two officers walked them to the village jail, where they were reunited with Danny.

Ellen and baby Ellie returned home. This was too much for Jimmy to handle, she thought; there was no way for him to save his brothers from the torture they would face in the labor camps. Michael was resigned.

Danny was certainly excited to see his brothers. All of them except Jimmy probably thought this would be a thrilling adventure. It certainly couldn't be any worse than starving in a damp, cold mud hole. Jimmy's mission had been to make sure that the four of them were all together. The court convicted the three boys of the same crime as Danny and issued the same sentence. The boys were headed to Australia for at least five years, and possibly a lifetime, if they survived. Jimmy knew something about what lay ahead. He was an outgoing boy and fully capable of holding a conversation with any adult. In his short life, he had covered a lot of territory and met many people in his daily excursions. What he had learned in those travels might just save all of their lives.

As the boys waited to board the convict ship, Jimmy whispered his plan to all of them. The ship's voyage would follow currents north and then west to the Americas. Before heading south and around Cape Horn, the ship would stop in Nova Scotia to take on supplies for the captain and crew. This was where Jimmy planned to jump ship. Jimmy knew Nova Scotia had many Irish families, and he hoped someone would give them shelter. Jimmy then prepared his brothers for what life would be like on the ship. They would be packed in very tight, the seas would be rough, and they'd soil themselves. Prisoners who did not survive were tossed overboard to the sharks. There would be little food or water. And if someone was sick, everyone could get sick. This adventure would be worse than anything they had ever imagined.

When the ship loaded, Michael and Ellen were as close as possible, but they could not get a glimpse of their boys' finals steps on Irish soil. They prayed for a miracle—for Jimmy to keep their boys safe.

The voyage was just as Jimmy had described—a rolling nightmare with seemingly no end. Fortunately, though, they had each other and they had hope. These two things helped them survive. Jimmy marked the days of their voyage on a wooden girder inside the hull of the ship. When his marks totaled forty, he knew that the time for their escape was near.

Jimmy had made friends with one of the crew and gained his trust. He told the rugged man several lies—that his brothers could not swim and were afraid of heights—in hopes that he would drop his guard. When the boys went above deck, they reinforced his story by staying clear of the ship's rails. They huddled nervously in the middle of the deck, waiting to return to the hold. The truth was that they were all excellent swimmers.

One of the few pleasures they had had in their short lives was spending time at the beaches of Spanish Point in County Clare. It was there they learned to swim in strong ocean currents and climb rugged bluffs.

When the ship reached Nova Scotia, a storm prevented the captain from safely docking at the pier, so he anchored the ship offshore to let the storm pass. Jimmy sensed this was their chance. He asked the crew if they could have some time on deck. Normally, the guards would have said no, because the captain was concerned about prisoners attempting to jump ship, but four little boys, none of whom could swim, and all afraid of heights, seemed to pose no threat at all. The crew agreed, and the Murray boys took one step toward their freedom.

Jimmy gave each of them instructions. The rolling boat told them that the current was going away from the starboard side, the direction in which they would swim. Danny would lead, with Timmy and Andy in the middle, and Jimmy swimming in the rear, close enough to help anyone in need and to yell out instructions. They would jump on Jimmy's signal.

Their time on deck was limited to five minutes, which would allow plenty of time for Jimmy to size up the situation, find a landmark on shore to target, and choose the best time to jump. When they emerged from the prisoners' hold, the three younger boys took their usual place in the middle of the deck. Jimmy crouched over them, acting as if he was protecting them from the weather. He would say two words before they jumped: mother and father. At "mother," they would be ready, and at "father" they would spring up and make a dash to the starboard rail. Jimmy picked his landmark and waited until the rail was clear of guards and sailors.

Three minutes into their time on deck, the rail cleared. Jimmy gave the signal, and they were off. The four young boys flew off the ship to the shock of the guards. The prisoners in the hold heard the splash. Then came the calls from the guards to launch a rowboat. The prisoners heard the guards' plan and started to shout and pound the inside of the hull. The captain, fearing he had a riot on his hands, had to let the boys go. He needed all hands on deck to quell the hostile prisoners who remained behind.

In the freezing water, the boys swam for their lives. They had ten, maybe fifteen minutes before they would succumb to the cold. Danny led them well, Timmy and Andy managed to keep up, and Jimmy was grateful that luck was on their side. There was no sign of the crew chasing them. The wind helped drive the currents in a favorable direction. Chopping waves repeatedly lifted the boys and hurled them forward. The shore grew closer by the moment.

When the boys reached shore, Jimmy took the lead. They had to scale a large, slippery bluff, about thirty feet in height, before they started their search for refuge. The bluff was not much bigger than the ones they had climbed in County Clare, but they were weakened by the long voyage, and the forceful winds chilled them to the bone. Danny took the lead again, with Andy and Timmy following. Danny and Andy made quick work of the climb, but Timmy struggled. He lost his grip midway up and fell to the rocks below. Jimmy could not break his fall. Timmy cried in pain and held his leg. Jimmy, fearing it was broken, picked him up and lifted him onto his shoulder. Slowly, he made his way up the bluff with Timmy hanging on for dear life. At the top of the bluff, Danny and Andy helped Timmy walk on his one good leg, as Jimmy started the search for a savior.

Jimmy and the boys walked by several houses. Timmy and Andy could not understand why they were passing so many, but Danny understood. Jimmy was looking for signs, as he had done when he was scavenging for food back home. He knew how to spot a charitable family. It wasn't the biggest house. It wasn't the one with the most spectacular garden. A home with heart had a weathered fence, a garden for food—not beauty—and a clothesline filled with children's clothes. He was looking for a house with just one or two children. They walked, barefoot and shivering, for more than a mile until Jimmy found the one. He said a prayer to himself before he knocked on the door. "Please be from Mother Ireland" was his only request.

The mother of the home opened the door. Jimmy smiled. The mother's long, beautiful, red hair ensured their safety. The children had found their savior. The mother hustled the boys into her home, gave them each a blanket, and sat them next to a fireplace. She put a pot of water on the fire to boil potatoes. Her two young children were excited to have guests and helped their mother attend to their needs. The father sent word for the town doctor.

Jimmy thanked his hosts for the kindness and told them that his parents would come for them. They just needed to get word to their church in County Clare.

Several months had passed since Michael and Ellen lost their four boys. One evening, a priest came to their small hut. He called out their names. He had news for the Murrays. Their boys were in Nova Scotia with a good Irish Catholic family. They were safe and waiting for their reunion. The priest knew nothing more. How they had come to be with this family was a mystery to him. Ellen cried at the news. Michael was happy as well, but his thoughts quickly turned to how they, too, might survive the treacherous voyage.[1]

The Murray family's tale ends there, with the boys safe in North America and the parents still in Ireland. In all likelihood, however, the parents and children suffered the trip together, not on a prison ship, but on a British logging ship returning to Canada for another payload, using Irish peasants as ballast. There are no records of children under the age of ten, let alone a group of children from one family, being transported on a British prison ship.[2] There are, however, records of millions of Irish refugees making the punishing voyage to North America during the famine years. This reality, though, does not convey the hope for Ireland's independence and is purposefully set aside by my ancestors for the more heroic and inspirational family story featuring harsh penalties, brothers sticking together, and a brave escape from the clutches of an unjust government. This tale provided hope to future generations of Murray children that Ireland, just like the remarkable Murray boys, could escape the tyranny of British rule.

Elizabeth Gurley Flynn, a prominent Irish American radical, reflected on such heroic stories in her autobiography, *The Rebel Girl*: "The awareness of being Irish came to us as small children, through plaintive songs and heroic story. . . . As children, we drew in a burning hatred of British rule with our mother's milk. Until my father died, at over eighty, he never said 'England' without adding 'God damn her!' Before I was ten, I knew the great heroes, Robert Emmet, Wolfe Tone, Michael Davitt, Parnell, and O' Donovan Rossa."[3]

The Murray family—whatever its route and method—escaped the harrowing conditions in Ireland in 1848 and settled in London, Canada.[4] Opportunities were much greater in Canada than anything afforded them in Ireland. A booming economy, with massive railroad and canal construction projects, provided ample employment opportunities for the Murray boys.[5] However, for the oldest son, Jim, it was not enough. He heard stories of the gold rush in California and the riches that could be won through perseverance and a little luck. At age eighteen, Jim hatched a plan to make his riches. He left town in the middle of the night to follow his dreams and didn't see his family again for twenty years.[6]

2

Trail to the Rockies

The creeks, rivers, and mountain lakes were filled with the choicest brook trout, food which the gourmand might envy. Antelope and deer roamed in great numbers over the hills and valleys around them.

—Edwin Purple, writing about the Montana Territory[7]

Jim Murray's plan to get to the goldfields was simple. He headed to the nearest port to find work on a San Francisco–bound steamship—the only type of ship headed to California on a one-way trip. The year was 1858, and steamers were needed to provide transportation around San Francisco Bay, and to and from Sacramento. He talked his way onto a crew as a fireman,[8] stoking the fire that fueled the ship. It was tough work, and when he wasn't enduring the stifling heat of the boiler room, he lived in cramped quarters, ate awful food, and tried to avoid the regular fights among crewmates.

The route to California for steamships was different from that for the sailing ships that also made the journey at this time. Sailing ships would follow the trade winds out into the Atlantic, coming within sight of Africa before returning to South America to round Cape Horn. Steamships hugged the coastline, stopping in ports along the way. When the engines shut down, Jim had an opportunity to visit the ports and watch his crewmates spend their wages on liquor and women[9]—a preview of what he would see in the mining camps of California. But he was disciplined and kept his wages for passage to the goldfields and for equipment for prospecting.

After several months and many ports, the steamship arrived in San Francisco. Jim took his wages and joined a long line of young men heading toward the foothills of the Sierra Nevada. Murray spent the next five years prospecting and working others' claims. He learned about rock formations, mining operations, and his fellow miners, all of which would serve him well in the years ahead. One thing he did not take away was much money. Despite his hard work and resourcefulness, he did not amass the wealth in California that he had envisioned when he left Canada. But he would not give up.

In 1863, Jim decided it was time to take his meager savings and try new territories. Waves of miners had come and gone over the preceding few years. Most were now heading to the Comstock Lode in Nevada.

Others set out for Colorado. Jim decided he would travel north to the Montana Territory. He had certainly heard of the harsh conditions and the high altitudes in the Rocky Mountains, but that did not discourage him. He liked the idea of prospecting in remote areas with the opportunity to find and stake his own claims.[10]

Jim made his way to Salt Lake City after winter broke and the mountain passes cleared. This leg of his journey was well traveled; just a couple of years earlier, it had been the route for the short-lived Pony Express. There were many relief stations along the way, and fellow pioneers were always within sight. He likely accompanied a wagon train returning to Utah to pick up more supplies imported from the East. Alone, or in a group, he would pass through the deep snow at the crest of the Sierra Nevada, spend several days on the wide-open desert of the Nevada Territory, and finally travel through forty miles of bright white salt flats into Salt Lake City, at the base of the Rocky Mountains.

Murray's next leg, a four-hundred-mile trek north into the Montana wilderness, had to wait until he found a party heading in the same direction. There were too few supply stations and too many risks to travel alone in this territory. The river crossings were difficult, and bands of Indians routinely intercepted travelers. The spring runoff swelled creeks and rivers, and some required great care and patience to cross. A single rider on a strong horse would cross first, setting up ropes and pulleys to guide others who followed. Wagons were carefully caulked to float in the treacherous river currents. Losing a grip on the guide would send a wagon or a passenger into the river, and such accidents forced other passengers to assist with the rescue or recovery efforts. The entire process could take four to eight hours, depending on the size of the river and the number of travelers.

Indians were another concern. This was Jim's first trip into Indian country, and he learned what to look for from experienced men in his group. Most Indians in these parts were friendly and looking for trade, a smoke, or a wager on a horse race. They would approach on horseback with great speed and usually halt thirty yards from the lead wagon and raise their hands, indicating they came in peace. It was the Indians who approached quietly who were more worrisome. They were looking for advantages in numbers so that they might steal horses, ammunition, or supplies. Murray likely served as the rear guard for the wagon train, as he was the perfect sentinel. He had no fear and gave no sign of weakness.

After several weeks of difficult traveling, moving just fifteen to twenty miles each day, Murray and his party reached the primitive mining camp of Alder Gulch. The handful of cabins that composed the town were built with logs or rough-hewn planks. All were cramped. The camp's saloon could handle only a couple dozen men—fewer if card games were being played.[11]

Despite the dearth of permanent buildings, the camp was booming. Murray had seen such camps before in California, and it was not where he would start prospecting. He was looking for areas less populated. While he waited for a team going farther north, Murray certainly heard stories about the miners in this camp. One in particular surely caught his attention. A diminutive Scot by the name of W. A. Clark was making a name for himself, running many businesses at the same time. He worked several mining claims and supplied the town with goods from Salt Lake City. A series of ditches, three miles in length, fed Clark's sluices.[12] Nearly every time he traveled, he imported or exported commodities for profit.

Jim eventually joined a team that was heading north through the Deer Lodge Valley to Gold Creek and beyond.[13] Murray would go as far as Gold Creek, a mining camp located on a major trail and in territory considered neutral by the surrounding Indian tribes. Five days into his trip, he reached La Barge City, the last trading post before his final destination.[14] It was a place where Murray could stock up on supplies, gamble a little bit, and hear what the miners were saying about the territory. After a day or two of rest, he likely set off to his final destination.

Murray arrived in Gold Creek in the late afternoon, as it was nearly a full day's ride from La Barge City. There, he set up his tent next to a group of prospectors in the makeshift camp that straddled the creek. Jim was certainly anxious to hike into the hills, but that would have to wait. He had to join the campfire meeting that night to learn the laws of this camp and learn the location of staked claims. Everything discussed and agreed to at the campfire was the law, as there were no courthouses, judges, or jails for hundreds of miles.[15]

When morning broke the next day, Murray loaded his supplies and started up the mountain along Gold Creek. After traveling nearly five miles and ascending 500 feet—to an elevation of 4,700 feet—Murray set up his camp near a temporarily abandoned town. This is where his empire would begin.

3
Pirate in the Wilderness

Had he lived in the days of Drake and Raleigh he would have been a buccaneer.

—P. A. O'Farrell[16]

The *St. Paul Globe* interviewed Murray about his early days in the Northwest and reported, "He dropped his pack and made his fire in the little placer camp of Pioneer.[17] Prospectors, for the most part, had abandoned Pioneer and Gold Creek the previous year after getting word of big strikes at Alder Gulch and Grasshopper Creek.[18] Murray likely saw several advantages to Pioneer's location. It was relatively safe from Indians and highwaymen, was close to trading posts, and had been recently cleared of competition.

The Flathead Indian tribe occupied the area to the north of Pioneer. Although not openly hostile toward settlers, they were known horse thieves. The Blackfeet Indians occupied the area several miles to the east, and they routinely killed pioneers caught trapping or prospecting on their lands. Both tribes shared hunting rights in the valleys on either side of Pioneer. Herds of grazing white-tailed deer dotted the valley floors, and the streams teemed with trophy-size trout.[19] The two tribes' neutrality in this country, while protecting pioneers from physical attack, did not extend protection for their horses. Smoke from campfires led the Flatheads to their potential bounty. However, a solitary fire in Pioneer, high in the hills above the Indian hunting grounds, likely did not attract much attention. There were much easier targets along the military's well-traveled Mullan Road, connecting Fort Benton in the Montana Territory and Fort Walla Walla in the Washington Territory.

Highwaymen were also a threat in the territory, though most were concentrated in the area between Salt Lake City and the booming towns around Grasshopper Creek and Alder Gulch (Bannack and Virginia City). Just about every prospector who tried to ferry his fortunes to Salt Lake City met with a band of thieves. A network of spies in both towns alerted bandits when gold was in transit.[20] Mullan Road and the path between Pioneer and Deer Lodge transported far less gold and were of little interest to roadside bandits.

Mullan Road provided Murray with access to goods and labor. Completed in 1862, the six-hundred-mile wagon trail established a link between

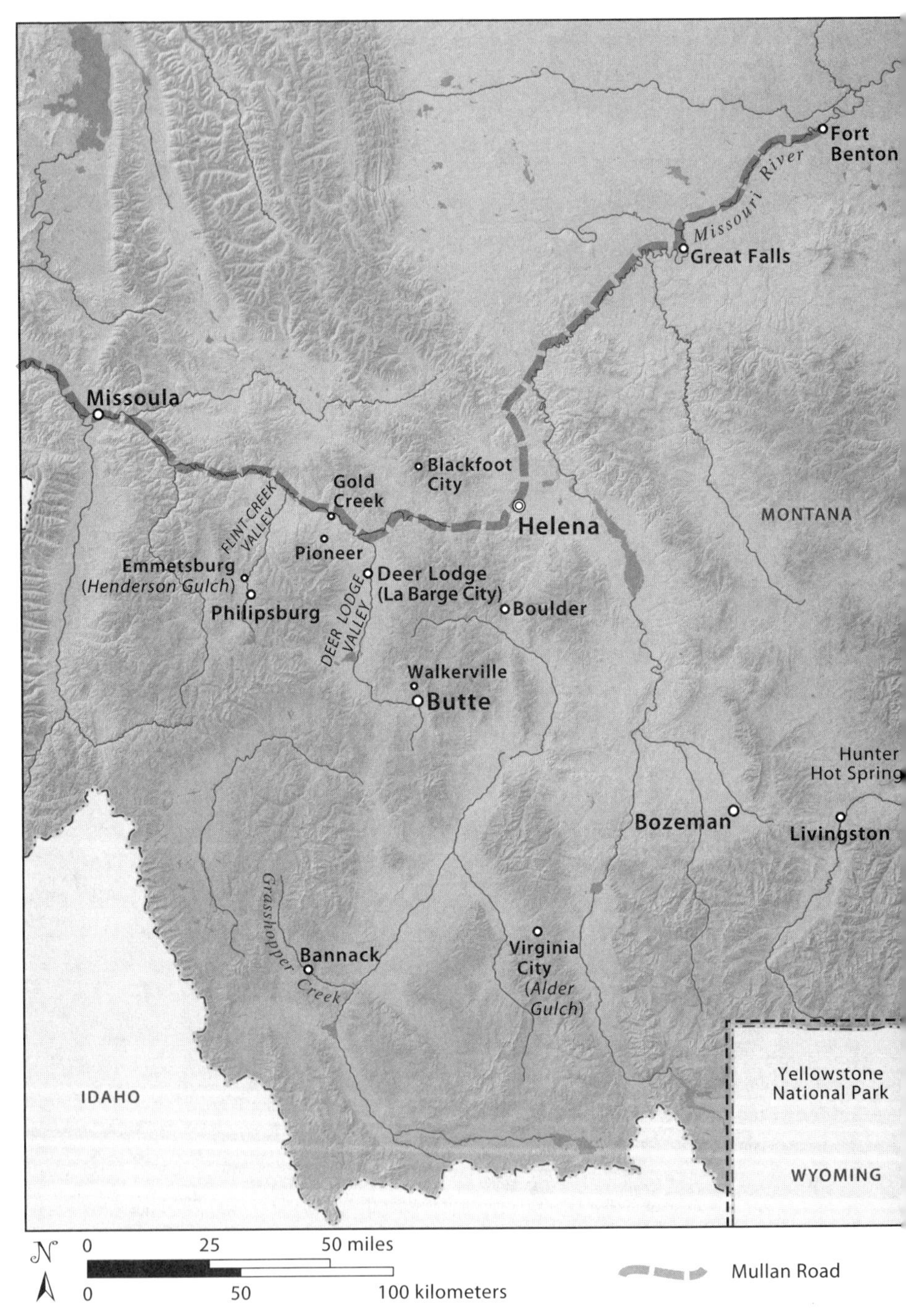

Western Montana in the mid to late nineteenth century.

inland seaports at the head of the Missouri River, near Fort Benton, and the Columbia River, near Walla Walla. Gold Creek became a rest stop along the route, and by 1865 the *Miner and Travelers' Guide* described Gold Creek this way: "wood, water, and grass at camp; supplies of all kinds to be had here, dry goods, groceries, fresh beef, animals, and possibly vegetables."[21] To the south, La Barge City and eventually the town of Deer Lodge provided larger trading posts. Murray certainly benefited from access to newcomers, or pilgrims, as they were commonly referred to by seasoned pioneers. He gambled to supplement his income, and pilgrims were easy marks. Those who stayed in camp and started prospecting became potential laborers once they had spent their savings or lost everything in a poker game.

Trade and Profits

The success that eluded him in California came quickly in his new environs. He recounted to a *St. Paul Globe* reporter that he "found 'pay dirt' and then got other men to work his claim for wages while he went in for trade and big profits."[22] This claim is borne out in contemporary reports from the first newspapers in the area. The *New North-West*, based in nearby Deer Lodge, reported that Murray owned a general store, saloons, real estate, a flume, and several mining claims just a few years after he entered the territory. Later reports indicated that he also lent money and bred horses during these early years.[23] Based on these various reports, Murray likely hit pay dirt shortly after arriving in Pioneer, hired others to work his claim, and started grubstaking, or lending money to prospectors for supplies. Horse ranching and expanded mining activities came next as he foreclosed on prospectors who could not make their loan payments, taking their horses and claims. When the Pioneer district started to bustle in 1868, he used his mining and lending profits to open a general store and two saloons. His store in Yamhill (adjacent to Pioneer) operated under the name of J. A. Murray & Company,[24] and he owned the Murray & Talbot Saloon in partnership with James A. Talbot.[25]

Sometime prior to 1875, Murray claimed ownership of the Tradewater Bar Flume[26] through purchase or foreclosure. The elaborate wooden structure played a critical role in the development of the Pioneer mining district. Water was the prospectors' first and least expensive method of parting gold from its earthen bonds. Wooden sluices fed with water separated gold from riverbed gravel, and high-pressure hoses blasted gold-bearing gravel deposits. While gold lay in wait in every gulch and riverbed, water flowed in just a few ravines. Flumes were essential to transport water to dry gulches and gold-bearing deposits. Trestles, some more than a hundred feet high, supported flumes delivering water to miners working claims in the Pioneer district.[27]

Murray piled up so much cash through all his ventures that he finally had to open a bank to store it all. His first of seven banks opened in Deer Lodge in 1868,[28] one year after W. A. Clark opened his first bank.[29] Murray attributed his early success to "just sticking to things," which, based on what is known of his business practices, included hard work, discipline, deception, and a fearless disposition. Murray built a reputation as "the most obstinate little man in Pioneer. He couldn't be bluffed, he wouldn't be cheated, and he didn't scare at anything."[30] He was constantly on the move looking for new opportunities, and he never squandered his earnings on liquor or prostitutes. He also earned a reputation for paying good wages to his employees. He claimed that high wages instilled pride in his workers and made them feel as if they were the "champions of the camp."[31]

Murray also earned an equally fierce reputation for holding on to every penny he earned or stole. Murray guarded his money with his personal arsenal and unwavering resolve. The *St. Paul Globe* reported, "He carried his weapons in sight and whenever anyone questioned his right he would simply say, 'What's mine is mine, and I'll have it if I go to hell for it.'"[32] When the US government established a court system in the territory, Murray added paper to his arsenal. He studied the law carefully, prospecting for loopholes, and then clogged the courts with filings to protect his mining claims and seize others. Murray also kept up with the territory's emerging government bureaucracy by participating in the political process. In 1874, Murray served as one of four representatives from Pioneer to the Democratic Convention.[33] W. A. Clark led the Democrats that year. Murray's involvement in politics, unlike Clark's, did not reflect any personal ambition. Murray simply wanted a hand in selecting the policy-makers who ultimately influenced his business prospects.

Hijinks and Shenanigans

Murray enjoyed an active social life in the early mining camps, much of which centered on gambling. He enjoyed all forms—high- or low-stakes poker, horse races, footraces, even betting on the number of planks in a carpenter's wagon—and he constantly looked for ways to ensure success. He played with marked cards, dealt from the bottom of the deck, fixed races, and rigged even the most casual side bets. Prospectors, fresh from a successful day in a gulch and full of liquor, were easy pickings for Murray.

One scheme at which Murray excelled involved a variation of the parlor game in which contestants guessed the number of beans in a jar. He would start by finding a merchant ferrying a load of items through town. It could be sacks of flour, planks of wood, or a pile of bricks. He would then buy the merchant a few drinks, count the items in his load, and direct him to park his wagon outside a designated saloon at a specific time. Murray would then proceed to the chosen saloon to ensure that he had plenty of inebriated, deep-pocketed prospectors ready to make a wager. Once the merchant parked his wagon, Murray wondered aloud about the number of items in the load and encouraged a friendly wager. He then proceeded to, in his words, "trim the suckers." On a good day, Murray walked away with several thousand dollars from these cinch bets.[34]

Although Murray enjoyed all forms of cinches, horse racing was nearest to his heart. In the early days of the mining camps, prospectors and Indians competed in two-horse races through town. Murray used to ride his own horse during these contests. As towns developed, they built racetracks to host standard races, harness races (trotters and pacers), and foot races. A typical day at the races in the early 1870s included three to four horse races (thoroughbreds and trotters) and a footrace between two or three local men.

Murray's stable of racehorses made its first appearance in the press on April 25, 1874, when the *New North-West* announced a two-horse race between Murray's Rowdy and Phil Evans's Nelly Grey. The match at Olin's Track in Philipsburg carried a $600 purse and a $50 forfeiture fee. Murray's horse won the mile race in 2:02.[35] Later that year, Murray was forty miles northeast, as the crow flies, in the small mining camp of Blackfoot City to race 7-up Pete, named after an English-pub card game.[36] In 1876, Murray's stable included the tandem of Caesar and Brutus. Caesar, a thoroughbred, raced for several years, traveling hundreds of miles to race in Missoula, Deer Lodge, and Butte. Brutus, one of Murray's trotters, earned notoriety for his owner without even setting hoof to track.

Murray entered Brutus in the 1879 Territorial Fair races at Helena, which opened on the first day of October, a Wednesday, and ran through Saturday, October 4. Splendid weather attracted several thousand people to the fair, with horse racing taking center stage. The racing started on the first day with a hundred-mile riding contest. Competitors, switching to a fresh horse every mile, rode more than four hours to complete the event. On Thursday, Friday, and Saturday, thoroughbreds and trotters took the field. Murray entered Brutus in the Saturday races, which carried the largest purse for trotters, with $400 going to the first horse to win three heats. Billy Grant, Live Oak, and Corrigan joined Brutus in the contest of endurance. After five heats, Brutus and Billy Grant were deadlocked with two wins apiece. In the sixth heat, Brutus bolted to the front and maintained a slight lead at the second pole. Billy Grant edged ahead at the next post, before Brutus charged to the lead, winning by nearly fifty feet. Murray took the $400 purse, and likely much more money from side wagers on his trotter.[37]

Claims surfaced shortly after the close of the fair that some of the races had featured "high games of rascality." Murray's horse drew attention from a keen observer who did not recognize Murray's winning entry. The horse, a blue roan with a star on his forehead and white hind feet, looked nothing like the Brutus the observer knew. He wrote to the *Spirit of the Times* in New York, the leading horse-racing publication of the day, describing the Murray steed that had shown surprising speed at the Territorial Fair. The editors surmised by the description of the horse that it was not Brutus, but rather Frank J, a blue roan recently sold to an anonymous party in the West.[38] Murray managed to escape any consequences for his apparent trickery and remained undeterred from engaging in similar shenanigans in the future.

Murray also enjoyed a good game of poker from time to time. He could easily cheat pilgrims and drunken prospectors, but when he ran up against professionals, he found it safer to risk other people's money. Most knew him to be wealthy and therefore assumed it was safe to lend Murray money for a short period. However, if Murray lost someone else's money in a card game, he simply skipped town without repaying his debt.[39] Few had the courage to try to collect from a well-armed pioneer. Another approach Murray used to profit from card games was to extend credit to players going up against the professionals. He lent only to those with valuable assets to post as security. If his borrower lost, which was usually the case, Murray profited by seizing his possessions. On one occasion, a gambler repaid Murray's loan and added a special bonus. News of the gift went viral, spreading to newspapers across the country all the way to the Atlantic seaboard.

The story begins with Murray lending an apostate Mormon $500 to call a hand held by the professional gambler Julius "French" Levy. Remarkably, Murray's borrower beat the pro and took down a pot of $1,300. It was likely a disappointment for Murray at the time, since he probably hungered for the man's collateral. Several years later, Murray received a gift that erased any disappointment. When the man died in Pioneer, he remembered Murray with a bequeathal of twelve bottles of wine with a sensational history. Murray never let the truth get between him and a good story, and his liquid bounty provided plenty of yarn with which to spin a good one.

According to Murray, the twelve bottles of wine that passed into his possession had started their journey in a sealed vault, deep inside a Jesuit monastery somewhere in Europe during the early eighteenth century. A war between religious fanatics destroyed the Jesuits' home, and vandals absconded with the precious wine. A merchant with a fine eye obtained many of the bottles and carried them into Poland. There, the merchant offered the wine to the king of Poland and was rewarded with a title and honors. On the engagement of the king's daughter to the heir to the French throne, the sovereign bestowed the wine upon his future son-in-law.

The French prince entrusted the wine to the Crown's stewards, one of whom was lying in wait for just this moment. The unprincipled steward, Bonforte by name, substituted the priceless bottles with inferior products and left for America with his royal bounty. Bonforte arrived in America in 1790 and confided to Henry Coatway the nature of his collection. Coatway became obsessed with the bottles and eventually killed Bonforte to seize them for his own. Fearing that the bottles could reveal his crime, Coatway buried them under an oak tree and never mustered the courage to reclaim his prize. Fifty years later, a Mormon uprooted the ancient oak and found the burgundy treasure; he soon traveled to Utah with the wine in his cargo.

Brigham Young heard stories of the ancient wine housed among his flock and convinced the owner that he was merely an instrument of God to shepherd the wine into Young's arms. But the bottles remained with the Mormon leader for only a short time before Murray's borrower and benefactor stole them and took them to Montana.[40]

Murray gave no indication that he ever enjoyed the fabled wine, but he certainly relished hearing that his tale appeared in newspapers in ten states, reaching all the way across the continent to the *New York Sun*.

Friends for Life

Murray's affinity for the working class, saloon side bets, rascality, and tall tales set him apart from other fledgling Bonanza Kings. So, too, did his friendships. He told the press once that he valued his friends over all the wealth he had accumulated.[41] Many of those friends, like James Talbot and Silas King, became trusted business associates, remaining out of public view. Other friends became well known in their own right, and their relationship with Murray was a source of colorful stories for the press. The most interesting of the lot were thespian John Maguire, trapper-turned-miner Frank "Sandbar" Brown, and drifter John "Fat Jack" Jones. Maguire would come to operate a string of theaters for Murray, Brown would run several of his mines, and Fat Jack would drive the rich and famous up and down the richest hill on earth for several decades.

Jim Murray loved the theater. Two of his racehorses, Caesar and Brutus, likely earned their monikers from Shakespeare's play *Julius Caesar*. Newspapers at the time, even in the remote wilderness, printed scenes from that and other classic plays. For prospectors living in Montana during the 1860s and '70s, these excerpts, often read by candlelight, were their only opportunity to become immersed in culture. That is, until actor John Maguire stepped off a stagecoach in the early 1870s.

Maguire, born in 1841, grew up in Ireland, in the town of Buttevant, a small village outside of Mallow in County Cork. He did not have to escape famine as Murray had, as his parents were middle-class proprietors of a large hotel outside a resort community. His earliest memories were of "gaily painted caravans" that appeared at the market square. As a young boy, he met many of the famous theater players from Ireland as they traveled between Cork and Dublin. His most cherished friend was Elizabeth O'Neill, a celebrated actress who later became Lady Becher. After studying theater at St. Coleman College in Fermoy, Maguire looked to America as the land of opportunities. In 1860, he traveled to San Francisco. There, he took small parts alongside many great actors of the day, including members of the Booth family. Maguire, unable to mask his thick brogue, struggled to find a place in the industry he loved, bouncing between stage and management, acting in a stock company in Virginia City, Nevada, and managing a rickety theater in the remote mining camp of Pioche in central Nevada.[42] Not finding solid footing in California or Nevada, he opted to follow the trail blazed by Murray several years earlier. In the early 1870s he entered the Montana Territory with a one-man act titled "American Flowers and Shamrock Leaves."

Maguire performed wherever he could find space for an audience to sit or stand. Sandbar Brown, writing a history of Henderson Gulch, near Philipsburg, noted Maguire's performances as early as 1871 in the town of Emmetsburg.[43] Two years later, in one of Maguire's most successful runs through the western frontier, he made a trip east to Fort Laramie, ninety miles north of Cheyenne, Wyoming. The soldiers in remote outposts cherished the performing arts, and many set up stages and cast garrison members in amateur productions. Lieutenant Major Andrew Burt arranged for a three-night engagement of Maguire to entertain his troops. It was so successful that Maguire began performing at other military installations in the area, and he spent two years traveling between forts and small towns in Wyoming and the Dakotas. His last stop before heading back to Montana was an engagement at Fort Lincoln, North Dakota, which was under the command of Major General George Custer. Maguire's performance impressed Custer so much that the general sat down on August 8, 1875—just eleven months prior to his final battle—and wrote Maguire a recommendation addressed to all commanding officers of military posts.[44]

Maguire remained in the Montana Territory for two more years, traveling hundreds of miles by stagecoach to entertain pioneers in Bozeman, Missoula, Deer Lodge, Butte, Blackfoot, Philipsburg, Pioneer, and anywhere else he could find a place for people to gather. He played in courthouses, dance halls, and churches.[45] Newspapers showered Maguire with glorious reviews at every stop. The *Helena Weekly Herald* wrote, "Mr. Maguire is a young man of great force and talent as a professional," and "his comicalities were laughable and amusing."[46] The Deer Lodge *New North-West* remarked, "His humorous recitations kept the house in a roar. His entertainment is worthy of good houses."[47] And the *Bozeman Avant Courier* penned, "His entertainment was received in the most enthusiastic manner, eliciting frequent applause. He displayed the accomplished artiste in the rendition of the most difficult pieces in a style we have never heard excelled."[48] During

MR. JOHN MAGUIRE, WHO WILL APPEAR AT THE OPERA HOUSE THURSDAY, MAY 25.

MR. JOHN MAGUIRE, the eminently popular actor-manager, appearing in widely celebrated entertainment, entitled "Begone Dull Care" or "A Cure for the Blues" in which he introduces his marvelous character impersonations, with lightning changes of costume, which have contributed to make his name famous as the greatest monologue artist on the American stage.

Prices, 25c, 50c and 75c. Seats on sale at Valley Clothing company.

1905 Playbill for John Maguire. —Library of Congress

Maguire's travels, and among all the adulation, word reached him about Custer's fate at Little Bighorn. He wrote a eulogy for his celebrity sponsor and returned to Fort Lincoln to raise money for the widows and orphans left behind by the soldiers who died in battle.[49]

In 1877, perhaps tiring of the long coach rides between performances, Maguire left the territory for a short spell to manage a theater in Portland, Oregon. He returned to Montana in 1880 and settled in Butte. There, a lifelong partnership between Murray and Maguire (described in detail in chapter 9) started in earnest.

Frank "Sandbar" Brown served in the Confederate Navy during the Civil War. He started his residence in the Montana wilderness in 1865, when he acquired trapping supplies at Fort Union. Brown treasured his first receipt and later donated it to the archives of the University of Montana. Riddled with spelling errors, it read in part: "Sold to Frank D. Brown two indian ponys one black and one a pinto for sixteen (16) dollars and one Winchester rifle and fifty cartridges for 77 dols, and 19 beaver traps for 43 dols, an a saddle and bridel for 34 dollars and a bil of grub for 14 dols, and 4 pair of moccasins and a buckskin shirt for 7 dols."[50]

After just one year in the backcountry, Brown earned his nickname, retelling the story to reporters on many occasions:

> It was in 1866, with two other men I was riding along the Missouri, about seven miles above the Marias [River]. One of the men was across a ridge and my other partner had crossed the river and had disappeared from view.
>
> I forded over a long sandbar, got the three horses hidden in some willows and backtracked, as we knew some Indians were following us. Hidden behind some sand, I saw three Bloods [Kainai Blackfoot] following our tracks. They had their guns ready, and you know Bloods never gave a white man a chance. They always killed from ambush. As the first Indian got over to the bar, I fired and he dropped. My partner heard the shot and came running back. I got the second Indian and my partner got the third. We scalped them and threw their bodies in the river. I guess that's how I got "Sandbar" tacked to my name.[51]

Later in his career, Brown turned to mining. Like so many pioneers, he had to hold down a second job to survive. He spent time as a rancher, officer of the law, and editor and publisher of a newspaper. His articles on early Montana history indicate that he met Murray in the formative days of the mining camps. The two became close friends over the years, and Sandbar operated several mines for Murray, providing meticulous reports, which he donated to the University of Montana archives. He also took on several odd jobs for Murray. He collected antlers to decorate the interiors of Murray's buildings, obtained sapphires for his wives, hired Murray's nephew, and on occasion solved problems for Murray's wayward associates. At Murray's request, Sandbar once arranged the release of High-Card Jennie, a prostitute notorious for robbing her clients, from jail. Murray provided the money and Sandbar posted bail to release High-Card back to her bordello.[52]

John "Fat Jack" Jones entered Murray's circuit of mining camps in the late 1870s. Fat Jack's nickname started as Flap Jack, because he was as skinny as a pancake. Somewhere along the way it changed to "Fat Jack." Standing six feet two inches tall in his boots, the skinny drifter cut an unusual figure.[53] He came to Montana from Deadwood, South Dakota, where he prospected for several years and claimed to be one of the founders of the booming camp, once telling a reporter, "I blazed the trail into the camp for those fellows. I was one of the first that discovered that place. I was in Deadwood when the trees stood in the streets as tall as them there telephone poles.[54] Before Deadwood, Jack had served in the Union Army for the entire Civil War, first as a drummer in the Thirteenth Maine Volunteer Regiment, and then as a private in the Ninth Maine Regiment.[55]

One of Murray's first encounters with Fat Jack occurred in Philipsburg around 1878. The town of 1,500 provided the best accommodations and services in the Flint Creek Valley and was a regular stop for Murray. From there, he could learn of happenings in Emmetsburg, German Gulch, and Granite.

Fat Jack ran a barbershop in Philipsburg, and this is where he and Murray had the first of their many comical encounters. Murray entered the barbershop and took a seat to wait his turn. After Fat Jack cleaned up his current customer, Jim took his turn in the barber's chair. Fat Jack lathered him up for a shave while his first customer was finding his payment. The man presented Jack with a ten-dollar gold coin for his four-bit shave. Jack had only a dollar in his till, so he had to step over to a saloon where his friend Brocky, a faro dealer, could make change. When Jack entered the saloon there was a game in progress. He reached over one of the men and flipped the gold coin onto the felt table to get his change. The coin bounced a couple times and landed on the queen just as the dealer turned the winning card—queen! Brocky swept away Jack's coin and pushed him twenty dollars in chips.

Back at the barbershop, Murray was sitting patiently. When ten minutes had passed, Jim cleaned himself up and walked across the street to see what had happened. A large crowd was gathered at the faro table and seated in the middle chair was Jack, partially hidden behind a large stack of red, white, and blue chips. Murray tapped his barber firmly on the shoulder. Jack turned his head just enough to see Jim out of the corner of his eye. Turning his attention back to the felt table, Jack said, "I guess you'll have to finish that shave yourself, Mr. Murray. I'm involved with a little transaction with my friend." Jim returned to the barbershop, shaved himself, and turned over the "Closed" sign for Jack.[56]

Jim ran into Fat Jack several more times on his circuit. Sometimes he would find him in Deer Lodge, other times in Emmetsburg, and almost always at a faro table. The two shared a love of gambling and became good friends. One day they came up with a proposition that was a sure thing. The sting was to happen in Murray's hometown of Pioneer, one of the few places Fat Jack had yet to visit. Murray traveled to Pioneer first, and Fat Jack lagged a day or so behind, his stagecoach scheduled to arrive in Pioneer at high noon.

On the appointed day, Murray headed over to Pioneer's coach stop. As usual, a crowd had gathered to meet the new arrivals. The stop was right next to the general store and across from the hotel. After the stagecoach came to a stop, Fat Jack stepped off wearing his large overcoat. He was an imposing figure and always drew attention in a crowd. Jim commented to the folks nearby, "That's the thinnest man that's ever stepped off in Pioneer!" Fat Jack didn't acknowledge his friend as he walked across the street to check into the hotel. About fifteen minutes later, Jack reappeared and stepped into the general store. Murray was nearby, taking in the scene. Fat Jack bought a plug of tobacco and, before he left, wandered over to the scales. With a few adjustments, he had his weight. Afterwards a few of the onlookers took a peek. The tall stranger weighed 143 pounds. Murray remarked, "I bet that man weighs no more than 120 pounds." One of the onlookers objected without revealing the evidence from the scales. Murray pounced, offering to back up his statement with a $100 wager. The crowd, sensing they had a sure thing, wanted in on the action. Murray obliged and covered $2,000 in wagers.

With all bets down, one of the eager gamblers went to retrieve Jack from the hotel. Jack walked back across the street. Someone in the crowd remarked that he might be mistaken for Abraham Lincoln if he discarded the cigar and wore a stovepipe hat. The crowd split as he made his way to the scales. A designated referee adjusted the weights. He double-checked his work and then announced the total to a disappointed crowd. Fat Jack tipped the scale at 120 pounds. Fat Jack made his way back to the hotel room while Murray kept the group distracted. Back in his room, Fat Jack reached under his bed and pulled out twenty-three pounds of sheet lead he had worn around his waist the first time he'd stepped on the scales. He tied it around his body again and took a nice long walk. About a mile outside of town, he discarded the lead in the bushes and then returned to get his share of the pot.[57]

Jim and Fat Jack split their winnings and went their separate ways. Fat Jack drifted off to another town and another faro table, but the two continued crossing paths and eventually became business partners in a legitimate, albeit unusual, endeavor.

The Hanging Judge's Daughter

Murray enjoyed a bachelor's life for fourteen years in the mining camps of California and Montana. He had no interest in raising a family, and marriage was far from his mind when he met divorcée Sallie House in Pioneer in 1870. A tough pioneer in her own right, Sallie came to Montana from Iowa when she was just a teenager. The day she arrived in Gold Creek, July 12, 1862, James Stuart noted in his diary, "With the emigrants today is

Mr. B. B. Burchett with his family, consisting of his wife, two very handsome daughters, one blonde and the other a brunette. Miss Sallie Burchett is sixteen years old and a very beautiful girl. Every man in camp has shaved and changed his shirt since this family arrived. We are all trying to appear like civilized men."[58] Ed House won Sallie's affection that summer, and they were married in the dusty mining camp. In the fall, they packed up and headed south to Bannack with their families, just one year before Murray passed through Gold Creek on his way to Pioneer. Sallie gave birth to a son, Freeman House, in 1863—one of the first children born to pioneers in the territory.

Sallie raised her son in one of the wildest towns in the West. The citizens of Bannack elected her father, B. B. Burchett, mining judge in 1862 and 1863. In that role, he presided over the first hanging in Montana and

Sallie (center) in a Burchett family photo, circa 1890. —Photo courtesy of Mryna Aldrich

worked alongside the notorious sheriff Henry Plummer.[59] After Sallie's parents returned to Iowa in 1868, she and Ed returned to Pioneer. They divorced shortly thereafter. As an attractive single woman, Sarah stood out in Pioneer just as she had when she stepped off the wagon in Gold Creek eight years earlier. The population of Pioneer numbered 522, roughly split between whites and Chinese. Her competition for the attention of Murray, and that of the other 215 single white males in camp, included only six single women, nineteen homemakers, and twenty-three prostitutes.[60]

Murray's attraction to Sallie was evident to everyone in town, and the couple's personal displays of affection brought a strong response. The townspeople expressed concern about the intimacy of their relationship and, according to Murray, compelled them to marry[61]—which they did in 1871. Married life seemed to agree with Murray, primarily because it ended up being good for business. When Freeman was old enough, Murray put him to work in one of his banks. He used Sallie as a shill in filing mining permits and hid properties under the name of her brother, Josiah.

The family moved to Deer Lodge in 1874, after the territory's Democratic Convention, and resided there for four years. Murray continued his relentless travel schedule, keeping abreast of which towns were on the way up and which were about to fold. In 1878, he decided the town with the best prospects was Butte, thirty-five miles and a full day's ride to the southeast of Deer Lodge.[62]

Next Stop: Butte City

When Jim, Sallie, and Freeman arrived in Butte in 1878, silver mining was heating up. Murray's main competitors for mining prospects in the area were W. A. Clark and newcomer Marcus Daly. Daly had come to Butte in 1876 as an employee of the Walker Brothers of Utah; he located several silver mines in camp and managed them for the Salt Lake City–based company.[63] Clark, the rugged entrepreneur, and Daly, the sophisticated corporate man, were polar opposites and repeatedly clashed in business and in politics. Murray stayed neutral in their feud and worked well with both men.

Murray made Butte his primary home for the next twenty-six years. His opened a bank in a rustic log cabin perched at the northwest corner of Copper and Main. There, he could look down on the grizzly mining town, with its wood-framed structures, muddy streets, and rickety plank sidewalks. On a clear day, he could see past the chaotic cluster of buildings that climbed the hill, down to the flats, where antelope grazed along Silver Bow Creek. John Maguire and Fat Jack joined him there in time. Together, they would see the town grow into what evangelist William Biederwolf called "the lowest sinkhole of vice in the West," where there was "enough legitimate vice to damn the souls of every young man and young woman in it."[64] Butte's slide into a moral abyss started in 1880, when Thomas Edison patented the light bulb, setting in motion a series of events that determined Butte's course for decades to come. Edison's invention, along with Bell's telephone, required copper—lots of copper—and Butte sat on one of the largest copper deposits in the world. Once cast aside as waste rock in the city's silver mines, copper ore became the resource that would hurl the mining camp into its destiny as one of the wealthiest and most notorious cities in America.

4
KILLING THE COMPETITION

Butte was simply an outpost of hell . . . [where] men lived by systematic robbery of people enticed into the camp by paid-for accounts of the fabulous richness of its mines.

—*Anaconda Standard*[65]

When Murray moved to Butte, the mining business had transitioned from placer techniques (sifting through surface deposits in streambeds) to hard-rock operations (carving out shafts and drifts[66] below ground). Developing a working mine required sinking a shaft, bracing walls with timbers, excavating or blasting drifts, and removing groundwater. Building stamp mills to process gold and silver and smelters for copper required a significant amount of capital.[67]

Murray approached this new era with discipline, using his own cash, or selling stock to passive investors, to fund development and processing operations. He never placed himself in a position where his capital source could remove him from his ownership position. Therefore, he never borrowed from banks or formed shareholder-controlled corporations to raise capital for development. If he did not have ready cash or willing investors, or see immediate potential in a mine, he allowed others to pursue development of his property through leases and royalty agreements. Murray was a keen raconteur and skilled at convincing other prospectors that only hard work and determination separated them from the great wealth buried beneath his claims. If the lessor failed to hit a productive vein of ore and quit the lease, there was always another miner ready to pick up the contract and take a turn extending the shaft farther into the hill. If a lessor found a productive vein, Murray could either collect royalty payments or contrive to evict his tenant and work the claim himself.

Murray's disciplined and diversified approach to funding development permitted him to manage a large number of mines. To build his portfolio, he spent a significant amount of time scouting for new prospects. Observers noted that "he went after ore systematically, and not only with a prospector's pick shovel. He set up a hoist and went right down to bed-rock to see what was there."[68] Murray's expeditions were not limited to finding new claims. He also searched for opportunities to jump the claims of others. The General Mining Act of 1872 required miners to work their claims to maintain ownership.[69] Individual owners, using their own cash for development, often suspended work on a mine until they had saved up enough money from other business ventures to continue excavation or setting timbers. Murray actively sought out partially developed properties that he could hijack from poorly capitalized miners.[70] And if Murray couldn't jump an abandoned claim, his other option was to steal underground ore by drifting into other miners' claims hundreds of feet below the earth's surface.[71] Murray's success at claim jumping and underground thievery led one old-timer, familiar with Murray's shenanigans during the placer mining era, to say, "Jim Murray, I knew you when you was a petty larceny thief, and now I know you when you are a grand larceny thief."[72]

Among Murray's earliest ventures in Butte was the acquisition and development of the Northstar and Salisbury Mines near Walkerville in 1881 with fellow Irishman Marcus Daly.[73] The partnership was capitalized at $2 million,[74] however, there is no indication the venture met with any success.[75] Later that year, Daly found the mother lode on his own when he obtained the patent for the Anaconda—a mine that held the richest veins of copper ore in the United States and drove Butte's rapid expansion for many years to come.[76] Murray would never hit one big strike like Daly. He collected, traded, and litigated several hundred gold, silver, and copper mining claims during his career, holding as many as fifty at one time in Butte alone. Each was unique, but four typify Murray's approach to the mining business. The Smokehouse Lode generated significant cash flow. The Blue Bird Mine sealed his reputation as a dangerous litigant. The Stella Lode, one of his biggest mistakes, showed he could forgive and forget (as long as it was in his best interest). And his acquisition of the Streicher properties demonstrated that great opportunity could arise from the tragedy of others.

Smokehouse Cash

Murray acquired the Smokehouse Lode in 1880, one year prior to Daly's big strike. The Smokehouse[77] blanketed the heart of Butte's soon-to-boom central business district. Three years later, in 1883, he patented the adjoining Arctic claim.[78] Initially, Murray allowed prospectors to squat on his claim, building shacks in which to live or operate small businesses. As the town started to prosper and lots became valuable, some of his squatters sold their buildings, claiming they held surface rights to the property. When Murray found out that people were taking advantage of his charity, he took them to court and invalidated their deeds. Merchants who wanted to continue operating on the surface of his claims had to enter into rental agreements with Murray, lest he demolish their buildings in his rightful pursuit of minerals underneath their foundations. Murray held the city hostage as well, forcing town officials to rent streets, sidewalks, and alleys on his property. Newspaper accounts reported that Murray earned between $420,000 and $657,000 per year with this scheme, making him one of the first millionaires in the state.[79] Fred Ritchie, a local theater manager, writing about the early days of Butte for a local paper, captured Murray's glee over his moneymaker in a stanza dedicated to the famed Smokehouse claim:

> Jim Murray he sat in a corner alone,
>
> A picture of comfort indeed,
>
> And a classical smile stole over his face
>
> As he thought of the great Smokehouse lead.[80]

Other entrepreneurs tried to replicate Murray's scheme in other portions of the central city, but defects in their patents allowed business owners to file a competing claim, the "Destroying Angel," which perfected the rights of building owners and allowed them to operate uninterrupted.

Headframe for Smokehouse Lode operating in Butte's central business district.
—Postcard from author's personal collection

Business owners operating within Murray's claims were not so fortunate, and they and the city sued repeatedly to strip Murray of the surface rights to his downtown mining patents. Their first effort, started in 1886, was defeated in a local court, and then appealed to the Montana Supreme Court. Murray, fearful that the supreme court would overturn the favorable lower court ruling, made a bold (and complicated) attempt to coerce the supreme court into letting the decision stand.

Murray directed a shill to engage a well-known Butte real estate agent in a wager on the outcome of the case. The shill gave the agent $250 of Murray's money and encouraged him to approach Murray and wager that his lower court victory would be overturned. Murray accepted the bet, and then leaked the arrangement to the press. He hoped that a press report of a powerful real estate agent betting on judges to overturn the lower court ruling would indicate the case was fixed in favor of Murray's opponents (the building owners squatting on his claim). Murray thought this would pressure the court to avoid the perception of impropriety and let the lower court ruling stand. The supreme court found in Murray's favor, but the judges made it clear they were not at all happy about the press reports of the wager.

The supreme court investigated the source of the news report and, finding Murray at the center of the scheme, fined him $800 for contempt of court. In their ruling, the judges wrote,

> It is seldom we find as many contradictions and as much falsehood in so short a record as the case before us contains. . . . [Murray] fabricated a falsehood, attributed it to other parties, and published it, to apprise the court of what had transpired, —to influence its decision in the suits then pending before it in which he was a party. . . . Must a court that sits to try causes be insulted by the very parties to the suits which they are trying, by a covert and cowardly insinuation of official corruption, and have no power to punish such parties for contempt?[81]

The press chipped in as well, writing of the contempt conviction that it "shows the sagacity with which that individual can concoct and carry out intricate schemes."[82] No doubt Murray took this as a compliment.

After the ruling, Murray prepared a long list of eviction notices and proceeded to file them in Butte's court,[83] placing the business community of the city under siege. It was a time when the central business district should have been blossoming. New rail lines were entering the city and outside money was flowing into the development of the city's mines. Business leaders implored Murray to settle with the merchants and grant them the rights they needed to advance development. It took more than a year for the business owners and Murray to strike a deal, but in September 1888 he took the shackles off the central city.[84] A year later, one paper looked back at the deal and concluded that it had been the "electric shock" the town desperately needed, resulting in "new and elegant structures . . . fast filling up the sites formerly occupied by unsightly frame structures."[85]

Murray may have let his fellow business owners and residents off the hook by removing the cloud over their buildings, but he did not offer the same reprieve to the city. For local officials, the struggle continued. It took decades of legal rulings to break Murray's control over city rights-of-way.[86] The courts in 1902 finally accepted the city's argument that the streets in the central business district had been laid out before patents were filed on the Smokehouse and Arctic claims. Murray was a millionaire several times over by the time the city won its case and easily absorbed the loss of revenue from his earliest moneymaker.

Clipping the Blue Bird

Murray saw plenty of shysters and charlatans roll through Butte with piles of cash from outside investors. Of all of these hucksters, Ferdinand Van Zandt stood above the crowd, both literally and figuratively. Before storming into Butte, his story and image were captured in a Western novel, *The Led-Horse Claim,* by Mary Hallock Foote. This made Van Zandt interesting fodder for Murray, who put the young man through a wringer so tortuous that the man put a gun to his own head and ended his life.

Van Zandt was born in California to a mining family of mixed fortune. His father died when Ferdinand was just a young boy. Upon his father's death, his mother ferried him and his two siblings back to New York, where he was educated at the Staten Island Academy. When he was in his early twenties he headed back west to Leadville, Colorado, hoping to recapture the glory days of his father. He struggled with prospecting, barely making ends meet, until his charm and good looks rescued him from backbreaking work with a pick and pan. Van Zandt was offered a sales job wooing investors for an industrial-scale farm in Colorado. His new employer arranged for several letters of introduction and booked Van Zandt's passage to England to mine the pockets of the wealthy.

Van Zandt quickly found his marks abroad, collected their cash, and took in a stunning $100,000 commission for his work. During his travels he also found a titled wife, the daughter of world-famous scientist Sir John Lubbock, 4th Baronet, 1st Baron Avebury. When Van Zandt returned to the United States, he parlayed his commission and the bank account of his in-laws to break into the expensive business of hard-rock mining and stamp mills.[87] He enjoyed a good run at the beginning of his new venture and became a popular subject for newspaper and magazine articles. Then he met one of Murray's partners.

Van Zandt stumbled into Murray's treacherous circles in Butte with his purchase of the Blue Bird Mine and the construction of a world-class stamp mill to process his ore. Pat Largey, one of Murray's partners and confidants, and a millionaire in his own right, was invited by Van Zandt to the grand opening of his new mill.[88] Largey and Murray followed up with Van Zandt about his possible purchase of their adjoining claims. He seemed like someone who might pay a handsome price for their group of mines, the largest being the Little Darling.

Murray and Largey came to terms with Van Zandt and gave him a short-term option on their mines for a price of $123,000, but Van Zandt failed to close the deal.[89] This may have been the first sign that Van Zandt was not as flush with cash as press reports had led readers to believe. Of course, Van Zandt would have needed funding well beyond the purchase price of the mines. He also would have had to raise funds to operate the mine and his existing stamp mill. Mining operation expenses were not inconsequential. Even on the off days, pumps had to continue running to keep groundwater out of the shafts. It was not unusual to have days, weeks, and even months when expenses exceeded revenues. Van Zandt reportedly employed five hundred men in his operation,[90] indicating a payroll of $15,000 to $20,000 per day. A string of unproductive drifts or shafts could drain his accounts and doom his operation. Murray had eyes and ears on the ground all over Butte, and he picked up their whispers at saloons and dance halls. If Van Zandt faltered, Murray might be the first to know.

Two years after Van Zandt passed on the option to purchase Murray's Little Darling, Murray and Largey moved to develop the mines surrounding the Blue Bird. As they proceeded to extend a shaft two hundred feet into the ground, Van Zandt reemerged as a suitor for the property. This time he offered the pair $200,000. Murray, perhaps sensing something was amiss, refused the offer and continued developing the mine.[91] Soon he discovered a productive vein that peaked inside his claim and spread to the adjoining Blue Bird. Murray and Largey had the legal right, as all miners did, to chase the vein beyond their stake, as long as its apex was within their claim. When they reached the Blue Bird's boundary and discovered that Van Zandt had already excavated their ore, Murray quickly filed an injunction to halt Van Zandt's operations and filed a $2 million lawsuit to reclaim the value of his stolen ore.

As Murray filed the suit, he boasted of hiring a dream team of lawyers to seal Van Zandt's fate. He listed Colonel Robert Ingersoll and Senator William Stewart of Nevada, both men of national reputation, as his lead lawyers, perhaps hoping to bluff his opponent into a settlement.[92] Van Zandt did not acquiesce but soon felt the financial stress of lingering litigation and dwindling cash reserves. Murray was granted his injunction, cutting off Van Zandt's cash flow, while leaving him with the daily expense of pumping water out of his mine. Van Zandt also had to spend money on security to fend off scavengers looking for timbers to sell to other prospectors.

The case languished on the court calendar for more than a year before a trial date was set. Elaborate three-dimensional models were prepared to illustrate how the silver veins peaked and dipped underneath the ground, juxtaposed with intersecting shafts and drifts. The models clearly showed that Van Zandt had stolen Murray's silver.

Van Zandt attempted to have the injunction lifted prior to trial in one last attempt to salvage some value from his investment. He had more than $3 million sunk into the mine and was on the verge of bankruptcy. He pleaded for permission to work portions of his mine that did not intersect with Murray's property. Injunctive relief was denied, and Van Zandt was forced to make a deal with Murray.[93] Murray agreed to accept a fraction of what he'd asked for in his suit, taking his payment primarily in notes secured by the Blue Bird claim.[94] This would prove to be the first step in a process that wrested control of the Blue Bird from Van Zandt and placed it in Murray's hands.

Twelve months after Murray negotiated his settlement with Van Zandt, the Blue Bird was in financial ruins, and the handsome tenderfoot could no longer hold off his creditors.[95] Murray was waiting in the wings with his secondary loans, ready to seize the Blue Bird for himself. Typically, Murray would have negotiated a settlement with Van Zandt and his senior creditors, but Van Zandt never returned to Butte. He traveled to England to explain his impending bankruptcy to the friends and family who held a rich stake in his crippled company. There he found no favor and no money to bail out his cherished mine. After failing to inspire his investors, he returned to his London hotel, pulled out his revolver, turned it to his head, and pulled the trigger.

Murray moved quickly after Van Zandt's fatal decision to make a deal with the widow Van Zandt and her father, Sir John Lubbock.[96] He gave the widow one year to reconstitute the financial footing of the mine,[97] but with the Great Panic of 1893 and plummeting silver prices, she had no chance at retaining control. Murray waited patiently, and when the year was up he took control of the Blue Bird, let the mine flood, and tucked away the patent for a later day when silver prices and advancing technology would again justify its operation.

Stella Misstep

Murray's reputation as an obstructionist and litigator reached a zenith with his methodical acquisition of the Blue Bird. A careless mistake with his Stella claim, however, proved that he was fallible. The Stella was one of the claims Murray leased out to speculators. In 1892 it was netting his operators $1,000 a day, according to one report in a Salt Lake City newspaper. In 1893 Murray switched horses and leased the mine to newcomer

Augustus Heinze. Murray's lease arrangement claimed a royalty from Heinze's revenues if the ore from the mine was of a certain quality. Heinze, a quick learner, made sure he never had to pay a royalty by mixing his ore with the waste rock that was a by-product of his mining operations. Murray sued Heinze over the practice.

During the Stella trials, Murray did what all good businessmen of the time would do: he used illicit tactics to convince the jury that his opponent had done something illegal. In this case, Murray payed the foreman of Heinze's operation to testify that his boss was running a crooked operation. The jury, however, remained convinced that Heinze's operation was on the straight and narrow. In one particularly compelling cross-examination, Heinze's attorney dumped a pile of copper ore and rubble on the witness table and asked Murray's expert to sort the good from the bad. It was a brilliant, high-impact visual that illustrated the difficulty of sorting ore prior to processing, and it doomed Murray's case. Murray lost his first trial, and lost again on appeal. He sued again and lost. Eventually, after the state supreme court refused to hear his appeal, Murray conceded a rare defeat.

So rare was defeat for Murray in the courts, the case was widely reported. P. A. O'Farrell, editor of Heinze's newspaper, memorialized Heinze's victory over Murray in his book *Butte: Its Copper Mines and Copper Kings*, writing,

> Jim Murray was one of Montana's old-timers, who knew, and was known by everybody. He had acquired a dangerous reputation as a litigant. Had he lived in the days of Drake and Raleigh he would have been a buccaneer. Had he succeeded in ruining Heinze, he would have boasted of his success to the last day of his life. But Jim Murray pitted against Heinze, was completely outclassed.[98]

John Maguire defended his friend in the *Anaconda Standard*, exposing Heinze's questionable dealings in Canada and labeling O'Farrell a "parasite" and "coward who only needs courage to be an assassin."[99]

While O'Farrell and Maguire feuded over the reputations of their champions, Murray and Heinze dismissed the Stella episode and struck up a cordial relationship. Eventually the pair worked on a number of deals together. Murray admired Heinze's treachery and held no grudge that would interfere with his future profits.

More Trouble with Germans

Hard-rock mining was a dangerous way to make a living. After you stepped into a cage-like elevator, you were lowered hundreds, even thousands, of feet down dark shafts to tunnels where dynamite blasts inched crews of workers slowly into seams of silver or copper-laden rock. When workers had a day off, or a holiday to celebrate, they often turned to their explosives to liven up the party. Drinking and dynamite was a deadly combination, and July 4th was a day when the pair frequently joined together. From these tragedies came opportunity, however, and Murray was always circling to seize the treasures shaken loose by a celebration with casualties.

The Fourth of July in 1892 proved to be a profitable one for Murray. The series of events that enriched his bank account started with the charity of a small operator. Frederick Isele had leased his mostly played-out claim on Silver Bow Creek in Butte to a group of Chinese prospectors. Every day he would weigh their meager pinches of gold dust and take his cut. A couple of days prior to the Fourth, the results were so slim that he let the prospectors keep everything for themselves. He knew they would need all of their small bounty to join the celebration to come. When the holiday came, the prospectors arrived at Isele's small, dirt-roof cabin, about a mile and a half outside of town, with cigars and a bottle of Hostetter's bitters as a gift of appreciation. Isele and his party—John Zehntner, W. J. Schmidt, and John Streicher—were already enjoying a keg of beer and firing off explosive cartridges. The bitters, at 94 proof, likely accentuated their recklessness in the hours ahead. The group continued to light cartridges, blowing out the window of one of their neighbor's homes in the process.

After midnight, Zehntner retired while Isele and Streicher continued their revelry. At about 4 a.m., Isele and Streicher planned their grand finale. Isele shook Schmidt out of his slumber, urging him to get up for the last explosion, "We are going to cap three giant cartridges of powder and set them off all at once." Zehntner was in the bunk behind Schmidt, and Isele and Streicher were wiring the charges at a table just four feet away. The next thing Schmidt remembered was being dug out from what was left of the cabin, his face and hands bruised and seared. Witnesses from the small cluster of flimsy cabins surrounding the explosion pieced together the fatal event.[100]

Isele and Streicher's three-stick finale never made it outside the cabin. When they attempted to throw their concoction outside the door, something blocked its path and it ignited inside the cabin. The explosion ripped Isele's body apart and tore Streicher's eyeballs from their sockets. If either survived the explosion, the loss of blood that followed quickly sealed their fate. Zehntner is the only one who survived unscathed, as he was protected from the blast by Schmidt's body. Isele and Streicher were both single and natives of Germany—Isele from Baden and Streicher from Württemberg. Both owned productive claims that were now up for grabs, thousands of miles from the German relatives who would attempt to lay claim to their legacies.

Word of the dead men's treasures spread quickly in Butte. Murray was likely familiar with the holdings of both, as they had been in Butte ten or so years before Murray settled into the camp. Streicher's claims were quickly tied up by an administrator appointed by the courts to act on behalf of his heirs. Murray was in no rush to make an offer. The administrator placed ads in the local newspapers detailing Streicher's ownership percentages in each of the mines: a half interest in the Humboldt and Narrow Gauge claims; a third in the Elba, North Pole, and Tiger claims; and a quarter interest in the Corona claim. All remained on the market for two years, while producing a few thousand dollars in royalties that were collected by the administrator. In the meantime, thirty-seven of Streicher's relatives in Germany organized and waited patiently for their payday.

In 1894, Murray made his move. He had his trusted shill, Silas King, initiate contact with G. A. Kornberg, who held power of attorney for Streicher's relatives. Kornberg, the German vice counsel in Butte, came into his position by working through Adolph Rosenthal, the imperial German counsel in San Francisco. When King started discussions with Kornberg, the estate holdings included the mining interests and $9,000 in cash from prior royalties. Silas King offered $8,000 for all of the assets, which Kornberg accepted on behalf of the relatives. Word traveled quickly to Württemberg that the relatives had effectively paid Murray's shill $1,000 to take their fallen relative's estate. Distance likely kept the relatives from causing much of a stir, until word came from Butte that Murray had partnered with Kornberg to pull $150,000 in ore from the Elba and Narrow Gauge Mines. The relatives then retained James Forbis in Butte to right what he claimed was "the greatest fraud that was ever perpetrated in this community."

Murray managed to stretch the proceedings over several years, finally submitting to a deposition, seventy-eight pages long, to tell his side of the story. Murray admitted to being the money behind the transaction and to striking a deal with Kornberg to work the Streicher properties. Murray took none of the cash from Streicher bank accounts, instead leaving the money for Kornberg to acquire the interests of others who held shares in Streicher's claims. The Germans continued their pursuit of Murray for several more years, but twenty-four years after their relative blew himself up, and weary of Murray's perpetual legal maneuvering, they failed to respond to a filing and their case was quietly dismissed. The "greatest fraud," which had started with a bang, ended with a *seufzer* (sigh).

5
Riding the Rails

We were run after by real estate men, exploiters, and others from the time we arrived in the city until we departed.

—Member, Courthouse Site Selection Committee, Seattle

Butte's boom could not have been possible without the construction of rail lines to the city. Copper was a high-volume, low-value commodity and required inexpensive rail transportation to make mining and processing operations profitable. The first rail line to reach Butte, the Utah & Northern, came from Salt Lake City and was set to be completed on Christmas Day, 1881.[101] Murray was in Butte for the occasion and celebrated the impending arrival of Butte's first iron horse at Silas King's saloon. King was a close friend and business partner of Murray's from their Pioneer days,[102] so both knew that even a drink in a friendly saloon could quickly turn dangerous. Murray took a seat at the end of the bar, near King's safe, where he enjoyed a clear view of the saloon's dubious clientele.

Soon after Murray's arrival, two locals occupying the middle of the bar, Joe Campbell and "Bodie" Joe Ralls, erupted into a heated argument. Ralls backed away momentarily as a friend pulled him aside. When he returned and had more words with Campbell, apparently trying to make amends, the saloon fell to a hush. Ralls's words only infuriated Campbell. Sensing Campbell's rage, Ralls stepped back and reached for his revolver. The silenced crowd split as someone yelled, "He's going to shoot." Murray jumped behind the bar, where his friend King was already crouching. Bodie Joe fired once at Campbell, and then both men's pistols misfired. As Campbell moved to point-blank range, the crowd knocked out the two front doors in its rush to escape. Campbell reeled off five shots while Ralls returned fire. When the thick gun smoke cleared, Ralls lay on the floor mortally wounded. King and Murray surfaced from behind the bar, and after Ralls's body was carried away on one of King's doors, they continued their celebration.

A shootout at one of Butte's saloons caused little stir. It was business as usual for a town built on violence. One reporter wrote of the early days in Butte, "Every business man in Butte and every miner is a walking arsenal. He carries a brace or two of pistols in his belt and a bowie knife in his right boot."[103] The arrival of train service was the real news that day, and a common saloon shootout was not going to dampen anyone's excitement. Murray was eager to ride the rails and expand his empire. He'd spent seventeen years moving between mining camps in southwest Montana with a horse and wagon. Rail would allow him to extend his business empire to the far corners of the American West, Mexico, and Canada.

Between 1881 and 1887, new lines connected Butte with eastern Montana, Pocatello, Salt Lake City, Tacoma, Seattle, Arizona, San Diego, and Mexico.[104] Rail service also ushered in a new business to Butte: hack drivers and their carriages. The stagecoach delivered customers to a central point in town, but the rail depots were all located on the outskirts of the city. Murray's friend from the mining camps, Fat Jack, thought driving might be the business for him, so he took a loan from Murray to buy a team of horses and a carriage. Murray, in exchange, secured a guaranteed ride for his frequent trips to and from the depot. Fat Jack was diligent about paying off his loan at first, but in time found better uses for the money, and then lost interest in the business altogether. He turned over his horses and hack to Murray and made the trek to the Coeur d'Alene district in Idaho, where a gold rush was underway. Fortune did not smile on Fat Jack in Idaho, and he quickly returned to Murray's bank in Butte looking for a second chance. Murray obliged and provided Fat Jack with a previously owned carriage Murray had purchased in Salt Lake City.

Early reports indicate that the prior owner of Fat Jack's fine rockaway was a judge, but over time the story stretched until Murray claimed its lineage started with Brigham Young himself. Fat Jack made the most of his second chance, eventually becoming ingrained in the history of the Northwest. Through the turn of the century he drove every famous businessman, politician, and entertainer that rode the rails into Butte. Political cartoonist Homer Davenport used Jack's image to prove the authenticity of anyone claiming an association with Butte. He would draw a picture of Fat Jack and ask the claimant to identify him. Anyone who had lived in Butte knew Fat Jack.

Murray's new circuit was initially limited to Pocatello and Salt Lake City to the south, and Seattle and Tacoma to the west. He was patient in his search for promising opportunities, and a significant expansion of his business empire did not occur until the 1890s. When he made the move, he needed more partners and employees to cover the new territory. For help in the Northwest, he turned to two nephews and a niece. James E., Marcus, and May came to Butte from Canada in 1897 with their mother after their father, Andrew, passed away. Murray put Andrew's children through college and placed them in operations in Pocatello, Salt Lake City, Seattle, Tacoma, and Butte. A third nephew, Alex, was a late arrival and succeeded Marcus in Pocatello, long after operations in that city were established. Alex, from

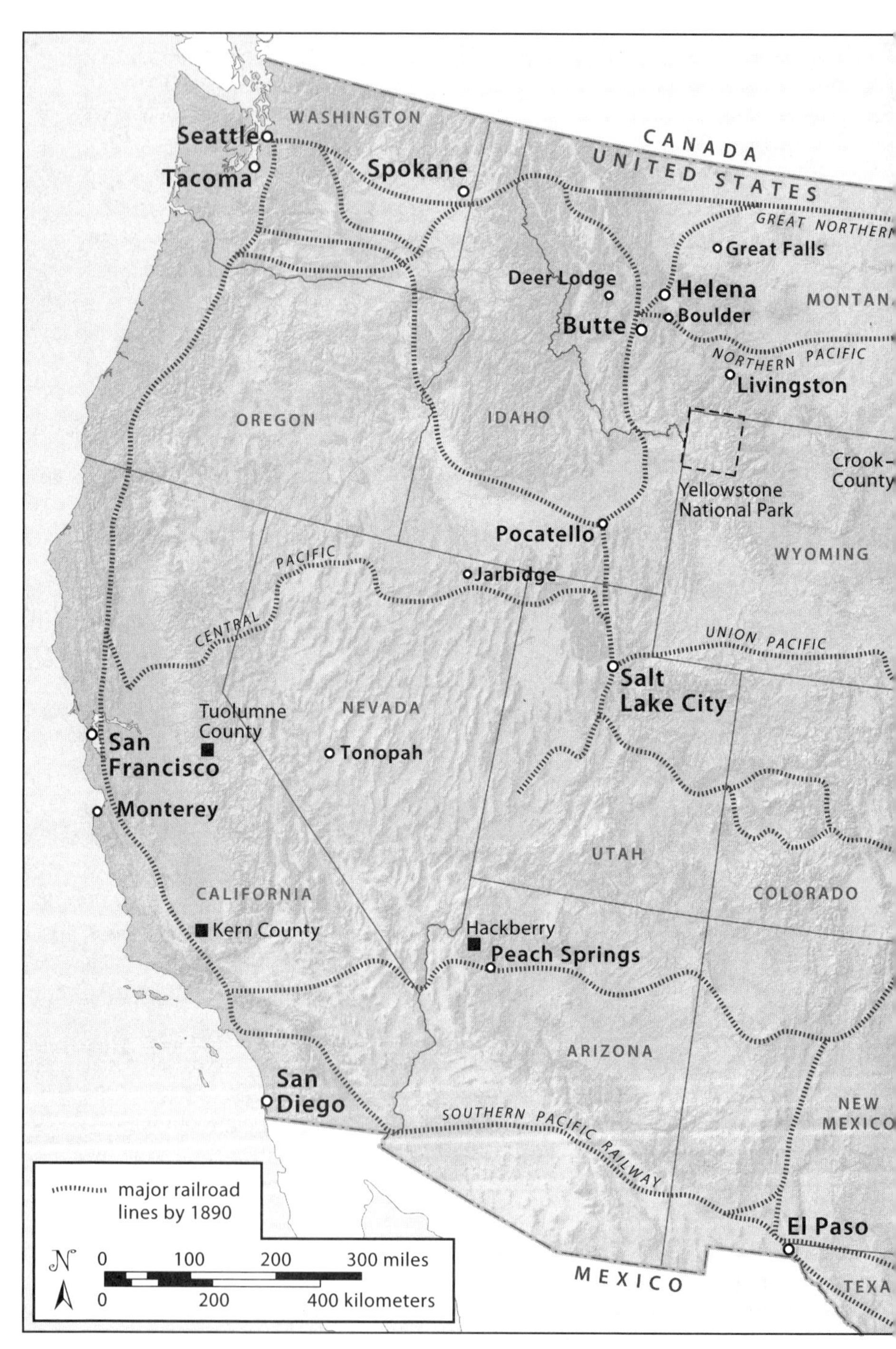
WASHINGTON
CANADA
UNITED STATES
Seattle
Tacoma
Spokane
GREAT NORTHERN
Great Falls
Deer Lodge
Helena
Boulder
Butte
MONTANA
NORTHERN PACIFIC
Livingston
OREGON
IDAHO
Crook County
Yellowstone National Park
Pocatello
WYOMING
CENTRAL PACIFIC
Jarbidge
UNION PACIFIC
Salt Lake City
NEVADA
Tuolumne County
Tonopah
San Francisco
Monterey
UTAH
CALIFORNIA
COLORADO
Kern County
Hackberry
Peach Springs
ARIZONA
San Diego
NEW MEXICO
SOUTHERN PACIFIC RAILWAY
major railroad lines by 1890
0 100 200 300 miles
0 200 400 kilometers
El Paso
MEXICO
TEXAS

Properties of James A. Murray

ARIZONA	
Hackberry	Mines
CALIFORNIA	
Kern County	Eucalyptus tree farm (D. B. A. Idaho Hardwood Company)
Monterey	Residence, land, newspaper, monument to Junípero Serra*
San Diego	Water company, land, office buildings, Murray Dam and Lake*
Tuolumne Co.	Mines
IDAHO	
Pocatello	Water company, newspaper, First National and First Savings Banks, theater
MONTANA	
Blackfoot City	Mines
Boulder	Resort (Boulder Hot Springs)*
Butte	Residence*, mining, private bank at NW corner of Copper and Main*, theater, office buildings, land, Clark Chateau*
Deer Lodge	Residence, private bank
Emmetsburg	Mines, Monument to Pioneers*
Great Falls	Theater, land
Helena	Broadwater Hotel and Natatorium
Livingston	Hunter's Hot Springs resort, water company, First State Bank, Murray Hotel (acquired through foreclosure by niece after Murray's passing)*
Philipsburg	Mines
Pioneer	Residence, mines, water company, general store, saloon
NEVADA	
Jarbidge	Mines
Tonopah	Mines
UTAH	
Salt Lake City	National Bank of the Republic, mines
WASHINGTON	
Seattle	American Savings Bank & Trust Co., land, office buildings
Tacoma	Banker's Trust Company, theater, office building
WYOMING	
Crook County	Oil wells

* Still standing

Murray's business empire spanned the entire American West and parts of Mexico.

Pennsylvania, was the son of Thomas, who was born in Canada after the other Murray boys arrived from Ireland. To supplement his family, Murray took in partners for his more complex ventures. Among these partners (and their locations) were George Winter in Pocatello, Frank Knox[105] in Salt Lake City, Gus Holmes[106] in Salt Lake City and Arizona, Jim Gleason[107] in Seattle, and Ed Fletcher[108] in San Diego.

One family member who would not be part of Murray's expanding team, however, was his wife. One of Murray's first stops on his rail travels was Las Vegas, New Mexico, where he filed for divorce from Sallie.[109] By all accounts, it was an amicable separation. Murray continued to employ Sallie's son at his bank and use her brother as a shill, and when Sallie remarried, he provided her with a generous wedding gift (a partial interest in the Blackfoot Mine).[110]

Pocatello, Idaho

Pocatello, a former trading post, was the first town on Murray's new circuit. It was a convenient stop on the way to Salt Lake City and connection to the transcontinental railroad, and the cash-strapped town needed a private capitalist to fund its water enterprise. Murray joined with two locals, F. D. Toms and J. J. Cusick, to bid on the franchise. The team bested the competition and was awarded the contract in 1892. As soon as construction began, Murray took action to oust his local partners. First on the list was the initial president of the water company, F. D. Toms.

Murray placed pressure on Toms to resign by withholding a cash deposit necessary to pay construction crews. Murray delayed his contribution by three months, leaving crews to sell their future paychecks for seventy-five cents on the dollar to a local saloon keeper. When that money was gone, workers appeared before the city council asking for food. The city obliged and fed the workers for several days. Murray struck the final blow by letting the workers know that his funding, and their paychecks, were contingent on Toms's resignation. The workers quickly turned on Toms, threatening a lynching if he did not resign. They even purchased a rope and set up a gallows using a chimney at the waterworks. Cusick was able to talk the vigilantes out of their plan, and instead arranged a meeting between Toms and a committee of workers. The meeting resulted in Toms resigning and transferring his shares to Murray. Murray took over the presidency and promptly settled all debts. He added Silas King to the board of directors to solidify his control of the company.

Now in complete charge of the water company, Murray employed an engineer, George Winter, to run the enterprise. Water service during the company's first few years of operations was barely passable until Winter completed construction of reservoirs to boost water pressure and system reliability. The expanded system was critical to provide fire protection for a Main Street packed with wood-framed structures. After the initial capital outlay, however, Murray tightened the purse strings on the operation to maximize his profits. In 1897, with new residents placing additional pressure on the system, Winter instituted restrictions on water used to dampen the dusty streets in town. City businesses responded to the restriction by rallying support for higher water rates and another round of capital improvements to expand the capacity of the system.

Pocatello had great promise, so Murray expanded his holdings. He sent his nephew Marcus to the city to oversee a newspaper Murray started to promote his interests in town, a bank to profit on development spurred by his waterworks, and a theater to build goodwill among community members and politicians.

In 1902, development pressure in Pocatello increased dramatically as thousands of acres were removed from the adjacent Fort Hall Reservation. Stress caused by population growth, economic development, and the need for water continued to increase. To help calm public discontent with his handling of the water system, Murray enlisted the support of D. W. Stanrod, a prominent judge in the area, and one of the first appointees to the Idaho Public Utilities Commission—a body that would adopt many new rules to control Murray's self-serving practices. Murray appointed Stanrod to the boards of directors of both the water company and Murray's local bank.

Stanrod's political connections, however, could accomplish only so much. It was left to Winter to use his commanding presence and stubbornness to fend off public demands. At one point, in 1911, Winter turned to his rifle to protect Murray's interest. J. M. Bistline, the mayor during part of Murray's reign as water czar, described the incident to Dr. Minnie Howard, a Pocatello historian:

> The water system at that time was a bone of contention. The franchise was owned by a millionaire Irishman of Butte, and his superintendent was an Englishman, George Winter, with a bull dog disposition. It was the first time I ever knew that an Irishman could tell an Englishman what to do and make him do it. It is usually the other way around.
>
> Murray seemed to bear Pocatello a grudge, and took pleasure in paying it off by having Winter make it miserable for the water users. The system was inadequate and kept the city from growing. He was in bad with every administration from the beginning, but really came to a climax in 1911. The city started a suit against the Water Company, and the legal papers placed in the hands of the Sheriff for service. A deputy, Jim Francis and Chief Ellis, went up to the upper reservoir to serve the papers and were forbidden by him to enter the grounds. The officers entered, and Mr. Winters fired a Winchester at them.

> That was the beginning of the end of the Winter regime.
>
> The officers came to the city and reported what had happened. There never was such a wave of indignation before or since. The news spread like wildfire. The people had taken enough from this bull headed John Bull. There was a movement from all over the city in the direction of the reservoir, many carrying rifles. I can still see Billy Trapp, a councilman, with his Winchester on his shoulder marching down Center Street. Billy was the kind who would use it. Hundreds of people joined in the march up the hill. The sight of such determined men awed Captain Winter, and he surrendered to the officers and was marched down the hill to Doc Snodgrass' auto and headed for the jail. At the Halliday subway a crowd had gathered and stopped the procession, and for a time it looked like a necktie party was in the making. While parleying, a shot was fired and it sounded as if hell had broken loose, but not as bad as that, as only a tire had been shot off.
>
> The officers' advice prevailed, and the procession headed for the Court House and jail. He was a badly scared man and was very thankful for the chance to break into jail. Even in jail he was not welcome by the inmates, as they promptly Kangarooed him for breaking in without their consent. The Kangaroo Court found him guilty, and he paid a liberal fine. He spent Murray's money freely, and became quite popular with the prisoners.

Mayor Bistline concluded his remarks about Winter, who was by then deceased: "It is my earnest hope that he may be occupying a high seat in Glory where water is not needed to quench a parched tongue. I also hope that he does not attempt to take charge."[111]

The struggle between Pocatello and Murray moved to the courts for several years after Winter fired his warning shots. The city won some cases but Murray won most. The city won the right to institute a rate commission, but Murray won the right to stack its membership to his liking. Murray brought in his nephew Alex, son of brother Thomas, to serve as a peacekeeper and replace Marcus. That bought Murray a few more years of precious cash flow. But like all encounters Murray had with local governments, the relationship was destined to get worse before the inevitable, messy divorce.

Salt Lake City, Utah

The next closest city to Butte on Murray's new circuit was Salt Lake City. He made a big splash in the city in 1897, backing $125,000 in downtown real estate loans. His borrower was prominent businessman Gus Holmes. Murray took a liking to Holmes, who served on the board of a Salt Lake City–based bank, the National Bank of the Republic. Two years later, Murray purchased property of his own in the central business district, buying a parcel at the corner of State and Fourth Streets. He immediately transferred the parcel to his nephew Marcus, who was still in Pocatello at the time (Murray enacted a dizzying number of property transfers among his shills, many times to avoid paying taxes).

After the turn of the century, Murray bought a sizable stake in the National Bank of the Republic. His purchase came with new restrictions on the bank's stock to protect his ownership position, along with a position on the board and the title of vice president. Murray transferred his nephew Marcus from Pocatello to work as a cashier in the Salt Lake City bank and watch after Murray's interests. There is no indication that Murray continued to invest in Utah, but with his frequent travels to the strategic city—Salt Lake City was the region's hub for rail transportation—he certainly gained intelligence about happenings throughout the West.

Fellow bank board members Frank Knox (president), John S. Phipps, and US Senator Thomas Kearns were important additions to Murray's business network. Knox was an accomplished banker and connected to every major initiative in Salt Lake City. Phipps was the son of a Pittsburgh millionaire and eventually sat on the boards of US Steel, Hanover Bank, and W. R. Grace and Company. Senator Kearns represented Utah between 1901 and 1905 and touted close relationships with presidents McKinley, Roosevelt, and Taft.

Murray must have gained important insights from his relationship with Knox, because many years later (1910), in a rare display of public appreciation, he gave Knox a custom Stevens-Duryea automobile. The press reported that the car had forty-six horsepower, could make better than a mile a minute, and was beautifully appointed with a rich wine-colored exterior. Before Murray's purchase of the car, it had been exhibited in New York and San Francisco. With the novelty of automobiles still strong in 1910, the gift was a significant status symbol for Knox to enjoy.[112]

Seattle, Washington

Turning to the west, Murray's next out-of-state investments landed in Seattle, at the terminus of the Northern Pacific Railway. Between 1899 and 1901, Murray acquired several lots in Seattle's central business district, spurred by the impending site selection for a new federal building. Along with a number of landowners, Murray entertained the selection committee often, leading one committee member to remark, "We were run after by real estate men, exploiters, and others from the time we arrived in the city until we departed."[113] As the committee focused its attention on locations along Third Avenue between Jefferson and Pike,[114] Murray purchased properties strategically, acquiring at least six sites along Third Avenue near several key intersections.[115] When federal officials unexpectedly selected a site on the southeast corner of Third and Union,[116] across from two of

Murray's properties, rumors circulated that he had unfairly influenced the selection process. Regardless, the new federal building was an undeniable boon to his portfolio. Every one of Murray's Seattle properties soon increased in value.

Murray preferred to have a banking interest in every community that was part of his business empire. In Seattle, he followed the same path he had taken in Salt Lake City, acquiring a stake in an existing bank. However, in this case his infusion of cash was sufficient to give him the title of president. The American Savings Bank had only $25,000 in assets before Murray and fellow Irishman Robert Tobin joined forces to bolster the institution's balance sheet, adding $175,000 in cash. The newly capitalized bank opened in a storefront at Second Avenue and Madison but soon moved into a high-rise built on a parcel at the same intersection. It was the second high-rise building in Seattle to be framed with concrete and steel, and it was featured prominently in promotional material for the city's Alaska-Yukon-Pacific Exposition in 1909. A gateway arch to the city was constructed adjacent to the bank's new building for the exposition.[117]

The board of directors for the revamped financial institution included Murray, several Seattle business owners, and Tobin, from San Francisco. Tobin was a founder of the distinctly Irish Hibernian Savings and Loan Society in the Bay Area. Murray installed W. V. Lawler, from Butte, as the head cashier. Murray's niece May Murray, a graduate of the University of Washington, also joined the bank as an employee. Marcus Murray, bouncing around many of his uncle's banks, joined his sister in the Emerald City in 1902 to handle his uncle's vast real estate holdings in the central business district.

The real estate side of Murray's business in Seattle was conducted in fits and starts, and it was characterized by the bluster and obstructionism common to his dealings in other parts of the country. Many of the properties he purchased were placed in his brother Timothy's name. After Timothy died, the properties shifted to Marcus, May, and James. All of these maneuvers made it difficult for outsiders to track which properties Murray held. Murray made the claim that he owned $3 million in Seattle property, but judging by various press reports, it appears the number may have been closer to $1 million—still a sizable stake in a city that he admired greatly due to its port and rail facilities.

Murray generated income from his Seattle real estate in a number of ways. He constructed his own buildings, sold parcels, and leased land on long-term arrangements. Two of his leased parcels were occupied by iconic buildings: the Arctic Building, adorned with numerous walrus heads, and the Vance Building, an excellent example of art deco architecture.[118] Both buildings remain standing today. Murray's own buildings included a modest low-rise office building, the Liberty Building, and a collection of hovels

Murray's American Saving Bank and Trust Company in the Seattle central business district, circa 1910. —Postcard from author's personal collection

unfit for humans. Murray-owned shacks at the corner of Third and Union included a saloon, a rooming house, and a laundry. The city's health commissioner, Dr. Crichton, issued a condemnation order for the lot, writing, "This is one of the worst places I ever saw." Boarders had to carry water to their rooms in pails because Murray would not repair the plumbing.[119]

Murray's first ten years in Seattle were extremely productive on the real estate front, but his control over the American Savings Bank slowly eroded, resulting in his ouster as bank president. Murray, as usual, did not go quietly. Just prior to his ouster, he filed a lawsuit to obtain bank records he believed would show improprieties by the rebellious faction. When he was voted out, he made a statement to the press so deposit holders would know he was no longer in charge. Fourteen months later he got even, organizing a syndicate to buy a majority of the bank stock and reinstall himself as the bank president.[120]

6
The Liveliest Town in America

On its crest the winches whine of millions in dividends. Under it 16,000 miners burrow out the precious copper, zinc, gold and silver. Digging the "tunnels of Babel!" And between catacomb and derrick lies ugly, romantic old Butte, once uncouth camp, now probably the most affluent little city in world and mother of millionaires galor.

—Jack Jungmeyer[121]

After extended trips to the far reaches of his new empire, Murray was always happy to be back in Butte and carouse with good friends, pick fights with old enemies, and on occasion, take part in the local court room theater. Butte changed mightily during the copper boom days. The town hosted as many as two hundred saloons in 1891, leading the *Denver Sun* to proclaim the mining camp the "Liveliest Town in America." With inspired names like Bucket of Blood, Graveyard, the Cesspool, Open-All-Night, and Pay Day, the saloon scene captured the imagination of readers throughout the West.[122] The presence of vigilante committees, organized to capture capital offenders, only added to Butte's Western charm. During one organized manhunt, the press reported that the hills next to Butte were "black with people" swarming over catacombs of abandoned mine shafts, ready to mete out immediate justice if the "cold blooded fiends" were captured.[123]

Murray did not have to sully himself with the masses when he returned to Butte. He and the rest of the well-heeled crowd could revel above the fray if they chose. The Silver Bow Club offered members-only accommodations on par with the best clubs in Chicago or New York. J. P. Morgan and George Hearst could be found at the Silver Bow when they were in town. Murray bent his elbow at the club as well, but he chose to spend most of his time making the rounds in the saloons, noodle houses, and hotel lobbies; playing freeze-out with Barney Lavelle, the town jailer, making proposition bets with Jack Enright, a professional gambler; and catching up with Fat Jack.

As Murray bounced around town, reporters were always anxious to catch the colorful multimillionaire for a quote or two. During December of

1900, a reporter from the *Anaconda Standard* caught Murray in his office and asked about a photograph that had come into the paper's possession.[124a] It was a portrait of Murray, sitting at a desk in a high-backed chair. On the back of the picture, Murray had written, "Ambition–A desire to live in the imagination of other people." Murray's reply gave the reporter insight into why a tycoon still wandered the dusty, smoke-choked streets of the dangerous city. Murray told the reporter of his disdain for ambition and asked rhetorically, "What are we all battling for anyway? Death is the sure winner and few there are who care much about you or remember you for long after Death has conquered you." He went on to say that he esteemed "more highly the few real friends I have than all the money I have or ever hoped to have." And Murray's friends from his early days in Pioneer and Deer Lodge were not holed up at the Silver Bow.

Another reporter, this one from the *Butte Inter Mountain*, wrote a story about Murray five months later, capturing the same type of humility. On May 6, 1901, Murray sat down by himself at a Butte café for breakfast. He ordered a batch of graveyard stew (milk and toast). The waiter knew the wealthy pioneer and struck up a conversation about the latest buzz about town. "Northern Pacific stocks are a little restless right now. They've jumped to $700 a share. You haven't got any of that stock have you Mr. Murray?" Murray replied that in fact he'd held a substantial sum, 1,000 shares in all, for several years. The waiter commented that the stock had started at $170 that morning, meaning Murray had cleared more than $500,000 in the run-up. He offered Murray a chance to celebrate his winnings with some of the diner's finer fare. As he set the table for Murray with a knife, fork, and spoon, the waiter suggested an upgrade to Murray's order of milk and toast: "We have some nice strawberries, some shad roe, and a crate of nice vegetables." Murray stood pat with his two-bit meal. "I don't want anything but that bread and milk and I don't want a knife and fork to eat it with. Take 'em away," chided the multimillionaire. The waiter cleared the place setting, save the spoon, and informed him the stock was now at $1,000 a share. Murray showed no emotion and waited patiently for his meal. When it arrived he ate slowly, with no apparent interest in cashing in his latest fortune. After his meal, he picked his worn hat off the rack and was about to leave when the waiter interrupted once more, telling the tycoon, "You have made a million dollars since you got up this morning." Murray was quick to retort, "I never mind a little thing like that. I made a million once before and it got away from me because I felt too good over it."[124b]

Reporters could also count on finding Murray at one of his regular hangouts, McGovern's saloon on Main Street, just four blocks down the hill from his bank building and apartment. It was a civil place, quieter than most, where you could have a conversation without concern that a gunfight would break out.[125] The owner, James McGovern, had operated at this location since 1883.[126] On one occasion Murray found his good friend Lavelle organizing a game of freeze-out. McGovern brought out some chips, took the gentlemen's cash, and the game began. Murray enjoyed a nice run, primarily due to his special deck of marked cards. Then he made a mistake. Murray turned away from the table for a moment to discuss a business arrangement with someone. Lavelle seized the opportunity. He quietly lifted Murray's deck and pulled out two aces to complement the two he already held. Murray turned back to play out the hand. Lavelle ran up the pot, much to Murray's delight. When the cards turned over, Lavelle revealed his four aces. Murray was incensed. "You're crooked! That ain't the hand I dealt you!"[127]

Mixing with his friends in Butte at street level meant Murray eventually crossed the men he bested with his legal maneuverings or underground thievery. Sam Sumwalt went looking for Murray one day and found his nemesis on Main Street. He accused Murray of jumping a claim he'd held for eleven years. Sumwalt certainly fit the profile of a Murray victim. He was an independent miner who owned a claim next to one of Murray's, and he did not have the means to actively work his property. Murray routinely crushed miners like Sumwalt in court, or by taking ore from the veins they could never afford to reach. In the heated exchange that followed, police were drawn to the scene. Murray, sixty-one at the time, threw a punch at the irate prospector but failed to drop him. Sumwalt drew his pistol and figured he could settle the dispute right there. As he raised his revolver, a police officer caught his arm just in time to spare Murray's life. As police escorted Sumwalt to the city jail, he shouted one final threat, "You will have to go to the graveyard or I will!" [128]

Sparkling and Vivacious

On one of Murray's return trips to Butte he came with a blockbuster announcement. During a trip back east, he had married for the second time—this time to the ex-wife of his most tortured lawyer.

Murray tied the knot with two-time divorcée Mary Coulter Haldorn on June 1, 1896, in Chicago.[129] Mary, twenty years Jim's junior, recently had divorced her second husband, George Haldorn. Mary was married for fifteen years to the local divorce-attorney-turned-passable mining expert. The two had a son together, Stuart Haldorn, who was ten years old on the day of Mary's wedding to Jim. Mary was described by the press as "sparkling, vivacious and pretty." The marriage to Mary marked the beginning of a transition for Murray's Butte operations. Mary was not interested in spending Murray's money in a glorified mining camp, where smelters dominated the skyline and belched thick, blinding smoke around the clock. Murray had a team of young relatives coming of age that could manage his

Mary Murray in 1906 appearing in Automobile Topics, *a national automobile publication.* —From the Collection of the Henry Ford (37.825.4/THF134350)

collection of cronies, lawsuits, and mining patents in the Copper City, and Mary was set on finding a new home. But first, her current husband and her second "ex" had to settle their score.

George Haldorn's animosity for Murray had built over many years, for both professional and personal reasons. Professionally, Murray took advantage of Haldorn's ardent desire to break into mining law. Murray promised Haldorn great riches in return for free legal advice or deferred billings, but in the end, all Haldorn received was a personal loan from Murray with a sky-high interest rate of 15 percent per year. On a personal level, the timing of Murray's courtship of Haldorn's ex-wife raised questions. Murray, traveling alone, had accompanied George and Mary on a cruise to Alaska a few years before the couple split.[130] It is not unreasonable to imagine this is where the romance began. Murray had a predilection for married women, a fact that came out during testimony in a trial where he sued ex-lover Emma Wallace. Wallace testified that Murray often boasted of his "great hankering for married women."[131]

Scorched by Murray professionally and perhaps personally, George Haldorn would certainly have been within his rights to file a lawsuit against Murray for all his broken promises—if nothing else, in retaliation for marrying his ex-wife. Instead, it was Murray who struck first, suing Haldorn for nonpayment of the $6,000 personal loan he had extended to his lawyer after receiving free legal advice. Murray went even further and attached Haldorn's house as security. Haldorn countersued for all his unpaid services, and the trial that followed revealed the many ways Murray extracted free time and services from his legal advisers.

Haldorn's countersuit against Murray totaled $22,000 and represented work on forty-five cases over a six-year period prior to his divorce from Mary in 1895. Perhaps not coincidently, Haldorn stopped representing Murray after he divorced Mary. Haldorn's reason for cutting ties with his client was that "certain matters occurred and I ceased to act as his attorney"—perhaps another indicator that Murray's hankerings extended to Haldorn's wife.[132]

Most of the forty-five cases that Haldorn recounted involved matters already known to the public, but in a few instances Haldorn revealed new information and an inside look at how a multimillionaire spends his time and energy. The most dramatic of these insights regarded Murray's obsession with finding the murderer of his friend and political ally William Penrose (see chapter 8), and his interest in buying juror votes in the Stella suit against Augustus Heinze. Murray met with Haldorn nightly, out of public view, to get daily updates on the hunt for Penrose's murderers. Murray was suspicious of the role labor union bosses played in the murder. Haldorn also explored potential financial relationships with jurors in the

Heinze case, but in the end Murray was not interested in providing the necessary payoff, settling instead on bribing a technical witness.

Other cases were less spectacular but nonetheless revealing. Haldorn represented Murray in a claim against a horseman who failed to deliver two horses, named Montana and Nevada, to the 1893 World's Fair in Chicago. Murray had planned to use the horses to fix a race and lost the opportunity to win a sure thing in their absence. Murray also used Haldorn to bluff one of his mine operators into making $18,000 in payments on a lease for the Stella when no payments were due. And regarding one of the few cases for which Haldorn received any compensation, he told the jury he billed Murray $1,500 after spending two months preparing a case that eventually was settled. Murray paid $50, or, in Haldorn's words, "less than swampers' wages in a saloon."

Haldorn was not proud of his role in handling Murray's sordid affairs but nevertheless felt he should be paid. The jury, choosing between a crooked millionaire and an attorney with no moral compass, sided with the attorney. The attachment to Haldorn's house was removed, and he was awarded $10,000 ($4,000 more than the note he owed Murray). Unfortunately for Haldorn, the verdict was subject to appeal, and Murray rarely dropped a case before his last appeal. In this case, the appeal process lasted more than sixteen years and twice rose to the Montana Supreme Court. In the end, the highest court in the state vacated Haldorn's award.[133]

Crazy Doc Larkin

Murray was a regular in the Butte courtrooms. Most cases of his were mundane affairs mired in complex contracts. On one occasion, however, Murray had an opportunity to add some levity to a proceeding where he was neither plaintiff nor defendant. The case involved an old nemesis, James "Doc" Larkin, a longtime prospector in the Montana Territory. In 1896, during the twilight of his career, Doc was committed to an insane asylum. He died there three years later.[134] Prior to being committed, Doc had sold a partial interest in two mines to the B&M Company. After his death, his heirs tried to sell the remaining interest to Augustus Heinze. But Heinze did not want a partner—especially the B&M Company. B&M was selling all its mining interests to groups tied to the Rockefellers, and Heinze did not want to end up with the Rockefellers as partners. The feeling was mutual. The Rockefellers wanted to control all the mining interests in Montana, and they would drive out any partner who had an interest in their holdings. The only way Heinze could work these two mines was to own them outright—and to do that he had to get the court to cancel Doc's sale to B&M.[135] The court battle over Doc's mental state at the time of the sale was considered the biggest trial in the history of the Northwest at the time.[136] The trial lasted four months, involved 215 witnesses, and generated more than four thousand pages of testimony.

Witness after witness told of crazy dealings they'd had with Doc. Some thought his mental state had begun to suffer when he took a hoisting bucket to the head in a Nevada mineshaft. Things seemed to get even worse after he shot and killed a man in a fight over water rights in German Gulch. There was no shortage of testimony about his erratic behavior, constant drunkenness, and penchant for going to blows. With this combination of craziness and potentially valuable mining permits, it was just a matter of time before Murray became entwined in the arguments.

James O'Brien, a local bartender, told the jury that Larkin had "a habit of carrying things to eat, ham bones, bread, etc., loose in his pocket, and would ask him to have lunch with him." Another witness, James W. Murphy, finally brought Murray into the fray. Murphy recalled a conversation with Larkin about Murray. Doc felt strongly that Murray was one of several people trying to cheat him out of his property. He was probably right. Murray, a partner of Heinze and an enemy to Rockefeller, was called to tell about the time he foreclosed on Doc in the early 1890s. When Murray arrived to testify, he found a packed courtroom. Previous news reports of testimony detailing Doc's crazy antics certainly contributed to interest in the trial. Murray took the stand and was sworn in by the clerk.

Heinze's attorney started the questioning: "Was Larkin competent to attend to business affairs from 1890 to 1893?"

"Well I would not have entrusted to him any of my business affairs," Murray responded.

Another attorney for the plaintiff, Mr. Forbes, followed up: "Would you foreclose a mortgage on a man who did not know what he was doing?"

"Well, I'm not in the habit of running around the country protecting men," Murray replied. The jury likely took that as a yes.

Forbes asked directly, "Do you think Larkin was sane enough to have papers served on him?"

Murray thought for a moment and responded, "I think he knew enough to go into the house out of the rain."

After a few more questions, Murray turned to the stenographer and asked, "Are you getting all of this foolishness down?"

As Murray stepped down from the stand, one of the attorneys stopped him. "Hold it just one moment Mr. Murray. I forgot one question. Were you ever in the employ of Mr. Heinze?"

To this Murray replied, "I worked for him for a time," referring to his Stella misstep, "but at present I am not in his employ."[137]

Murray's humorous testimony brought a smile to the observers in the courtroom but did nothing to tip the scales in Heinze's favor. Heinze eventually lost the case and his appeal. It was a rare loss for Heinze and a big setback for independent mine owners in Montana.

Fat Jack's Fame

Murray's trips to and from Butte almost always started and ended with a carriage ride from Fat Jack. While in town, Murray and Fat Jack, far removed from their pranks in Pioneer, continued to generate comical news for the press. A young Jack Jungmeyer, years from gaining fame as a movie critic and publicist for Walt Disney, captured one of the most-often-told stories from their days in Butte.

Fat Jack carried his love of faro from Pioneer and Philipsburg to Butte. During a difficult run at the tables he turned to his best customer for a short-term loan. Since Murray already held a note on his hack and horse, Fat Jack offered up his false teeth as collateral for a few chips. Murray obliged and Fat Jack quickly lost the money. Jungmeyer picks up the story a few days later with Fat Jack mumbling a request to Murray for special consideration: "Shay Jim, for goonish shakes, lemme have my teef back again; jush lemme borrow 'em for an hour or two. I can't eat a blame shing, and I'm shtarving to deash!" The heartless Murray roared back, "Aw go on! Eat soup if you must eat!" Jungmeyer reported that it took two weeks for Fat Jack to pay off the loan and return to solid food.

Jungmeyer also praised Fat Jack for his stature in Western lore, dubbing him "the most famous Jehu of the West." Fat Jack's celebrity came from ferrying the most famous and powerful people though the wealthy metropolis, and the most famous of these trips was in 1903 and involved a sitting president, Teddy Roosevelt.

Fat Jack had given Teddy a ride or two when he was Governor Roosevelt and a vice presidential running mate with William McKinley. The crowds on the streets were enthusiastic, but the boys working in the mines below were firmly in William Jennings Bryan's camp those years.[138] Fat Jack was thrilled to be selected for the honor of driving Roosevelt around town for his 1903 visit. He bought a new $15 persuader[139] and practiced driving the rough road between town and the Columbia Gardens, where President Roosevelt would give a speech. Fat Jack committed to memory every rock and divot along the route to make sure the president had a good ride.[140]

The city was also prepared for Roosevelt's visit. Red, white, and blue bunting decorated every building. City officials braced for huge crowds. The railroads offered special fares and extra trains to get residents from nearby communities to the festivities. The local papers published the president's schedule for everyone to see. He would arrive at 3:43 p.m. at the train depot. The procession through town would start at 3:55 p.m. He would give a speech from a temporary balcony at the Finlen Hotel at 5 p.m. Following his speech, the president would dine at the Thornton Hotel at 6 p.m. At 7 p.m. he would travel from the Thornton to the Columbia Gardens to meet with labor officials and miners, and then return to the train station at 9:15 p.m. Fat Jack would be his transportation to the Finlen, the gardens, and back to the train depot.[141] On the day of the president's arrival, the crowd swelled along the procession route. Every balcony and rooftop was filled with spectators. A few adventurous souls sat atop telephone poles to get a good view.

Fat Jack was ready.

The president's train arrived ten minutes early. This gave the president extra time to meet with and greet local dignitaries and old friends John Willis and Seth Bullock. When Roosevelt was ready to proceed, Fat Jack opened the door to his carriage and was greeted with a warm smile from the president. Fat Jack beamed with pride that the president remembered him from his last trip to Butte. Fat Jack mounted the driver's seat and used his brand-new whip to guide the horses into a slow walk up Main Street. There were thousands of people waiting to see the president. Fat Jack would give them a good look that day.

Fat Jack ready to drive President Roosevelt (second from right). —Smithers.32.056.04, C. Owens Smithers Photo Collection, Butte-Silver Bow Public Archives

With Seth Bullock riding next to the rear wheel of the carriage, Fat Jack drove the president through the throngs of well-wishers. The Butte Police Department had forty officers on duty that afternoon, and the president's secret service detail kept a keen eye on the crowd. McKinley's assassination had everyone, including the president, conscious of potential troublemakers. Ropes kept the crowds off the street, but as Roosevelt passed the lines were broken and the masses followed the president on his trip up the hill.

Roosevelt later shared his thoughts on the ride in a letter to his secretary of state:

> The ordinary procession in barouches was rather more exhilarating than usual and reduced the faithful secret service men very nearly to the condition of Bedlamites. The crowd was filled with whooping enthusiasm and every kind of whiskey, and in their desire to be sociable broke the lines and jammed right up to the carriage.[142]

After a couple of short stops to visit with schoolchildren and accept souvenirs, Fat Jack delivered the president to the Finlen Hotel. Roosevelt proceeded to a temporary platform high above the crowds to deliver a short speech and receive more gifts from neighboring communities. Fat Jack then drove the president three blocks to the Thornton Hotel. Here the president attended a dinner with a hundred invited guests. The guest list was equally split between the town's warring pro- and anti-Heinze factions. The president's visit occurred during the time that officers of Standard Oil, organizing a new company, were attempting to monopolize the city's mines. Heinze was the largest of the remaining private operators in town at the time.

Roosevelt also included his thoughts on the dinner party in his letter to the secretary of state:

> In Butte, every prominent man is a millionaire, a professional gambler, or a labor leader; and generally he has been all three. Of the hundred men who were my hosts I suppose at least half had killed their man in private war, or had striven to compass the assassination of an enemy. They had fought one another with reckless ferocity. They had been allies and enemies in every kind of business scheme, and companions in brutal revelry. As they drank great goblets of wine, the sweat glistened on their hard, strong, crafty faces. They looked as if they had come out of the pictures in Aubrey Beardslee's Yellow Book. The millionaires had been laboring men once; the labor leaders intended to be millionaires in their turn or else to pull down all who were. They had made money in mines; they had spent it on the races, in other mines, or in gambling and every form of vicious luxury. But they were strong men for all that. They had worked and striven and pushed and trampled, and had always been ready, and were ready now, to fight to the death in many different kinds of conflicts.

> They had built up their part of the West. . . . But though most of them hated each other, they were accustomed to take their pleasure when they could get it, and they took it fast and hard with the meats and wines.

Fat Jack waited patiently in the lavishly decorated lobby. He had never seen the Thornton quite like this. It was completely transformed for the president's visit. Timbers framed the hallway to the dining room, creating the look of a drift inside a mine. Just before the entrance to the main dining hall, large baskets overflowed with firearms checked by the guests. The dining room itself was arranged as a stope, a large underground clearing. Buckets designed for carrying ore were scattered around the room and held ice and magnums of champagne.[143] Fat Jack had a feeling his party would be in a good mood for the ride out to the Columbia Gardens.

At 7 p.m. sharp, Fat Jack returned to his hack and pulled up to the side entrance of the Thornton Hotel. The crowds were gone, and no other coaches would follow on this trip. The president was joined by longtime friend and hunting partner Jack Willis. A group of mounted cavalrymen would ride along for security. After the president took his seat, Fat Jack turned and asked with a smile, "Are you all ready Teddy?"

"Let 'er go Gallagher," responded the president. And with that, Fat Jack cracked his whip and his team proceeded to a fast trot. Along the way, the president asked Jack to slow down for a military unit that was marching along the route. He spoke briefly to the soldiers. As they continued onto the flats, Jack Willis recalled what happened next:

> "Drive faster, Jack," he [the president] ordered; and the horses were urged into a canter. That suited him better, but not for long. In a few minutes he called out: "If you don't go faster, Jack, I'll climb up there and do the driving myself!" Jack then whipped his steeds into a gallop. That was what Roosevelt wanted and he was happy. At intervals, in the exuberance of his spirits, he would stand up in the wildly swaying hack, extend his arms, and turn loose a "YIPP-EEE" that could have been heard for a mile in the stillness of the night.[144]

Jack made the trip to the Columbia Gardens in fifteen minutes that night. It was twice as fast as a normal trip—but he had the original Rough Rider in his carriage, and Roosevelt enjoyed every minute.[145]

Fat Jack waited patiently through the president's event at the Columbia Gardens to take him and his party back to the train depot. This time, he drove his team at a trot. The president was ahead of schedule and no longer under the influence of his dinner drinks. When they arrived at the depot, Jack jumped to the ground to open the door for his passengers. After everyone was off, Roosevelt shook Fat Jack's hand and invited him to the White House. "Jack, if you ever come to Washington, if you ever do, you go down to the stream and pull out half a dozen of those nice trout and wrap them up in some grass and bring them along, and you bring them to the White House and you and I will fry them for ourselves."[146]

Murray had a strong attraction to eccentrics like Fat Jack. The cast of characters that decorated Murray's life while he built his wealth was a unique aspect of his personality. Another was how he chose to spend his fortune. There were hundreds of hinterland millionaires in the American West, but few demonstrated the odd pecuniary habits of Jim Murray.

Part II

Wealth and Leisure

7
THE RICHEST MEN IN THE WEST

There were a lot of queer characters rolling around [New York City] in those days. High up on the list of human oddities was old "Pearl Jim" Murray, who used to hang around the Waldorf Bar and Rector's when the theater crowd was at its height.

—Parker Morell[1]

Millionaires were a sensation in this country at the turn of the century. There were so few, about two thousand out of a population of eighty-six million, that newspapers could print every one of their names on just a few pages.[2] The millionaires from western mining states, Murray's peers, totaled just over two hundred, and with Murray being a millionaire ten or fifteen times over, he was near the front of this elite class. Reports from the era indicated that only W. A. Clark had more ready cash at hand—and Clark was likely one of the five richest men in the nation's history.

Studying how these millionaires made and spent their fortunes gives us important insights into how our current economic system developed, for even amongst our country's first millionaires, there were many opinions on key aspects of capitalism, including risk, liability, and labor relations. Today, the entrenched American business model[3] favors the corporate form, featuring no personal liability or risk for managers, adversarial labor relations, and a focus on shareholder value. During the dawn of industrialization, however, many capitalists shunned the corporate form and felt risk and personal liability were necessary elements of a free marketplace. They also recognized the value of paying good wages to bolster local economies. Adam Smith would certainly have sided with the merchant capitalists over the corporate capitalists in this regard, for his "invisible hand" that guided free markets did not contemplate the irrational behavior induced by limited-liability corporations, nor the careless use of other people's money.

Peterson's Bonanza Kings

Richard Peterson, a professor of history at San Diego State University, studied mining tycoons, also known as Bonanza Kings, of the Trans-Mississippi West for more than seventeen years. His work was based on a sample of 50 individuals, balanced geographically, from the pool of 207 who made their fortunes in California, Nevada, Idaho, Montana, South Dakota, Utah, Colorado, and Arizona. His findings appeared in two books, *The Bonanza Kings*[4] and *Bonanza Rich*.[5] In *The Bonanza Kings*, he explored social mobility, motivation, education, business strategies, labor relations, and use of capital. *Bonanza Rich* featured the spending patterns of the wealthy mine owners.

Peterson found that most of his subjects were born in America, built their wealth in cooperation with labor, partnered with technical experts (for example, engineers and geologists), used lenders and investors to finance their ventures, and operated with strong ethical standards. Peterson contended that the Western millionaires in his study were not the cutthroat robber barons who built the railroad systems that activated industry in the West. Murray was excluded from Peterson's sample in part because he did not have a contemporary biography—an element Peterson obviously needed to understand the personal history of his subjects. Murray's profile is compared here with Peterson's findings to illustrate how his background and interests corresponded to his peers in both the East and West.

LINEAGE

Seventy percent of Peterson's fifty subjects were born in America, and the overwhelming majority, 88 percent, traced their lineage to the British Empire (England, Ireland, Scotland, Wales, or Canada). Eastern capitalists shared the same pattern of parental lineage but had a higher percentage of American natives in their ranks, with more than 90 percent born on American soil. In classifying class origins, the occupation of the tycoons' fathers reveals a greater contrast between coasts. Three-quarters of the Eastern capitalists came from a family in which the father was a member of the professional class. For the Bonanza Kings, this is true of just over 50 percent. East Coast capitalists also had the advantage of higher education, another indicator of class, with 78 percent having high school or college educations, compared to just 55 percent of the Western mining millionaires. Lacking the class and status of their Eastern counterparts, a good share of the future Bonanza Kings had to overcome financial hardships to travel West and stake their claims. Murray, who lacked American roots, formal education, and class advantage, clearly started at the back of the pack amongst his future peers.

BUSINESS TYPE

Most future mining moguls, including Murray, arrived in the West prior to the industrialization of mining. They operated surface claims for a period but then had to scale up and diversify to compete and survive. They had to acquire and retain productive claims, finance development, hire employees, ship ore to processors, extract minerals, and get their product to market. Peterson considered all of his subjects entrepreneurs for making this transition, but he missed an important distinction by placing them in one category. Only a handful of Peterson's fifty subjects worked alone in the classic sense of an entrepreneur: making decisions and risking their own money. Most worked in partnerships or as part of corporations, a few were inventors or hit one big strike, but only a handful were true entrepreneurs working alone and unaided to build and retain their empires.

Eleven of Peterson's fifty fit the definition of an entrepreneur, building a successful business independent of others, and of this group, just three were immigrants. The three immigrant entrepreneurs in Peterson's study were Joseph De Lamar (Dutch), Henry Newell (Irish), and Dennis Sheedy (Irish). Of these three, only the Dutchman equaled Murray's level of success. No Irish immigrants within or outside of Peterson's sample matched Murray's success, either—giving Murray the distinction of being the most successful Irish entrepreneur in the American West.

LABOR

Labor relations under Peterson's Bonanza Kings were mostly peaceful. The period he reviewed was 1892 to 1904, which included some labor disruptions following the Silver Panic of 1893. Much of the labor peace is attributed to the fact that the mining tycoons, including Murray, had known and previously worked beside many of their employees for several years. Another factor, although Peterson found this less important, is that the Bonanza Kings often lived in the communities where they operated. These connections between owners and communities facilitated communication vital to providing labor a voice on operations and wages. Several of the tycoons, notably George Hearst and W. A. Clark, went beyond fair wages and made significant contributions to their communities. Hearst built libraries and schools to support his employees. W. A. Clark built the Columbia Gardens on the outskirts of Butte to provide workers and their families a magnificent retreat. Murray also contributed to community facilities, secretly financing the first major hospital in Butte, and publicly working with Clark to build an orphanage for the children left behind by worker fatalities.

CAPITAL

Capital was necessary to access and process ore. Ready cash in local bank accounts was relatively scarce in comparison to the vast number of potential headframes, shafts, drifts, mill stamps, and smelters that could cover and penetrate the countryside. This combination of limited cash and unlimited opportunity quickly eviscerated most of the fledgling Bonanza Kings' patience and discipline and sent them scurrying for financing from outside sources. Clark, Murray, and a handful of others chose not to set up corporations and borrow from others, and instead used their own cash.

These few merchant capitalists, who used their own money, had the independence to transact business instantaneously, without the approval of others. Unfortunately, what their corporate competitors lacked in mobility they made up in recklessness, tilting the market at times by overpaying for claims and inflating demand for labor by pursuing marginal prospects.

ETHICS

Peterson claimed his subjects were not cutthroat capitalists like the robber barons who built the railroads in the West. He illustrated the ethical standards of his group by quoting Thomas Walsh, a progressive mining tycoon from Colorado, who said, "Honest wealth is a badge of honor." It is unfortunate that Murray was not part of Peterson's study, for he provides a stark contrast, having once stated, "There isn't any honest money in the world. I've got $10 million and if I had an honest dollar in the bank roll I'd throw it away."[6] Murray's business ethics were undoubtedly a product of his environment. In Ireland, he experienced the overwhelming force of Britain's economic power. The British government was invasive, corrupt, and worked against his family and countrymen at every turn. In his early days prospecting in the Rocky Mountains, he lived freely under a handful of rules established by his peers. Everyone was equal in the mining camps, if you weren't afraid to draw a gun to protect your rights. In time, small mining camps transformed into cities, territories became states, government power concentrated, and powerful Eastern corporations displaced virtually every individual mine owner. Murray fought hard to maintain and expand his wealth in the face of concentrating power in government and business. Murray used any tactic necessary to beat back government and corporate influence on his empire—while he continued to outmaneuver and pummel his fellow merchant capitalists.

Among Peterson's Bonanza Kings, and even among those not included in the study, Murray was clearly an outlier in terms of his background and his business model. He was an uneducated immigrant entrepreneur competing against mostly educated, American-born individuals who pooled their money and risk with others. And to add to the disparity, he carried a deep resentment of government power and reckless corporate business practices. P. A. O'Farrell was right to label Murray a "buccaneer."

In spending his mostly ill-gotten bounty, however. Murray fell right in line with most everyone else of great wealth during the Gilded Age, spare a few idiosyncrasies.

Spending a Fortune

In *Bonanza Rich*, Peterson found that most of his fifty Western millionaires spent their wealth in a fashion similar to their Eastern counterparts. Spending usually involved lavish dinners and entertainment in New York City, a stable of racehorses, mansions, grand tours of Europe, sending children to the finest colleges, collections of European art, and charitable donations to educational institutions. Murray did much of the same, and with regard to his party habits in New York City, he certainly topped the list.

NEW YORK NIGHTLIFE

The allure of New York City captivated more than just mining tycoons. Hinterland millionaires of all types added a splash of bravado to New York City during the Gilded Age. Railroad barons, timber titans, and silver and copper kings filled lobster palaces and Broadway theaters. They mixed freely on Peacock Alley and in the Waldorf Bar with J. P. Morgan, Henry Clay Frick, and countless Wall Street millionaires, telling stories of Indian raids, gunfights, and great riches. Murray, who earned the moniker "Pearl Jim" by carrying a cache of loose pearls in his pockets, joined "Bet-a-Million" Gates and "Death Valley Scotty" as the most garish of the outsiders. Gates was a successful salesman who bet freely on the horses, and Scotty was a con artist who claimed ownership in gold mines in California. When Murray was out on the town, he was often joined by New York's own James Buchannan Brady, best known by his nickname "Diamond Jim." Two published biographies and one motion picture captured the lavish spending and outlandish jewelry collection of Brady, who made his fortune selling passenger cars to the railroads.

Parker Morell wrote the first Brady biography in 1934, in which he recounted Murray's relationship with Diamond Jim. He wrote that Murray "owed his nickname to his passion for pearls, nearly two hundred of which he carried around in his pocket at all times." Morell added that Diamond Jim thought Murray was "slightly cracked," but "because Murray carried nearly a million dollars in pearls on his person, and because he steadfastly refused to part with any of them, no matter what he was offered, Jim gave him the benefit of the doubt."[7] Morell credits Murray with goading Brady into adding pearls to his expansive collection of jewelry. Restaurateur George Rector, in his autobiography and cookbooks, also recalled stories of Murray. He wrote about Pearl Jim spreading his pearls across a table in full view of other restaurant patrons, and the stress this caused Rector maître d's. Murray, having spent most of his adult life surrounded by thieves, seemed to have little concern for the urban variety, although Rector noted that Murray never let his carriage driver lead him into Central Park.

Murray's penchant for flashing jewelry carried back to the early days of Butte, where he was known to be the first to wear diamond-studded jewelry in the mining camp.[8] Across the West Coast, stories were also told of a pouch of diamonds and sapphires that Murray carried in his coat pocket. Ed Fletcher, a tortured partner of Murray's, confirmed the newspaper accounts of the legendary pouch in his memoir.[9] As with everything,

Murray likely had a purpose with his gaudy displays of wealth. First, no one desperate for money in the Wild West approached a poor person for a loan, and second, he probably enjoyed fooling the crowds, as many of the jewels in his collection were fakes, a secret revealed only in the accounting of his assets after his death.[10]

Murray's frequent trips to New York were not only to amuse the crowds with his faux pearls. He also traveled there for the horse shows, to watch his racehorse Collector Jessup at the Saratoga track, to book productions for his theaters, and to visit his nephew James E. Murray, who studied law at New York University between 1898 and 1901.[11] Nephew James claimed that some of his fondest memories from law school were of dining with his uncle, Diamond Jim Brady, and actress Lillian Russell.[12]

Known as "Pearl Jim" Murray to the theater crowd in New York City, Murray often dined with Diamond Jim Brady (right) and actress Lillian Russell (left). —Library of Congress

HORSE RACING

Horse racing, the sport of kings, was a favorite of wealthy capitalists on both coasts. Murray's friend and mining partner Marcus Daly was at the top of the class in this sport. When he passed away, Daly had more than 350 horses in his stables. Joining Daly in horse racing's upper echelons were his financial partners James B. Haggin and George Hearst. Murray was a solid member of the horse-racing community, as well, and probably one of the few Bonanza Kings who rode his own horses. Murray liked to ride and drive himself in the early days[13] when races through mining camps pitted just two horses in head-to-head competition.[14] He first purchased a horse bred for racing—the quarter horse Texas Dan—in 1884 in New Orleans.[15] Murray boasted several times about starting a large stable, but it appears he kept no more than three or four horses at a time.[16] His best horse was Collector Jessup, a thoroughbred stakes-winner that raced in New York and other parts of the United States in the early 1900s.[17]

MANSION MANIA

East and West Coast capitalists shared the impulse to build lavish mansions in exclusive neighborhoods. San Francisco's Nob Hill and New York's Millionaires' Row on Fifth Avenue were ideal for primary residences, and Newport, Rhode Island, and the north shore of New York's Long Island were preferred summer retreats. Mining moguls from the Rocky Mountain states, chasing status and financing, joined the mansion mania on Fifth Avenue in New York. They were led ably by W. A. Clark's monstrosity—a 121-room, 31-bath home featuring four art galleries at the corner of 5th and 77th Streets.[18]

Murray avoided the expense of a large mansion for most of his life. When he wasn't living out of his suitcase, he lived in a modest apartment above his private bank in Butte.[19] Talk of a grand estate finally surfaced when he married Mary Coulter Haldorn. Murray boasted about a possible mansion for the first eight years of his second marriage—potential locations included Hudson Bay in New York[20] and a site next to his resort at Hunter's Hot Springs in Montana.[21] Finally, at sixty-four years of age, Murray gave in and purchased a compound in Monterey, California, fit for one of the wealthiest men in the West.[22] Hugh Tevis, the son and heir to one of Marcus Daly's original investors, Lloyd Tevis, had completed the splendid estate, which fronted more than one thousand feet of coastline, in 1901 for his fiancée. The newlyweds planned to move into the complex after their marriage, but tragically, Tevis died on his honeymoon, and his bride elected not to make the seaside mansion her home. Murray, always flush with ready cash, picked up the home for just $20,000 in 1904.[23] His wife was certainly the driving force to secure a new home outside of Montana, for reasons that became clear some years later (see chapter 11).

Murray's Monterey mansion (circa 1920) covered one thousand feet of shoreline. The main residence is on the far left and stables are on the far right. —California History Room, Monterey Public Library

The architectural style of Murray's mansion was unique among those of his fellow millionaires. The home featured a Spanish-style exterior, in contrast to the Victorian stylings of nearly every other mansion of the era. On the interior, he seemed to favor Arts and Crafts motifs, combined with animal skins and mounts as accents.[24]

THE GRAND TOUR OF EUROPE

Virtually all the mining tycoons spent time abroad. Some went in search of cultural riches that were nonexistent on the western frontier, a few made religious pilgrimages, and many were simply doing what was expected of the nouveau riche.

Murray made the grand tour of Europe and points beyond in 1900. Murray loved to tell stories, and with no one to verify the events of his trip, it is difficult to know what really happened. His adventure started with a slightly exaggerated purpose: "I took a trip around the world for the purpose of seeing if I wanted the earth and how much lumber it would take to fence it."[25] His travels took him to the Himalayas, Russia, Scandinavia,

Central Europe, and Ireland. During his time in Germany, he claimed to have dropped in on Emperor Wilhelm II while out on a stroll, and he remarked that the potentate extended his party a cordial welcome.[26] Remarkably, Lamar Cecil, a Wilhelm II biographer, did not discount Murray's account, remarking that Wilhelm II "liked Americans and could be very casual in his social contacts."[27] Murray rounded out his trip with a final boast about his mother country. After staying at a resort on the Lakes of Killarney in Ireland, Murray shared that he might buy the lakes and all the hills that surrounded them.[28]

CHILDREN AND COLLEGE EDUCATIONS

The wealthy mining kings, as well as Eastern capitalists, took great pride in sending their children to the top institutions in the United States and Europe. For the lesser-educated Western capitalists, it likely represented their first opportunity to have their offspring mixing with the upper classes of society. Murray had no children of his own, but after he took financial responsibility for two nephews (Marcus and James E.) and a niece (May), he put each through fine colleges.[29] After they completed their studies, he put them to work in his banks or attending to his legal affairs. Marcus and May worked in banks in Montana, Washington, Idaho, and Utah. James E. Murray, who went on to serve as a US Senator for twenty-six years, had the most education and ended up with the largest share of responsibilities among the nephews and nieces. His education included a law degree from New York University. During his studies, he lived in luxury; his uncle provided season passes to the theater and open credit lines at the finest restaurants.[30]

ART

The Gilded Age millionaires spent a good share of their fortunes on art, and most focused on the famous European painters. The grand tour of Europe was often spent purchasing art to be shipped home. Murray spent some of his fortune on art, but his collection was modest compared to those of his counterparts. He converted a bowling alley in his Monterey mansion into a gallery[31] and filled it with the work of Western artists, including Francis McComas and William Keith.[32]

CHARITY

The millionaires of the Gilded Age, from both coasts, gave extensively to universities, often in return for naming rights to buildings and a permanent legacy. Murray's charitable donations are difficult to catalog because of the conditions he imposed on his benefactors. He had no interest in his legacy, insisted on anonymity, and swore his benefactors to secrecy. Despite these conditions, stories of his generosity have emerged in bits and pieces over the years. Murray's primary philanthropic interest seemed to be hospitals and orphanages. His donation in 1890 to fund the first hospital in Butte remained a secret for eighty-seven years—the gift was finally revealed by Tom Murray, son of the hospital's founder, Dr. T. J. Murray (no relation to Jim).[33] His support of orphanages was more public. He teamed with W. A. Clark to fund an orphanage in Butte, and he made provisions in his estate planning to donate a significant property near Helena for the same purpose.[34]

Murray's charity also extended to the many miners he worked beside in the early days of prospecting. One of Murray's bank employees said, "Whenever an old-timer would come in there with an honest desire to get ahead he could get almost any amount of money from Mr. Murray without staking a thing for security." When Murray reviewed these loans, he'd pick up each note and wonder aloud if the poor old fellow was making it. "Never a word about any desire to see the money repaid," the employee claimed. News reports indicate that Murray burned more than $700,000 in outstanding loans at his Butte bank before he passed away.[35] Murray's estate documents indicate that there may be some truth to reports of Murray's munificence because he still held more than $1 million in private loans at the time of his death. Some of these notes were for small amounts, made out to unknown figures, and showed no sign of efforts to collect (see appendix for a listing of these loans).

8
Irish Rebel

The object is to aid the Irish people in the attainment of the complete and absolute independence of Ireland, by the overthrow of English domination. . . . It shall prepare unceasingly for an armed insurrection in Ireland.

—Constitution of the Clan na Gael

While Jim Murray's crooked business dealings did not necessarily distinguish him from his peers, he nevertheless stood out in one key respect: his politics were decidedly radical. From the Irish Land League protests of the 1880s through the Easter Rising of 1916, Murray was a steadfast champion of an independent Ireland. At the same time, he supported workers' efforts to gain fair wages. In Butte, a town where there existed, in the words of historian Dave Emmons, an "ideological seam . . . where the rights of the Irish and the rights of the worker were joined,"[36] a millionaire capitalist could become a fierce champion of labor during a period of extreme class-based tensions in American politics.[37]

Murray's sympathies for his mother country emerged in the early 1880s as he turned his attention to the land reform work of Charles Stewart Parnell. Murray, like other Irish immigrants, followed newswire reports and editorials about Parnell's agitation in local papers like the Deer Lodge *New North-West*, the Fort Benton *Benton Record*, and the *Helena Weekly Herald.*[38] Enthusiasm for Parnell's efforts swelled in 1880 as he conducted an American fundraising tour covering sixty-two cities over three months. Support continued to grow with Michael Davitt's missionary efforts the following year.[39] Butte's large Irish population rallied to Parnell's cause, forming chapters of the Irish National Land League,[40] the conservative Ancient Order of Hibernians (AOH), and the radical Clan na Gael, which operated as the Robert Emmet Literary Association. Each organization had a distinct focus: the Land League funded Parnell's diplomatic efforts, the AOH—a Catholic organization—raised funds for a local benevolent association and lobbied Congress and the president to recognize home rule for Ireland, and the Clan funded militants using physical force to extricate the English from Ireland.[41]

Membership in Land League, AOH, and Clan na Gael chapters throughout the United States was almost exclusively the province of working-class miners and merchants. Butte's copper aristocracy provided some of the few exceptions. In addition to Murray, Marcus Daly, Cornelius "Con" Kelley, and other mining executives with Irish ties joined working-class immigrants to support the Land League and AOH.[42] Murray's involvement, however, extended beyond these moderate groups. In 1883, he accepted nomination into the militant and secretive Clan na Gael. During the seven years he was a member of the Butte organization, the national Clan na Gael sponsored several dynamite attacks in Britain.[43] Tellingly, Marcus Daly was also nominated to the order but refused to join, suggesting just how polarizing the Clan's radical activities were even among those sympathetic to and supportive of the larger cause.[44]

Outside of secret Clan na Gael meetings, Murray made no effort to hide his loyalty to his mother county and his disdain for power brokers in the Catholic Church who conspired to perpetuate British rule. Murray's views became public shortly after Pope Leo XIII directed the Irish clergy in 1883 to suppress support for Parnell.[45] Murray, working with close friend John Maguire, organized a meeting to fashion a public response. Maguire convened a group of Butte Irish at his Renshaw Playhouse and placed three items before the group: a resolution supporting Charles Parnell, a proposal for the formation of a local chapter of the Irish National League to raise money for Parnell's living expenses, and election of trustees to lead the chapter. Murray headed the committee that drafted the resolution supporting Parnell but took the opportunity to send a broader message. His words implicitly supported both land reform and home rule movements, praising the work of Parnell in "all of his efforts to alleviate the sufferings of Ireland and the Irish people," and explicitly denouncing the Pope's support of an English strategy that "starves, coerces, and exterminates the people of Ireland." The group unanimously adopted Murray's fiery language, formed a chapter of the Irish National League, and selected Maguire and Murray to serve as two of seven trustees of the organization.[46] Joining Murray in the leadership of the new group were local Land League activists James Mathews and Sam Mulville. Within a week, the group raised $250 to send to Parnell. Murray and Daly led the donations with contributions of $25 each.[47]

Three years later, in the summer of 1886, Murray joined Marcus Daly and W. A. Clark as the largest donors to a $2,500 campaign to support joint efforts by Britain's William Gladstone and Parnell.[48] Later that fall, Murray, Mulville, and another National League founding member, James Lynch, joined several Butte Land Leaguers and Daly as official hosts for Michael Davitt's visit to Butte. Davitt set aside his radical views on land reform (Davitt advocated nationalization of land ownership) and spoke to an

Renshaw Hall, circa 1890 in Butte. —PH002.82, C. Owen Smithers, Butte–Silver Bow Public Archives

enthusiastic gathering at Murray and Maguire's Grand Opera House about the fight for home rule. He concluded his remarks, to prolonged applause, with these words: "The policy pursued at home may bring about trouble, reverses may have to be sustained, many worthy persons may be evicted, some may receive the Queen's hospitality in English or Irish prisons, but the cause will prevail at last."[49] Davitt left Butte and the United States with a sizable war chest, but he feared continued support for Ireland's cause would be hampered by a biased press. Murray shared this concern and would later make a bold move to ensure the Irish cause was not silenced in America.

Populist Politics

Murray's participation in the radical wing of Irish American organizations coincided with his shift to a decidedly radical politics in domestic affairs. In 1884, he was elected to the Silver Bow County's People's Party Central Committee. Also elected were his business partner James A. Talbot and Irish labor leader Patrick Boland, president of Butte Miners Union and a fellow member of Clan na Gael.[50] In Boland, Murray once again was working with a radical and dangerous element of the Butte community. The People's Party national platform in 1884 supported antimonopoly legislation, a progressive income tax, reduced hours for workers, abolishment of child labor, a woman's right to vote, and better treatment of veterans.[51] In Butte, the party addressed local concerns, denouncing the emerging political "syndicates" that controlled the Republican and Democratic conventions, lavish spending on elections, and the disturbing trend of mine owners combining capital in large quantities "for their own aggrandizement and the oppression of honest labor." The convention closed with Sample H. Orr, chair of the party's platform committee, calling for labor to strike for its rights before capital had it under its heel.[52] The likely targets of Orr's comments and the party platform were businesses headed by Murray's fellow capitalists Marcus Daly[53] and Samuel Hauser.[54]

In 1888, Murray shifted his allegiance to a newly formed Workingmen's Party. This short-lived party was led by a newcomer to Butte, firebrand William Penrose. When Murray stated that "he who never made an enemy was not worth having as a friend,"[55] his inspiration may have been Penrose. Irish radicals Maguire and Mulville joined as well. The formation of the Workingmen's Party, like that of the People's Party before it, was a response to alleged corruption in the two major parties (Democrat and Republican). The platform focused entirely on city services such as an improved water supply for domestic use and fighting fires, new equipment for the fire department, removing politics from the police department, and reducing the use of violence by police officers. The local bent was certainly of great interest to Murray because he was in the midst of his dispute with the city over his Smokehouse Lode claim. The Workingmen's Party offered eighteen candidates for local election. Murray took the chair of the City Central Committee, and Penrose represented one of the city's seven wards. The party won only two seats and later disbanded.

Murray and Penrose joined the Democratic Party the following year and developed a strong bond.[56] Penrose, eighteen years Murray's junior, became a frequent traveling partner of the wealthy capitalist. Local newspapers reported the pair traveling to Chicago together and returning with matching black silk shirts, attending the state fair in Helena, and visiting the east coast on at least one occasion. Their strong friendship became so apparent that one paper referred to them as Pythias and Damon in a poem about local politics.[57] Murray was not the only one Penrose won over. It seemed as if the entire community was caught up in his charms. The only groups that seemed reticent to embrace the budding politician were Irish factions in the local unions. It certainly didn't help Penrose with this group that he was born in Cornwall, England, and had been a member of the Republican Party.

Penrose's popularity with most of the citizenry likely started with the reputation he built before coming to Butte in 1885. When he was just twenty-four years old, he showed that he was not someone to back down, a trait admired in the raucous mining camp. While he was working in Nevada, an article appeared in the paper of a nearby community denouncing him. He immediately traveled to that town, Eureka, hunted down the editor on Main Street, and confronted him. The editor drew his revolver, but Penrose snatched it before a shot was fired. Penrose then proceeded to "beat him over the head with it, inflicting severe wounds."[58]

In Butte, Penrose gained broad community support as an editor of a local paper that sympathized with Irish and labor causes. He formed a chapter of the Sons of St. George, which gave him connections across the political spectrum.[59] He was relentless in his efforts to establish connections at all levels. He once invited a local marching band (the Boston and Montana) into his house after it had performed for a funeral, asking if they would play at his funeral as well. "That we will," was the hearty answer, "and we will give you the biggest band that ever marched in Butte!"[60] In 1887, Penrose's political networking paid off when the territorial governor appointed him to be one of three arbitrators to settle labor disputes. Two years later, in 1889, he captured a seat in the state legislature.[61] In 1890, working with Murray, who then chaired the Silver Bow County Democratic Central Committee, Penrose helped guide the Democrats to a sweeping victory in Butte's local elections.[62]

Murray's alliance with Penrose was cut short in 1891, when his friend did not heed labor's call for state legislation limiting work days to eight hours. Labor wanted the eight-hour day and had counted Penrose as a solid vote in its favor. However, when the roll was called in the legislature, Penrose voted against the bill. He tried in vain to explain his reasoning to the union bosses. He felt the restriction would ultimately cost thousands of jobs. Labor heard none of it. Pro-union businesses pulled their ads from Penrose's paper, and in turn, Penrose used his editorial column to launch savage personal attacks on Butte's labor leaders. Murray stood by his friend politically but could not guarantee his safety.

On the evening of June 10, 1891, Penrose left his home to quell another matter. His mistress, Belle Brown, was making threats against his wife. Penrose went to persuade her to stop the harassment. He left her place shortly before midnight to return home. He never made it. Penrose was found shot to death shortly after midnight. The police officer working the beat saw a woman with a man's build leaving the scene of the crime. The labor leaders targeted by Penrose's poison pen were also nearby.[63] Penrose left police with many suspects to consider. But first, a community needed to mourn.

The citizens of Butte packed a local church to hear final tributes to the controversial man who had quickly charmed a community. The procession to his burial site required every carriage in town. The marching musicians he had once hosted kept their word and led the procession to his grave. They passed his home, the spot of the murder, and the jail cell where his lover was being held as a suspect. His faithful dog Jerry ran alongside the wagon carrying his casket and watched sadly as the casket was buried and covered with sod.[64]

Penrose's killing was testament to the dangerous nature of the radical characters and political contests in which Murray had grown inextricably involved. In a rare show of emotion, Murray commented to the press after his friend's funeral, "I have been looking all over town today for Penrose. I expect to meet him on every corner and I cannot conceive of his being laid away in the ground."[65] Murray hired private investigators to find the killer, but they came up empty. One of the labor leaders suspected of the crime confessed years later and told of a warning given to Penrose to leave town. When he failed to heed the warning, a group of labor leaders drew straws to choose his executioner.[66]

For the remainder of the 1890s, Murray continued to serve the Democrats as a delegate to state conventions[67] and was appointed by the governor to represent Montana at various national mining conventions.[68] In 1893, he accepted his most significant appointment, as Montana's representative in the Trans-Mississippi Congress.[69] Late in the decade, Murray, like most people with an interest in the mining industry, turned his attention to reinstating the silver standard to the nation's currency system. He placed his hope for this change with presidential candidate William Jennings Bryan, a fusion candidate of the Populist and Democratic Parties, who denounced monopolies and championed worker protections.[70] Murray's support for Bryan gained national attention when Joseph Pulitzer, editor of the *New York World* and an opponent of a bimetallic standard, published Murray's name alongside those of thirty other multimillionaires, including Marcus Daly, W. A. Clark, and silver magnate John Mackay. Pulitzer pegged the capitalists as members of a secret "Silver Trust" that controlled Bryan.[71] The list was reprinted in papers across the country, often in conjunction with articles contrasting the wealth of these Bonanza Kings with a recent reduction in miner's wages in Leadville, Colorado, from $3.50 to $2.50 per day.[72]

Defying popular assumptions, Murray responded to Pulitzer's charges and spoke out firmly on the side of labor. When cornered by a reporter in Tombstone, Arizona, shortly after the publication of Pulitzer's critical piece, Murray proclaimed, "No matter what may come, I will not reduce the wages of any man in my employ. Why should one man who does very little work be able to roll in luxury and have more money than he knows what to do with while thousands of men whose labor produced the wealth are practically penniless?"[73] To another reporter, he highlighted the importance of his local connections, adding, "If I lived in New York I might feel different, but I intend to always live in Butte and pay good wages."[74] Murray apparently kept his word and maintained a spotless record with labor. He never had a strike at his mines, even as strikes flared up repeatedly across the West during this period.[75]

Murray's name surfaced again in the national press in 1900 as controversy erupted regarding the contest over William A. Clark's seat in the US Senate. Murray's good friend John Maguire, a Republican, informed the New York press that Murray was a consensus pick to replace the scandal-plagued Clark.[76] Several papers picked up the story, but only the editors of the *Denver Post* accurately assessed Murray's interest in the Senate: "Mr. Murray wouldn't be bothered by such a bauble. He's too busy making millions. . . . He would rather stay at home bossing the Butte water works and shaking dice for mines when he requires relaxation from more serious affairs."[77] Murray also downplayed his friend's statement, saying, "I consider the honor of being appointed to an office doubtful, because appointments are made usually for the future political benefit of the appointee."[78] Governor Robert B. Smith eventually tapped former congressman Martin Maginnis to fill out Clark's term,[79] leaving Murray to continue his dice games at McGovern's Saloon on Main Street.

Murray's political affiliations up until the turn of the nineteenth century—the People's Party, the Workingmen's Party, and eventually the Democratic Party—likely grew out of his desire to protect his own form of proprietary capitalism and to maintain a level playing field in the competition for new business. Murray could clearly see that concentration of large amounts of investment capital under corporate control resulted in managers spending other people's money without discipline and driving up the cost of property.[80] Shortly after the turn of the century, however, Murray appears to have transitioned his involvement in party politics to nephew James E. Murray. The pull of the railroad to new parts of the West and geographic diversification of his empire likely pushed Murray to delegate his political activities in Butte.

9
John Maguire's Opera House

John Maguire will have a theater in Butte even when hell freezes over.

—James A. Murray[81]

Murray and his fellow Bonanza Kings piled up significant cash in the 1880s and 1890s. Most shared a portion of their wealth with their communities through the construction of public facilities that could be enjoyed by employees and local residents. Marcus Daly used his wealth to build two horseracing tracks, one in Butte and one in Anaconda.[82] W. A. Clark built the sixty-eight-acre Columbia Gardens, an oasis of greenery outside of Butte (where toxic smoke from smelters killed nearly every tree and blade of grass).[83] Jim Murray spent his extra cash on a world-class opera house for his close friend John Maguire, using a complicated financing scheme that relied on outside funding but gave Murray the upper hand in guiding the venture through challenging times in the entertainment industry.[84]

Murray and Maguire knew each other well. The two had frequented the same circuit of mining camps in southwest Montana during the 1870s and worked together on Irish and national politics in Butte in the early 1880s. Maguire proposed a theater project to Murray in 1884, and one year later he opened the best theater in the West outside of San Francisco. What followed, however, was twenty years of dramatic ups and downs in every aspect of the venture, most of which played out in newspapers across the West. The drama emanated from a complex combination of forces that led many writers of the period, as well as historians, to throw up their arms and attribute the plight of Butte's Grand Opera House simply to Murray's idiosyncrasies. Few took the time to unravel the complexities of the theater business, with its rapidly changing market conditions and technology, or understand the play between Maguire's unbridled optimism, Murray's penchant for litigation, and their love for each other.

Maguire was one of two people for whom Murray publicly expressed his affection, and the only partner he paid a salary or allowed to lose money.[85] Their relationship evoked the same type of close bond that Doris Kearns Goodwin suggested Abraham Lincoln and Joshua Speed shared, as well as William Seward and David Berdan.[86] None of these relationships violated the mores of the day. Historian E. Anthony Rotundo described such relationships as "a common feature of the social landscape" at the turn of the nineteenth century.[87] The saga of the two men's Grand Opera House is a fascinating story of life imitating art, with Maguire and Murray costarring in a Greek tragedy.

The First Grand Opera House

The tragedy began with a meeting in Murray's simple, single-story, wood-framed bank in Butte. Maguire was of a mind to build a permanent theater to replace leased space, where he operated a theater above a local store. He found a perfect site inside the stakes of Murray's Smokehouse claim. Maguire needed to acquire property rights from two parties to have clear title to the site. Murray held the right to enter the site for mining purposes. Another group held the right to occupy it for nonmining purposes, subject to Murray's right to remove anything that interfered with access to his claim. The owners who held rights to use the site for nonmining purposes asked Maguire for $2,500 for their interest in the property, and another $3,000 to pay Murray for rights to his surface claim. Murray counseled Maguire to offer $1,800 for the lot and return to him when the deal was struck.

Murray's interest in helping Maguire was likely the result of several factors. Beyond their common passion for politics and Irish nationalism, Maguire was single and had no competing interests that could compromise his focus. He was dedicated, fanatically in fact, to a career in theater management, as his acting skills, although adequate, could not provide the income or status in the industry he loved. He had a track record of perseverance and success in attracting performers to remote locations. He was able to get acts to travel to Butte by steamboat and wagon train, and before that, he had convinced troupes to endure horrific conditions traveling to his theater in Pioche, Nevada. [88] This success was made possible by an extensive network of individuals who liked and respected Maguire as a manager. Finally, Maguire brought with him a very special artist as part of his team.

Edgar S. Paxson, who would become one of the most revered Western artists, was in charge of producing all of Maguire's scenery. Paxson's work often received its own glowing reviews by critics of the theater. Paxson also had credibility as a tough pioneer, having spent time in Emmetsburg when Murray was gambling and Maguire was performing his one-man act in the 1870s. In his diary, Paxson remembered those days as being filled with violence and shootings.[89] It was rather remarkable that all three would endure that milieu to form a team that would take some of the wild out of the West.

Maguire was successful in getting the lot for the lower price, and when he returned to see Murray, he received a quit claim for the surface rights in exchange for $1. The pair then turned to financing, constructing, outfitting, and booking the new theater. Murray structured the financing, following the convoluted schemes he used for mining properties. The objective was to use other people's money while maintaining full control of the property. This should have been a challenge because Maguire was

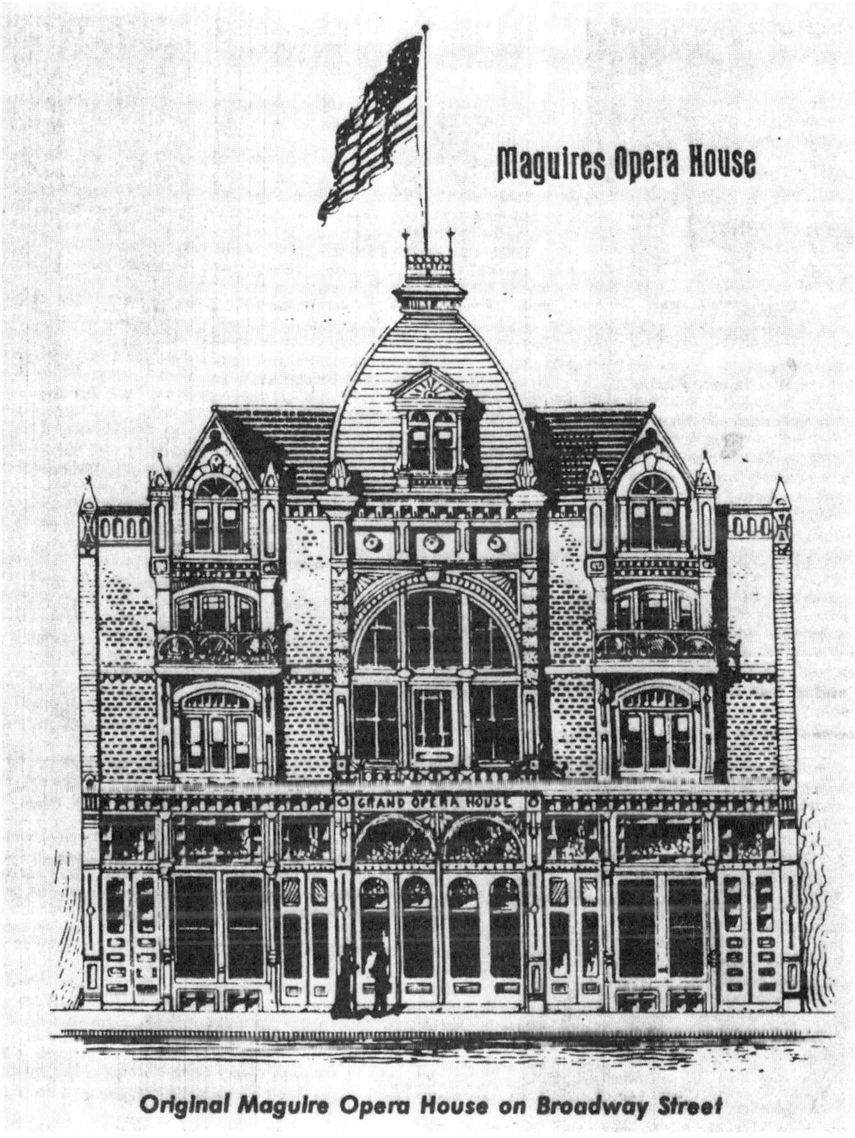

John Maguire's first opera house —*Montana Standard*, August 6, 1978

seeking financial commitments from people who knew most of Murray's financial gymnastics. Fortunately for Maguire, the strong desire to have a stamp of civilization allowed Butte's elite to look the other way when they handed over their money to the new Opera House Company.

Theater was very important to civic pride in the Wild West. New towns were popping up everywhere in the late 1880s, and they all wanted theater. It provided entertainment and a connection to the more civilized parts of the country.[90] Murray invested $1,000, Marcus Daly was in for $1,000, W. A. Clark wrote a check for $500, and a long list of Butte's upper class donated the balance.[91] The corporation collected $22,000 in all to build the new opera house, and Murray was elected president of the company that would oversee all operations.[92]

After construction was underway, Maguire worked dutifully to acquire management control over a string of theaters in the Northwest, leverage he needed when he traveled to New York to book the 1885 season.[93] Once his circuit was intact, he and Paxson headed to New York—Maguire to book acts, and Paxson to learn the latest trends in scenery design.[94] Murray chipped in as well. He took on the responsibility of ensuring the fabrication and delivery of eight hundred cast-iron folding chairs to the new theater from a manufacturer in Racine, Wisconsin.[95]

While in New York, Maguire spoke to the press about his success booking shows for Butte's Grand Opera House and his circuit of theaters. He negotiated an exclusive arrangement with noted producer and advance man Gustave Frohman "to play all his attractions west of Colorado to California by way of Montana and Oregon." The deal with Frohman ensured forty weeks of engagements. Maguire booked several of the remaining dates directly by securing popular performers Nellie Boyd, Rose Eytinge, and Frank Mayo. The one regret Maguire had with his inaugural season is that he failed to book Lulu Hurst, a popular teenage magician of the time. Hurst, who would have commanded great prices and packed the opera house, suddenly retired after just two years as a performer.[96]

Maguire, Paxson, and Murray completed their respective tasks on time. With the acts booked, scenery painted, and chairs in place, Maguire planned a grand opening to rival any in the country. Programs for the evening were printed on satin, and Montana Territory Governor Samuel Hauser was tendered an invitation and expected to attend.[97] Anticipating strong interest, Maguire charged premium prices for opening night in the new facility. A correspondent for the *Helena Weekly Herald* captured the events of that evening. His words guide us through the front doors and into Butte's Grand Opera House, where Paxson's magnificent artistry was on full display.

> A spacious entrance with boards for hangers on either side gives a metropolitan aspect to the building and proclaims it at once a temple of drama. Entering these portals, one passes the box office on the right, and arrives

> at the first door of the theater. Here the door keeper takes his stand, prepared to usher those attending either into the main auditorium or the gallery.
>
> Stair cases to the gallery lead up either side of the door, but are completely separated from the theater by a partition, which effectually shuts out the noise made by persons going up or down stairs. A door through the partitions at the foot of the gallery stairs forms the entrance to the dress circle and parquette. It is on entering this door that one gets the first glimpse of the interior of the theater.
>
> Handsomely upholstered, folding chairs, with a frame of iron and cushioned seats and backs, extend around the building in arcs of circles, occupying all the available space on the floor and affording a much larger seating capacity than one would at first sight imagine. . . . Indeed, the gallery, parquette and dress circle will seat altogether 900 persons. . . . the consequence is that there is not a bad seat in the house. Every chair, even those farthest from the stage, affords its occupants a good point of observation.
>
> The interior decoration of the theatre is what constitutes its chief beauty. The walls and ceiling are beautifully frescoed with elegant designs in soft tints and fine coloring. . . . everything is neat, tasty and simply elegant. The frescoing in itself is sufficient to proclaim its executor an artist, but the opinion of his abilities is doubly heightened by the drop of the curtain, his chef d'oeuvre. It is a marvel of beauty and skilled execution. When it is lowered to the sight of the audience and its manifold beauties were unfolded to their gaze, their enthusiasm knew no bounds, and vented itself in loud applause, cheering and calls for the artist who had originated and executed it. Nor would the audience be quiet until he appeared before them and bowed his acknowledgement. The artist is Mr. Paxson, a resident of Butte, of whose abilities the Silver City may well be proud.
>
> The stage is large, excellently arranged, and provided with complete and beautiful scenery, prepared by Mr. Paxson. The boxes, four in number, are situated two on each side, and in their construction and decoration add no little to the interior beauty of the theatre. They are made with curving fronts, each provided with upholstered railings in front, Brussels carpets and lace curtains.
>
> As whole, the new theatre is a gem, and one of the most brilliant in the cluster of architectural beauty of the Silver City. . . . It is one of the prettiest theatres in the West.

The evening's program was introduced by Butte's mayor and, in turn, Maguire. Attendees wore the finest fashions from New York City. Murray watched from one of the boxes. Another was occupied by Helena millionaire and theater owner John Ming. The general seating was about half full according to the *Herald* correspondent. Two boxes were empty and the governor was not in attendance. The lack of attendance could have been pinned on several factors, Maguire's optimistic ticket pricing and a play without a major star being two chief reasons. The play for the evening was *Victor Durand*, which *Life* magazine critics had given high marks, and which had just come from a stop in Helena. It appears that Paxson, the set designer, received the highest praise of the night.[98]

During the next few years, the Grand Opera House was the foundation for a renaissance of culture in the Rocky Mountains. Maguire led the revival with Murray's financial backing. He lived in an apartment built into the theater and earned a monthly salary independent of the company's success or failures.[99] Paxson also benefited from a unique arrangement, operating his side business from a studio in the basement of the opera house. When thick smoke from the smelters did not block his light, Paxson used his spare time to work on what would become his signature work—*Custer's Last Stand*.[100] Murray maintained an active role beyond writing checks for equipment and operating expenses. He often joined Maguire on trips to New York to book acts and enjoyed mixing with the celebrities of the day. Over time, Murray developed important relationships in the industry, establishing close ties to composer Victor Herbert, producer Augustin Daly, and popular stage actress Ada Rehan.[101]

Two years after opening the theater, Murray called for shareholders to add $50,000 to the company's coffers for future capital improvements and perhaps emergency reserves to cover operating deficits. It is not entirely clear that he had only the theater company's best interests at heart, because this was one of Murray's tactics to squeeze out weak partners in his for-profit ventures. Shareholders had two choices when a capital call was issued: they could stand pat and see their ownership percentage reduced, or they could put in cash proportionate to their existing stake and maintain their ownership position. After the dust settled on Murray's first capital call, he and Marcus Daly each increased their ownership position and committed $7,000 to the new round of financing. The pair's increased funding indicates several casualties among the weaker partners.[102] Maguire personally bought out $4,000 in stock from shareholders who chose not to respond to Murray's cash call.[103]

The following year, disaster struck the Grand Opera House. During a summer performance in 1888, warm weather and stifling smoke from the copper smelters prompted Maguire to open the backstage door and encourage a breeze for the relief of his patrons. As he went on to attend to the opening scene, high in the rafters, one of the many curtains started to sway from the gentle draft. As the play started, gas jets were lit to illuminate the stage. The curtain gently rested against the flames. At first, the fabric smoldered and smoke wafted through the air. Then, with a burst, the fate of the magnificent building was sealed.[104] Seeing the flames, Maguire ushered out the performers and guests without incident. Sifting through the charred remains the next day, he found little of his library, manuscript collection, and personal effects. He had lost virtually everything. Fortunately, his most prized possession, a letter of recommendation from Major General Custer, was out for framing at the time.[105]

Maguire quickly shuffled whatever was salvageable to a nearby building and within days was open for business again in a makeshift theater. The town rallied behind the popular showman and held a benefit to rebuild the theater. Mine owners shut down for a day while a fundraiser was being held at Daly's racetrack.[106] It was widely reported at the time that the event raised upwards of $30,000 for the theater, enough to rebuild and reopen the Grand Opera House.[107] This was likely Maguire's spin to put a good face on the community's efforts, because in reality only $4,000 came to his coffers from the event.[108]

The Second Grand Opera House

Most of the wealthy shareholders, including Marcus Daly, tore up their stock from the first two rounds of funding, clearing the way for a fresh start on financing Butte's second Grand Opera House. The shareholders who held out for some return on their investment transferred the land underlying the Grand Opera House to Maguire but recorded a $17,000 mortgage against the property. Maguire was on the hook to pay these shareholders approximately $1,000 every six months. To build the new opera house, Maguire cobbled together a fragile financing plan that included the Daly fundraiser ($4,000), cash on hand prior to the fire ($6,000), a bank loan secured by his shares in the opera house ($8,000), and Murray's checkbook as a last resort. The rebuild took just six months and the grand reopening was set for January 1888.[109]

Maguire's optimism and limited financial experience affected the launch of the second theater. He spread himself thin by accepting an offer from John Mackay, the Silver King from Nevada, to run Mackay's theater in San Francisco. While Maguire was focused on booking Mackay's theater, construction costs soared in Butte. Maguire had to pledge his revenue from future performances at all of his venues to make up the shortage. This was of little value when both San Francisco and Butte suffered crippling winter storms that kept patrons away from the new facilities. He fell behind on his mortgage payment to the Butte shareholders and never caught up. Fortunately, Maguire had Murray at his side to cover his losses. Unfortunately, Murray's tactics to keep the opera house afloat required several stops in the local courts, an occasional visit to Helena and the Montana Supreme Court, and several disruptions to the theater's schedule.[110]

The litigation that plagued the second Grand Opera House started almost immediately with unpaid contractors and unpaid property taxes.

Murray settled a lawsuit brought in 1890 by purchasing the outstanding contractor liens.[111] It was a strategic move on Murray's part to keep these obligations ahead of the shareholders' mortgage. Four more years passed and the original shareholders, not having received any payments on their note for nearly six years, filed for foreclosure. Murray battled the shareholders for several years, using both the construction liens and unpaid property taxes to keep the group from getting a clean shot at recapturing the property. It took the shareholders two years and several court trials to win their first battle with Murray and finally take possession of their land in 1896. But Murray was not done with the nascent profiteers. The shareholders held title to the land but not to the building or the improvements inside.

Murray seemed to enjoy the cat-and-mouse negotiations because he vowed to clear the brick structure off the site if the shareholders did not sell their land to him, or buy his building.[112] After the shareholders and Murray failed to agree on a price for the land, the tycoon made good on his vow and started removing everything inside the theater. The shareholders sued Murray to stop his gutting of the building, but eventually the Montana Supreme Court affirmed Murray's right to remove everything from the site. The press observed the sometimes comical proceedings as Murray emptied the theater, removing various props: the deep sea, a corner grocery store, two banks, rocks and icebergs, Gothic arches, picket fences, a steamer, a Venetian city, a palace, and a rocky pass. He also took the mundane drapes, chairs, wastepaper baskets, candlesticks, and stepladders.[113]

As Murray proceeded to demolish the structure itself, at least one observer noted that Murray's "demolition" looked much like he was simply preparing for a renovation. Nevertheless, the presence of a construction crew removing pieces of the building brought everyone to the table to clear the outstanding debts of Maguire's opera house. To close the deal, Murray wrote a check for $75,000 to regain full control of the theater. In the fall of 1896, Murray restored the Grand Opera House and handed the reins back to Maguire.[114] During the short interruption, Maguire used nearby facilities to house his performances, showing the same flexibility he demonstrated as a traveling showman when the territories were in their infancy. The litigation years, from 1890 to 1896, did nothing to slow down Maguire's bookings. In fact, these years reflect the height of his success, when bookings included Mark Twain, Sarah Bernhardt, Emma Juch, and Emma Abbot, and he enjoyed partnerships with theater owners in Denver and Oakland.[115]

In appreciation for his friend's financial and legal support, Maguire renamed the third incarnation of his theater the Murray Opera House. This lasted for just seven months until the name reverted back to Maguire Opera House,[116] most likely because Murray was superstitious about having his name on buildings.[117] He claimed that a setback early in his career taught him never to get so full of himself.

The following year, after all the legal dust had settled, Maguire and Murray faced strong headwinds in their attempt to make a profit. One factor was the loss of high-income jobs in Butte as independent miners sold out to eastern corporations. However, the strongest challenge came from powerful syndicates that took control of marquee entertainment throughout the country. These monopolies exerted tight controls over performance dates and eventually relegated the role of theater manager to, in Maguire's words, "that of a janitor."[118] Murray and Maguire came to terms with the new order in 1897 and leased Butte's Grand Opera House to a management company the following year. A retirement benefit was held by the Butte community for Maguire to give him a small cushion for life outside the theater.[119]

Maguire's run, from the early one-man shows in the mining camps to presenting headliners in his palatial Butte opera house, made a distinct mark on the history of theater. Maguire's impact was recounted in histories written about theater in the West by M. B. Leavitt and Frederick Warde, two of the era's great promoters. Warde, writing in *Fifty Years of Make-Believe* about Maguire's early career, said this:

> John was a man of many eccentricities, generous to a fault, loyal to his friends, fond of good company, and ready to recite at every opportunity. His favorite selections were Tennyson's "Charge of the Light Brigade," Hood's "The Bridge of Sighs," and "Shamus O'Brien." All of which he gave with intense earnestness in his native accent. John's resourcefulness and ready wit to meet emergencies were keenly developed by his experience in the early days of Montana when he traveled from camp to camp as an entertainer.[120]

Leavitt, writing about Maguire's post-wilderness career in *Fifty Years in Theatrical Management*, shared similar thoughts:

> John Maguire was a money getter, but not a saver. He was the soul of honor, and no man in his profession west of the Rockies enjoyed a wider circle of friends, or was more charitable. He gave to the needy to the end of his resources. He was never married. For many years, beginning in the seventies, John and I carried on extensive business relations in the Northwest, and our earnings in the end were exceedingly large. And while he represented my interest and handled the finances, he always squared up to the penny. For more than forty years he was prominently identified with the theatrical business of Montana and the Pacific Coast.[121]

Life after the Syndicates

Life after relinquishing Butte's Grand Opera House was a challenge for Maguire. Much of it he spent working in concert with Murray, exploring opportunities as a writer and editor, and occasionally testing the waters to reenter the volatile entertainment business. He spent some time in New York, looking at the possibility of building a theater for Murray near Longacre Square.[122] In 1901 he briefly took back control of his Butte opera house when no one else could make the numbers work in their favor. He and Murray toured nearby cities looking for theaters to create a circuit and re-create their success of the late nineteenth century.[123] After just one season they gave up, and Maguire turned to part-time work as a solo performer and stringer for the newspapers that used to review his plays. In a clear signal that his career as a manager was over, he donated two of his prized possessions to the Montana Historical Society. The first was the recommendation letter he received from Major General George Custer.[124] The second item was his life-size bronze bust, which occupied a spot in the Grand Opera House for many years. It was a gift to him from a childhood friend from Ireland, noted New York sculptor Dennis B. Sheahan.[125] Although the life of a manager was behind him, his friendship with Murray continued. The pair had a few more adventures to play out in the years ahead.

10
Hot Springs and Grand Resorts

Where the bark tepee then stood, the summer cottage now stands among the same old trees; where the Indian trails once threaded the hill and forest, the white man's roads and railways now run.

—*Wonderland* promotional pamphlet, 1902[126]

Murray's ceaseless rail travel, for business and pleasure, took him to every corner of North America and Europe. Like many of his Eastern counterparts, he also found his way to Hot Springs, Arkansas, where a string of resorts piped steaming water to lavish bath houses the equal of any in the world.[127] Murray seized on this concept and partnered with Jim Hill's Northern Pacific Railway to develop equally grand resorts in the Rocky Mountains, at gateways to Yellowstone and the future Glacier National Park. These resorts, in function and design, combined Murray's passion for physical and psychological fitness with the revival of California Mission-style architecture. They also provided a venue for entertaining friends, politicians, and business partners. Murray's endeavors in this business line paralleled his experience in the theater business, as changing technology and concentration of economic power in the East made it difficult for resorts to remain profitable. Nevertheless, Murray tolerated the ups and downs of the resort business, eventually counting three hot spring resorts in his real estate portfolio.

Prior to Murray's investment in resorts, railroad barons promoted passenger travel in the late 1870s and 1880s to attract well-heeled investors to buy land the railroads had received as compensation for the capital they risked on steel, timber, and construction crews. One Northern Pacific Railway advertisement that ran in *Harper's Weekly* guaranteed that travelers would not be subjected to riding with "undesirable company," because only wealthy, high-society people could afford such a trip. Following the recession of 1893, the railroads took a broader view of their potential market, promoting tourist trips to Yellowstone and Yosemite in partnership with hotel and resort owners.[128]

The Northern Pacific Railway, stretching from Seattle to St. Paul, where connections were made to Chicago, St. Louis, and New York, was a common carrier for Murray's business travels. The railroad had stations near Yellowstone Park and Lake McDonald in northwest Montana (the future site of Glacier National Park). The rail stop for Yellowstone was in Livingston, Montana, which served as the northern gateway to Yellowstone. Local hotels were often full of Eastern visitors taking the stagecoach to and from the nation's first national park, where visitors were entertained by the park's hot springs, geysers, waterfalls, and scenic vistas.

Dr. A. J. Hunter was Murray's forerunner in the hot springs business, founding Hunter's Hot Springs outside of Livingston in the 1870s. Hunter had first observed the hot springs in 1864. He was traveling on the Bozeman Trail at the time, en route to the Alder Gulch gold diggings in southwest Montana. Romanticized versions of his first encounter tell of hundreds of colorfully marked teepees representing several Indian tribes. This version claimed the Native Americans treated the springs as neutral territory, allowing the elderly and infirm to peacefully take in the waters.[129] Other versions place only the Crow Indians at the springs, with occasional hostile incursions by Sioux and Blackfeet. Either way, Hunter returned to the area in 1870 after finding no luck in the goldfields. He extricated the natives by claiming squatter's rights to the springs. In 1883, when rail first came to the area, he successfully fended off a legal challenge to his ownership claim from the Northern Pacific. Hunter built rustic accommodations near the springs and operated on a seasonal basis until 1885, when he sold the springs to an investment group.[130] The new owners had big plans for the springs, but little money. Murray provided the group with $50,000 to finance their expansion plans.

Murray wasn't particularly interested in meager profits from the ownership group's loan payments. He wanted their collateral—the small hotel and the land that they provided as security. In 1897, as his borrowers struggled financially, he moved to strike the final blow on their business.[131] He started a rumor that he was forming a partnership with the Northern Pacific Railway to build a competing hotel. The phantom property was just two miles from the hot springs and adjacent to the train depot in Springdale that also served his borrowers' hotel. Murray planned to tap the hot springs and pipe the water to his hotel, following a model used by resorts in Hot Springs, Arkansas. He and the Northern Pacific would each chip in $50,000 to build a grand hotel and spa.[132]

The suggestion of well-funded competition was enough to cause his borrowers to give up their dreams and surrender the property at a foreclosure sale. Murray bid the amount of his loan and took title to the resort. His ambitious plan for the Springdale rail stop was never mentioned again, and he turned his attention to consolidating more property on which to expand

Hunter's Hot Springs resort. Murray bought the adjacent Mendenhall Hotel two years later, in 1899, completing the footprint for his grand scheme.[133] Over the next nine years, Murray added a three-hundred-room hotel, a golf course, tennis courts, an indoor swimming pool, a gymnasium, and a salon to the hot springs complex. To promote the resort, he struck a joint marketing deal with Northern Pacific. Hunter's Hot Springs was one of just two Montana resorts mentioned in the railroad's promotional literature.

A reporter attending a convention at the resort described the architectural design as "the modified Moorish type common to Spanish America," and made the bold claim that it was the "most complete hotel building west of St. Paul." The reporter described the lobby as possessing "an air of homelike, refined hospitality" with its "soft brown tones, its beautifully paneled and beamed walls and ceilings, its alcoves, its cheerful fireplace, and its rich upholstered furnishings." He noted that the rooms featured brass bedsteads and furniture made of solid mahogany, Circassian walnut, birdseye maple, and oak. Continuing his tour, the reporter expressed amazement at the back-of-house fixtures, noting that "the kitchen, pantries, store rooms, cold storage, laundry, and other essential departments are all fitted with the

Murray exported the California mission-style architecture to other parts of the country. He used the style in the expansion of two major resorts in Montana. Pictured here is Murray's grand resort at Hunter's Hot Springs. —Postcard from author's personal collection

newest and best equipment—labor saving devices that are, many of them, too intricate for the average layman to understand." The scribe was likely talking about the earliest versions of machinery to assist with laundry, dishwashing, and food storage.[134]

Promotional material from the railroads extended beyond the quality of the resort to the comforts, and implied safety, of surrounding population centers. In *Wonderland*, a publication written by O. D. Wheeler for the Northern Pacific, potential tourists learned that "the railways have revolutionized the region. Instead of towns composed of log huts and tents, there are now found cities with elegant residences, fireproof business blocks, public libraries, fine churches, school buildings, electric lighted streets and homes, and all the addenda of any modern city."

Murray's strong interest for the fledgling resort industry, much like his interest in the theater, seemed personal, as neither provided financial rewards. Murray was keen on matters involving physical and psychological fitness. He spoke to the press with enthusiasm about his visit to Olympia, the New York fitness farm of wrestler William Muldoon. He saw Muldoon's regimen transform stiffened weaklings into athletes with renewed vigor. Muldoon combined time on the punching bag with summersaults, footraces, wrestling, and sparring to rehabilitate his clients. Murray also noted that Muldoon never turned away the infirm for lack of money. Murray followed this policy, keeping an open door for those down on their luck. It was widely reported that he allowed many of his pioneer friends to stay at the resort free of charge if they were suffering through a rough patch.[135]

Murray's attention to the psychological benefits of resort living was evidenced in his correspondence with his partners. Writing in June to Ed Fletcher, his partner in San Diego, he proclaimed it the "Psychological Season," and with some self-deprecating bullying, encouraged his partner to spend some time away from work to renew his spirits at the hot springs. "Don't get it into your head that things would not go along without your presence," Murray wrote. "Things will go along all right if we are both dead." He encouraged his partner to take a four-week trip that included a stop at Hunter's Hot Springs and a tour of Yellowstone, eventually returning home to "the land of sunshine and liars by the Clark Road."[136]

Murray's interest in physical conditioning was likely a response to his own medical history. He suffered many strokes during his lifetime and needed the aid of a cane later in life.[137] At one time he hired a personal trainer to accompany him on his travels. His choice of trainers, like many of his choices, was unique. Murray hired Abdullah Ben Tahar Sahib Mohammad—A. B. Tahar for short—to serve as his physical culturist, or personal trainer. A. B. claimed to be the son of an Arabian sheik and, prior to his work as a physical culturist, had worked as an acrobat and circus performer. He pulled many of his exercise routines from circus acts and had his clients improve their balance by walking on a slack wire strung between posts, or jumping rope while standing on two-foot-diameter wooden balls.[138]

The medicinal value of hot springs was also part of the marketing focus of Murray's resort. Murray's promotional material echoed that of Dr. Hunter, with claims that cases of rheumatism were typically cured in two weeks. Murray also touted the healing benefits of the waters for arthritis deformans, stomach disorders, chronic constipation, liver and kidney diseases, sciatica, and skin diseases. He piped the mineral water into fountains located in the hotel lobby to give customers easy access to their beneficial qualities. Murray also kept a physician and a team of nurses on staff and suggested medical examinations upon arrival at the resort. For those who could not make it to the resort, he bottled the water and distributed it for sale in nearby cities.[139]

The renovation and expansion of Hunter's Hot Springs also gave Mrs. Murray a stellar platform for entertaining Butte's high society. On a number of occasions, Mrs. Murray rented private rail cars to ferry loads of socialites and their husbands to the hot springs for weekend parties. On one occasion, she hired an orchestra to accompany the group on the half-day trip. Augustus Heinze, both rival and partner to her husband, attended at least one of her parties.[140]

As Murray completed the expansion of Hunter's Hot Springs, he added another resort to his portfolio. He purchased an interest in the Boulder Hot Springs between Butte and Helena. It was an ideal stop for those traveling to Lake McDonald and the future Glacier National Park. He eventually bought out his initial partners and expanded the resort, adding the mission-style architecture he'd brought to Hunter's Hot Springs. He also added fixtures and design elements influenced by the Arts and Crafts movement.[141]

Much like his theaters, Murray's resorts faced increasing pressures from changes in the national and local economies. As the nation's transportation system evolved, and roadways were paved alongside railways, hotel stays became shorter as tourists were no longer tied to fixed train schedules. The convenience of automotive travel also meant tourists could bypass Murray's resorts altogether. Another blow to the local resort industry was the takeover of many mining operations by eastern corporations. This resulted in fewer well-heeled travelers inside the state, as high-paid industry jobs moved east where the money was centered. To counteract these trends, Murray turned his marketing efforts toward regional events and business travelers. He hosted tennis tournaments and conventions to reduce the drag on his balance sheet. He also started investing in real estate and businesses in Livingston, which was well suited to capture automobile traffic to and from Yellowstone National Park.[142]

Despite the countervailing forces impacting his two existing resorts, Murray added a third hot springs resort to his portfolio in 1917, telling the *Ronan Pioneer*, "I've been in Montana fifty years and I haven't noticed the Lord making any more of them." The Broadwater Hotel, located just outside Helena, came with a checkered past, having passed previously through the hands of three millionaires—Colonel Charles Broadwater, Augustus Heinze, and James Breen—before Murray took title.[143] Despite indicating that it would be reopened, Murray made no immediate move to invest in the aging property. It seems Murray had other plans for the well-positioned property—plans that would be revealed in a few short years when he started work on his last will and testament.

Murray's Boulder Hot Springs resort located between Butte and Helena, circa 1910.
—Postcard from author's personal collection

11
Murray's Monterey

Alas for the little town! It is not strong enough to resist the influence of the flaunting caravanserai, and the poor, quaint, penniless native gentlemen of Monterey must perish, like a lower race, before the millionaire vulgarians of the Big Bonanza.

—Robert Louis Stevenson[144]

Monterey was a special place for Jim Murray. He conducted little in the way of business in the community. All his activities in Monterey were rather charitable. If he ever had an inkling of writing an autobiography, it is here that he could romanticize his life. Amongst the adobe ruins, windswept cypress trees, and rocky shores of the Pacific, Murray was at his best, unsullied, for the most part, by the fistfights, litigation, and double-dealing that colored every other community he touched. In Monterey, Murray lived in a grand mansion set amongst an eclectic group of artists, wealthy vacationers, fishmongers, and military officers. Here he took a keen interest in the life of Junípero Serra and his Carmel Mission, the artists who captured the area's beauty on canvas, and the Spanish architecture that defined the region. Monterey is also where he laid John Maguire to rest, and where he made plans to stay by his friend's side for eternity.

Monterey became a fashionable resort in 1880 when the Southern Pacific Railroad extended passenger rail service from San Francisco to the seaside community, built the lavish Del Monte Resort, and carved a seventeen mile scenic trail for carriage rides along the coast.[145] The location was equally attractive to Murray as a business headquarters because of his increasing interest in Southern California and Arizona. A residence in Monterey would place him in the center of his vast network of businesses and a short train ride from San Francisco, where he had established several strong relationships in the city's Irish Catholic community. Eighty percent of the city's population was Catholic, and a good share were Irish,[146] including Robert Tobin, a founding member of the Hibernia Bank who sat on the board of Murray's Seattle bank. The timing of the move, just after the turn of the century was also good for Murray because his nephew James had returned to Butte from New York University with a law degree and was fully capable of handling most of the elder Murray's business concerns in Montana.

The Murray Hacienda

There was only one mansion in Monterey at the time that suited a multi-millionaire, and as fortune would have it, the seaside palace was on the market. The Tevis mansion encompassed more than one thousand feet of undulating coastline. The new Monterey city plan, surveyed in 1886, laid out fifty-six residential lots in what is now Cannery Row. Hugh Tevis bought seventeen of the lots to accommodate a 15,000-square-foot mansion. The bookends of the estate were expansive living quarters to the south and a large horse stable to the north. In between were guest and servant quarters, a greenhouse, and a bowling alley. Tevis, the son and legatee of Lloyd Tevis, a financial partner of Marcus Daly, spared no expense. The mansion featured silver fixtures and redwood paneling, and the latest in technology. The home had hot water throughout, a battery-powered backup electrical system, and ice-making machines.

Hugh Tevis built the mansion for his fiancé between 1900 and 1901, but he died shortly after they were married, and before they occupied the house. The widowed bride may have used the house occasionally as a winter retreat for a couple of years, but she then sold it to local real estate developer David Jacks in 1904. Jacks held the home for a few months before selling the estate to Murray. It is likely that the Murrays were the first permanent occupants of the residence. Murray transformed the bowling alley into an art gallery and decorated the home in the style of his resorts, with bearskin rugs on the floors and plenty of mounted animal heads on the walls. Murray eventually added a windmill, modeled after one in San Francisco's Golden Gate Park, to draw his own water and avoid municipal charges. He also bought several lots across the street to create a buffer between himself and other residents.[147]

Junípero Serra Tributes

Shortly after moving into his seaside compound, Murray got caught up in the renewed interest in California's missions and put in motion his first tribute to the legendary Junípero Serra. For this project, he commissioned the most popular sculptor of the day, Douglas Tilden. California born and Paris trained, Tilden was both deaf and mute from an early age. In Tilden's view, both disabilities, the results of a bout with scarlet fever, accentuated his artistic and creative talents. San Francisco's mayor, James Duval Phelan, appointed Tilden to that city's beautification committee in the 1890s, and the result was a string of significant sculptures beautifying the urban landscape. His iconic works include *Admission Day* (1897) and the *Mechanics Monument*

(1901). These spectacular works earned him the title of Father of San Francisco Sculpture. His commission from Murray was to create two important elements for a granite monument to mark the location of Serra's first mass in America. The first element was a profile of Serra to be placed in the center of a cross that would adorn the monument. The second was a relief of the Carmel Mission to sit at its base. Willis Polk, best known for his architectural designs, coordinated the fabrication of the monument with stonecutters M. T. Carroll and Sons at the Holy Cross Cemetery in Colma, California.[148]

The site of Serra's first mass was less than eight hundred yards from Murray's residence, just inside the front gate of the Presidio, a military installation that bisected "old" and "new" Monterey. The famed oak tree that purportedly served as the backdrop for Serra's mass was still standing, although just barely, at the time. The only indication that anything special had occurred at the location was a small wooden cross marked "June 3d 1770."

Serra had come to this location in dramatic fashion. On May 31, 1770, sailing aboard the *St. Antonio* from San Diego, he knew he had arrived in Monterey by the sight of three large bonfires—signals that scouts traveling by land had found their destination. The *St. Antonio* acknowledged the scout's signals with a volley of cannon fire. The next day, the scouts joined Serra on board the *St. Antonio* and celebrated the impending founding of Mission San Carlos Borromeo, today commonly known as the Carmel Mission. On Pentecost Sunday, June 3, 1770, the parties from land and sea converged at the oak to bury a casualty of their travels, conduct mass, establish the mission, and take possession of the land in the name of their Catholic majesty, the king of Spain.[149]

The sacred site was owned by the city of Monterey, a gift from a private historic preservation group led by George Hearst. The group, the Landmark League of California, acquired and donated several historic sites in the Monterey area and planned to install improvements as funds were available. Murray seized on the opportunity presented by the league. In the absence of any funds for improvements, Murray took control of the design, funding, and placement of the memorial.[150]

John Maguire soon joined Murray in Monterey for reasons unrelated to the Serra tribute. Murray needed his good friend after a medical emergency, and Maguire answered the call. On January 11, 1905, eight months after moving to California, Murray had suffered a massive stroke while staying at the St. Francis Hotel in San Francisco. News reports placed him at death's door, and the doctors in attendance "entertained little hope for their patient's recovery." Murray, however, managed to stave off death for another day, and Maguire was a welcome addition to his recovery efforts.[151]

Maguire stayed with Murray for several months and reported his friend's condition to a Butte newspaper, writing that in just a few short months Murray had regained perfect health. He also gave Butte readers his first impression of the Murray's new residence, writing, "The Murray home here excels anything I have ever seen. It is such a combination of grandeur and simplicity harmonized into a poetic entity as to remind one much of Irving's Spanish descriptions of all that is most chaste in the Alhambra, and its greatest adornment is the old Montana hospitality of its owners." Maguire noted that the Chautauqua, a series of lectures and presentations on art and literature, was in town, and that he planned to stay awhile and work on a book.[152] Several months later he wrote again, but only to share a poem he was inspired to write while sitting on the Murrays' seaside terrace. The poem (reproduced in the appendix) offered his explanation for the Irish origins of the hummingbirds in Monterey.[153]

As Murray's health returned, he started work again on his Serra tribute, and Maguire returned to his solo plays and work as a stringer. Murray made steady but slow progress that year, gaining approval from the war department to construct a foundation on its property.[154] The local press noted the pouring of the foundation and reported for the first time Murray's intention to replace the simple wooden cross "where practically the history of California began" with "a handsome cross of Vermont granite, twelve feet, in height."[155] To make room for the monument, construction workers laying the foundation removed the last of the branches of the now-dead oak. Onlookers quickly snatched up the historic limbs.[156] The following year, little progress on the project was evident, as a natural disaster turned everyone's attention to much greater needs.

The Great Earthquake

On April 6, 1906, Mary Murray and her son Stuart were sleeping in the Monterey hacienda when, just past 5 a.m., they felt the earthquake (eighty miles to the north) that felled San Francisco. Stuart Haldorn recounted the events to the *Washington Post*:

> I was asleep in my home when the shock came on Wednesday morning and was awakened by the rocking of the building. I felt as a man does when he is on the ocean and the ship careens as great waves roll under it. It all came too suddenly to make me much frightened, though I heard the timbers cracking under the strain. The shock lasted several seconds, some of the plaster in my room falling, and then stopped, only to start again for another few seconds. I heard the doors flying opening where the shock had pulled them away from the latch, and now and then a crash outside. At the second shock I jumped from my bed, then very much awake, and hurried to the windows. I knew what it meant by this time, and I rushed downstairs in my night robe and out into the street, where I saw many people in like attire—some of them quite ridiculous—and a

> great deal of debris about the houses, where the cornices and the chimneys had fallen down. The most scared creature was our family cat, with its hair standing out straight and mewing pitifully.[157]

The recovery efforts that lay ahead for the City by the Bay were daunting, and opinions were sought from all quarters. Reporters caught up with Murray in Salt Lake City, where he suggested the city think big—really big. He noted that among the heap of ashes, several well-built buildings survived. He called on city leaders to issue $500 million in one-hundred-year bonds and adopt new ordinances to remodel the city in its entirety. He asked them to "picture the city with streets not less than 80 feet in width." He discouraged skyscrapers and called for boulevards to sweep around the waterfront all the way from North Beach to the iconic Cliff House restaurant, and parks throughout the city. Both his building height and street width suggestions were likely made to prevent another city-wide fire like the one that followed the earthquake. He also wanted to level Goat Island (today known as Yerba Buena Island) in the middle of the bay to an elevation just above high tide and make it the terminus for all railroads. He concluded his remarks by predicting, "I believe that the most modern city in the world will spring up on the ruins of old San Francisco."[158] Although urban planners took a different path than what Murray prescribed, many would concur that his prediction about the future prominence of the city came true.

Until then, San Francisco was in desperate need of money and shelter. Maguire did his part, hosting a fundraiser in Salt Lake City with his extensive network of entertainers.[159] Murray contributed as well, providing cash to support artists left homeless by the quake. Murray and his wife had grown close to the artists of the region. After converting the bowling alley in their mansion to an art gallery, they actively collected the works of several California artists, including Francis McComas, Gene Francis, and William Keith. Murray provided his financial support through Charles Rollo Peters, an artist with an international reputation and a thirty-acre estate at the edge of Monterey known as Peters Gate.

Murray gave Peters $10,000 in 1906 and another $5,000 in 1907.[160] This allowed Peters to take in artists displaced by the earthquake and then later open a gallery at the Del Monte Hotel to sell their works. It was the first gallery dedicated exclusively to California artists.[161] This was a significant amount of money in that period. It would have taken a blue-collar worker thirty years to earn that amount, and a white-collar worker ten years. Murray recorded the gifts as mortgages on Peters's property but made no effort to recapture the money. This was a standard practice with many of Murray's charitable gifts. He structured them as loans to make sure his beneficiaries did not misappropriate the gift. If they did, he could make their lives very unpleasant through the court system. Peters must have used the money in accordance with Murray's wishes because when the notes came due after a year, Murray made no effort to collect.

During the chaos of 1906, the stonecutters working on Murray's tribute to Serra likely turned to much grimmer tasks. Nevertheless, Murray found yet another way to celebrate the location of the first mass. Murray sought out a canvas capturing the event painted by Frenchman Léon Trousset. The painting was produced circa 1877[162] while the artist was in California and making frequent stops in the Monterey area.[163] Trousset, as he did with many of his works, raffled the painting in San Francisco to earn money.[164] Given the concentration of wealthy Catholics in the city at the time, it is likely that he sold many tickets. Reportedly among the ticket purchasers were several noted clergy, including Father Montgomery, who later rose to become an archbishop. The winner of the raffle was French capitalist Louis Dutertre.[165] When Dutertre left San Francisco to operate a large hot springs resort in Golconda, Nevada, the painting found a prominent spot in the drawing room of his hotel. John Maguire found the painting on his travels between Salt Lake City and Monterey and acquired it for Murray at a "handsome price."

Maguire's eloquent description of the artwork's homecoming underscored the importance of the piece to the Catholic community in Monterey. Upon its arrival in Monterey, he wrote,

> Securely packed in a case measuring nearly eight feet long and six feet high, Trousset's painting, "The Landing of Junípero Serra," and the celebration of "The First Mass" under the live oak tree at Monterey arrived here by express from Golconda for me yesterday.
>
> The canvas is nearly seven feet wide and five and a half feet high, and is mounted in a heavy walnut frame. The subject is the celebration of the first mass on the spot ever since marked by a cross under the branches of the live oak, where a temporary altar was erected for the ceremony. Over the altar and secured by common ship rope fastenings to the branches of the tree is a canopy of ship's canvas. In the center of the altar is the well-known crucifix now in the Mission church at Monterey, and which Father Junípero always held in his hand when preaching to the Indians.
>
> On the stout arm of the tree are suspended two of the mission bells. The picture is taken at the supremely impressive moment during the elevation of the chalice, which is uplifted by Father Junípero, while the little congregation are on their knees bowing in adoration of the holy sacrifice. The father is being assisted in the celebration by the two padres who arrived with him on that memorable 3d of June, 1770.
>
> There are more than sixty figures in the picture. Facing the altar, but at a respectable distance, are three rows of Spanish soldiers in their leather jackets and military accoutrements; immediately backing them in their picturesque garb are the sailors of the frigate which is seen at anchor close

> to the shore. While at either side of the altar are the superior officers, military and naval of the expedition.
>
> A central figure is the Indian boy, mentioned by Father Junípero in his diary, who is "serving mass", while on the one side is a group of converted Indians who accompanied the expedition. On the opposite are some Monterey Indians curiously peering between the rocks at the strange ceremony.
>
> There is a magnificent view of that portion of Monterey harbor sweeping around the old townsite and the hazy brown view of the further shore.[166]

Shortly after the arrival of the Trousset, Murray may have contemplated, for at least a moment, changing his plans for the granite monument featuring Tilden's work. The *San Francisco Call* reported Murray's intention that "one of the historic crosses that was taken to Ireland from Spain more than 100 years ago will mark the spot where Father Juniper Serra landed." Adding a bit of bluster that likely came from Murray himself, the

LANDING OF PADRE SERRA AT MONTEREY, CAL., June 3, 1770

Painting owned by Mr. J. A. Murray — By courtesy of the owner

Léon Trousset, Father Serra Celebrates Mass at Monterey, 1877. —As it appeared in *Views and Legends of Monterey and Surroundings*; now in collection of Carmel Mission

report added, "The importation of the historic relic will attract visitors to Monterey."[167] As it turned out, the historic cross, if it ever existed at all, did not find its way to Monterey, and Murray continued with his plan to use Tilden's work.[168] As for the potential visitors, Murray found another way to promote the significance of the site. He allowed J. K. Oliver, a prominent Monterey-area photographer, to capture an image of the Trousset painting for a promotional brochure, *Views and Legends of Monterey and Surroundings*, which was distributed in local shops.[169] This was just the first of many photographs of the iconic painting that made its way into publications. Today, full-color images of the painting adorn virtually every publication associated with Serra or the Carmel Mission.

Maguire's delivery of the painting to Murray marked a new chapter in the pair's relationship. Murray, wanting to ensure Maguire had means and substance in his life, started a daily newspaper in Monterey, the *Monterey Daily Cypress*, and installed Maguire as its associate editor.[170] The first edition rolled of the presses in January 1907. Maguire's new title and his background gave him opportunities to meet some of the nation's literary greats because Charles Stoddard, Jack London, and others were frequent visitors to the area. Tragically, however, Maguire's time in his new position lasted less than three months. He died on March 22, 1907, from heart disease. His long and eventful life was memorialized at a high mass performed by Father Mestres at the Carmel Mission. Heartfelt tributes to Maguire's life appeared in papers up and down the West Coast. Universally, writers mentioned Maguire's historic efforts pioneering theater in the West and his selfless concern for others. A passage from a Salt Lake City paper was typical: "John Maguire was a whole-souled-generous-hearted Irishman, ever ready during his days of prosperity to dip deep down into his pocket to relieve the financial condition of anyone who appealed to him for assistance."[171] Murray's paper in Monterey shared a view of Maguire's stature in the industry as "one of the best known managers in the United States. No man in the profession was thought more of. Many of the leading stars in the country today owe their rise to him."[172]

Murray arranged for the burial of his closest friend on the Catholic side of the Monterey City cemetery, just over a mile from his mansion. Murray marked his friend's grave with an elaborate monument, nearly six feet tall and four feet wide, incorporating the stage of Butte's Grand Opera House engulfed by rough-hewn granite. The inscription at the top of the monument reads, "Ring Down the Drop, Life's Fitful Play is O'er," which, combined with the partially carved theater stage, expressed Murray's sorrow that his friend had not gotten all that he had hoped for out of life. With nothing more to do for his friend in life, Murray purchased another plot in the cemetery, looking forward to a time when he could provide comfort to his friend in the world beyond.[173]

Headstone for John Maguire, commissioned by James A. Murray.
—Photo by Kevin Bransfield

The loss of his dearest friend was certainly a major blow to Murray, but he showed no signs of slowing down in work, or with his passion projects. In fact, he redoubled his efforts in memorializing Serra's life, taking on a major renovation of Serra's Carmel Mission. Efforts to restore the deteriorated mission had begun in the 1880s with the construction of a new roof. Murray's work was the next significant improvement to the mission, which was badly in need of interior improvements. The tile floors from Serra's day were all but gone, and only a few wood planks partially covered the mission's dirt floors. An article published in Murray's newspaper detailed the scope of his restoration of the historic church. The article, titled "Restoring of Church Floor: Carmel Mission Is Like When Indians Attended There," was published on March 29, 1908, and is reprinted below:

> The work of restoring the floor of Carmel Mission, undertaken by James A. Murray of this city, has been completed. As it is now the lower part of the church is almost the same as when thousands of Indians went there to attend services.

A cement floor has been laid all over the church, which is 49x125 feet. The floor is laid in diagonal blocks and is colored red to represent the old mission tiling. A new floor has also been placed in the chapel and sachristy [*sic*].

Inside the chancel the floor was laid with old tile which remained unbroken on a bed of cement.

The tombs of Junípero Serra and the several of his fellow priests were raised and the old stones that covered them replaced. Leading to the altar massive cement steps have been built.

The old stone stairway leading up to the little pulpit has been repaired with the identical stone that the builders of the Mission used. Stone for the purpose was quarried on the Gregg Ranch a couple miles away and brought to the church and cut. It would take an expert to determine whether the steps had been repaired.

The stairway leading up to the old belfry tower, which was built of chalk rock, has been repaired with the same material.

For about four months this work of restoration has been going on under the direction of Charles W. Meader. Instructions from Mr. Murray were to replace the work as nearly as possible to the original, and this has been carefully done. Over 5000 square feet of cement work has benn [*sic*] laid.[174]

Murray funded and directed the first interior renovation of the Carmel Mission.
—Postcard from author's personal collection

Meader, the project manager, was the son of another well-known pioneer who made his mark in California and Montana. Charles T. Meader was elected mayor of Stockton, California, in 1865, prior to pulling stakes and heading to Butte, Montana. There he is credited with locating the first copper mine in that city and building the first smelter.[175] Unfortunately, as many who pioneer a town, it was those who learned from Meader's mistakes that attained great riches.[176]

After Murray's renovation, the next significant restorations of the Carmel Mission were conducted after 1920 by Harry Downie—much of which replaced Murray's work. The stair work to the small pulpit and the outside stair to the belfry are likely the only remains of Murray's contribution at the mission. Meader's completion of the renovation work coincided with the delivery of Murray's monument to Serra. On March 23, the granite shaft arrived in Monterey. Heavy trucks and a team of sixteen horses were employed to move the monument into place,[177] after which it was covered pending the official unveiling. The official dedication of the monument took place on June 3, the anniversary of the Franciscan father's landing.

When the cover was pulled from the great shaft of granite and the monument was revealed, the public saw for the first time Murray's design. The shaft was adorned with a large Celtic cross, featuring the bas-reliefs sculpted by Tilden. The Celtic cross featured intricate knot-work patterns without beginning or end, symbolizing the knots that "bind the soul to the

Murray commissioned a Celtic cross to mark the location of Junípero Serra's first mass in northern California. —California History Room, Monterey Public Library

world."[178] This form of cross, certainly unfamiliar to Serra, was immediately recognizable to Irish Catholics in the community. It had recently been revived as a symbol of Irish nationalism in their mother country. The Sinn Féin party was using the image on postage seals to raise funds and protest English imperialism.[179]

Murray's selection of the Celtic cross was more than likely a reflection of his ardent Irish nationalism, but he also could have been recognizing the support the Irish gave to the Spanish missionaries. The only public expression of his motivation came in the form of a poem, "The Passing of an Oak," commissioned by his wife in 1909. The poet, Mary Sullivan Spence, was the daughter of Irish pioneer John Sullivan, one of the founders of the Hibernia Bank in San Francisco, and wife of Monterey land baron Rudolph Spence. Sullivan Spence's words offered a Eurocentric view of the Serra's legacy and, in part of one stanza, captured the significance of the first mass to the Catholic community, declaring it the moment when the "Western empire's spirit woke, In the name of God and Spain."

Sullivan-Spence offered a laudatory stanza about Murray's role in commemorating the site of the fallen oak tree, adding an asterisk and footnote to ensure future readers understood her reference:

Vacancy–where once it rose

Centuries beneath the sky;

'Til came *one** who saw, and chose

That a memory should not die,

And a white shaft guards the fame

Of a little oak at rest–

Cenotaph that yet shall claim

Kinship with the old world's best;

But for this there would not be

(In a world which can forget),

Aught a memory of that tree;[180]

*Mr. James A. Murray

The dedication of the monument in 1908 marked the culmination of Murray's work to commemorate Serra and the places he worshipped. It is also the year Monterey's influence on other parts of Murray's business empire was revealed. High in the Rocky Mountains, Murray was completing the rebuild of one grand resort (Hunter's Hot Springs) and beginning the expansion of another (Boulder Hot Springs). Both featured the mission-style architecture that surrounded Murray in his new hometown. At Hunter's Hot Springs, near the gateway to Yosemite, and at Boulder Hot Springs, on the roadway to the future Glacier National Park, the rooflines of his hotels featured multiple arches, similar to the one prominent on the Carmel Mission. By exporting his favorite stylings, Murray introduced thousands of East Coast tourists traveling on the Northern Pacific Railway to the beautiful designs featured in virtually all of Serra's missions.

Murray flirted with continuing his charitable works in Monterey but, for one reason or another, nothing ever came of some bold proclamations. In 1910, he claimed he would completely rebuild the Carmel Mission. His boast was repeated by multiple papers in the Bay Area, with a reporter writing that the "Carmel Mission will not only be rebuilt, but it will be restored inside and out to its former grandeur by James Murray, the millionaire clubman whose summer home, the Hacienda, overlooking Monterey Bay is one of the show places of the country." Murray reportedly was in touch with the "proper authorities" to "revive the mission to all its former glory" under his direction. "No expense will be spared in paintings, vestments or altar linen; everything will be looked into, as well as the necessary replastering, reprinting and repainting." [181]

There is no doubt that Murray had the cash to execute his bold vision for the mission. He had nearly a million dollars on hand, and he needed just upward of $50,000 to finance his proposal. A likely factor in derailing the project was the control he demanded over every endeavor. Murray was the consummate micromanager, and he never spent anything of consequence without control or strings in place—something Charles Rollo Peters would soon realize for himself. Father Mestres likely did not give Murray free rein to conduct the renovation project, and Murray would never write a check without conditions that would allow him to recapture his money if he did not like how it was spent. Mestres was wise not to give Murray a mortgage on the mission in return for his donation toward any renovations.

After his blustery musings about renovating the Carmel Mission, Murray's public displays of charity were not seen again by the community. His diminished interest in community betterment may have been due to the passing of John Maguire, or perhaps it was the withdrawal of artists from the community. In either case, he took on no other grand projects in his adopted hometown. Murray's next appearance of note in Monterey history occurred in 1912, in a place where he was very comfortable: the county's superior court. In 1912 and 1913, Murray filed suit against his former beneficiary, Charles Rollo Peters. The artist left the Monterey community shortly after opening the Del Monte Art Gallery and never returned. His son, writing about his dad several years after his death, indicated that Monterey carried too many sad memories for his father to remain at his legendary estate. Peters had suffered the loss of children and his wife to tragedy between 1900 and 1908. Sometime between 1909 and 1910, Peters cut all ties to the community and sold his estate to Sarah Todd, a local rancher.[182]

Murray was apparently caught off guard by the transaction because Peters did nothing to address the mortgages held by Murray on his property. There is also no indication that Peters sought permission from Murray to retain all the proceeds from the sale of his estate. Given Murray's reputation, Peters's oversight is understandable. The wealthy miner had issued hundreds of thousands of dollars in personal loans that went uncollected. Peters likely felt that if Murray had not asked for repayment for three or four years, then he was of a mind to forgive the loan entirely. Not so in this case. Peters likely ran up against another tenet of Murray's partnerships: no one could get rich on his money. Partners could live a modest lifestyle, but they could not enrich themselves with Murray's money.

Murray filed lawsuits to assert the validity of his mortgages on Peters Gate and to foreclose on the new owner's interests. It appears he succeeded in his effort to gain title to the property, as Todd entered into a mortgage with Murray after the lawsuits were decided in his favor. Whether any money exchanged hands for the clouded title is unclear. Murray probably did not receive much, but the foreclosure process allowed him to go after Peters for some compensation. Court records indicate that Peters was forced to sell two paintings hanging at the St. Francis Hotel in San Francisco in order to make at least a symbolic payment to Murray. Paintings by established California artists at that time sold for $50 to $500, indicating that Murray's lawsuits were not so much about the money as the principle of transaction.[183] If Peters had held on to his property until Murray passed, he would have joined the company of many others who had their loans forgiven, as Murray's estate found itself swamped by such loans.

Mrs. Murray's Big Move

Mrs. Murray found the move to Monterey much to her liking. She had every intention of outliving her husband and providing a rich life for her son. She wasn't sure that was possible if her primary residence remained at the apartment over her husband's bank in Butte.[184] The city was full of her husband's confidants, a brother's widow, two nephews, and a niece continually weaving their way through her husband's business affairs. Mrs. Murray needed her own power base, free of her husband's cronies and relatives. Past controversies limited her choices, particularly on the East Coast, but her husband's choice of Monterey aligned nicely with her plans.

Mrs. Murray's desire for a home far from the Treasure State's mining towns was not unusual—it was in fact the norm for the wealthiest capitalists. By 1900, Murray's fellow Copper Kings and partners W. A. Clark and

Marcus Daly had both acquired residences on Millionaires' Row along Fifth Avenue in New York City. Silver baron John Mackay joined the pair as well. Clark was interested in breaking into New York society; Daly benefited from proximity to his new partner and employer, the Rockefeller syndicate; and Mackay had left the decision to his wife. She, like W. A. Clark, was very interested in breaking into the upper echelons of New York society.[185]

Murray was a frequent visitor to New York, and once boasted of plans to build a mansion on the Hudson, but he had no interest in high society and would never be an employee of a New York syndicate. Mrs. Murray had no interest in a permanent home in New York, either. Twenty years earlier she had been involved in a scandalous affair that started just one hundred miles away in Reading, Pennsylvania, and spilled over to Philadelphia. The only person in Butte who knew all the details was her ex-husband, George Haldorn. Mrs. Murray, it turns out, was a woman with many last names—Coulter, Smith, Haldorn, and Murray—each with an intriguing story.

Mrs. James A. Murray was born Mary Hammond Coulter on June 26, 1860, and was raised in Minersville and Reading, Pennsylvania. Her parents were both deaf mutes and teachers. Her father died when she was young, and her mother eventually moved to Philadelphia, where she taught at the Institute for the Deaf and Dumb, which still operates today as the Pennsylvania School for the Deaf. During Mary's mother's tenure, the school operated near downtown on Broad and Pine Streets. Mary attended boarding school in nearby Pottstown, between Reading and Philadelphia. She graduated when she was nineteen, returned to Reading for a brief spell, and fell in love with a local physician. The happy couple was engaged and set a wedding date. Three days before her wedding, however, Mary was presented with a significantly better opportunity. Frederick Smith, grandson of a Pennsylvania Supreme Court justice, and the only child of a wealthy lawyer, offered a competing proposal. Smith had a moderately successful legal career of his own but was under no pressure to make a living for himself. He had plenty of wealth in his family and was primarily interested in producing an heir—an ambition that eluded him in his first marriage. Smith, forty-eight, was nearly thirty years Mary's senior.

Mary chose money over love and married Smith on July 2, 1879. Wedded bliss, if it ever existed, ended for certain after just a few short weeks. Smith noticed his vivacious bride and former US Senator Roscoe Conkling exchanging flirtatious glances. Shortly thereafter he found a cache of letters from the doctor his bride had left at the altar. Smith's jealousy quickly soured the relationship, and Mary left Reading to be near her mother in Philadelphia. She moved into a boarding house in which she had lived before her marriage. The proprietor there was in a relationship at the time with a young divorce lawyer by the name of George Haldorn. She connected the two, perhaps hoping to gain some benefit from Mary's potential windfall. Haldorn filed Mary's divorce papers only to find that Smith had beat him to the courts by a few days. The lawyers then proceeded to engage in a series of failed entrapment schemes, each trying to prove their opponent's infidelity. Mary soon found out she was pregnant with Smith's heir and, even as she brought the pregnancy to term, continued her efforts to end the marriage. She named her daughter Marie Carroll Smith. At some point during the legal proceedings, and certainly before a settlement was reached, Haldorn fell for Mary and dumped his boardinghouse flame. In return, the spurned proprietor turned against Mary in court testimony. The titillating drama played out in East Coast papers over a two-year period. The episode ended with a divorce for Mary and Smith, an heir for Smith, and a second marriage for Mary.

The newspaper reports were merciless to Mary. Her husband successfully cast himself as the jilted one and Mary as a gold-digging deserter. Upon the couple's separation, a reporter wrote that Mary was "only nineteen years old and practically as inexperienced and unmatured as a school girl." When divorce papers were filed, Washington, DC's *Evening Star* reported that Mary's "face was her fortune." Finally, when Mary wed her divorce-attorney-turned-lover, the Reading paper wrote that Mary "possessed a pretty face and was bewitchingly seductive" and, regarding her second nuptials, "Such events have transpired before and will probably happen again." With their reputations in tatters, George and Mary Haldorn decided to make a new life in the West, leaving her baby daughter behind for Smith to shower with riches.[186] After stopping briefly in Fargo, they moved to Butte, where Haldorn began his quest to become the attorney to the Bonanza Kings.[187]

The Haldorns made the right choice to go west, and Mary made the right choice never to return home. Monterey was the perfect location for Mary to build her own network to seize control of Jim Murray's wealth when the time was right.

Mary's first opportunity to break any hold Murray's blood relatives had on her future inheritance came when her husband suffered a massive stroke. While John Maguire came to Monterey to help his friend recover, Mary worked to accelerate control of her financial future. She convinced Murray, with Wells Fargo bank officials as her allies, to transfer title to the Monterey mansion to her name. The transfer included ownership to all of the furniture, two carriages, and two automobiles.[188] Likely using Murray's poor health as justification, she also pushed Murray's cashier in Butte, E. L. Chapman, to dissolve Sandbar Brown's partnership with her husband. Chapman wrote to Sandbar offering little comfort for the financial strain the disentanglement placed on the pioneer. "Mr. Murray does not want you to go bankrupt," Chapman offered.[189] He might have added, "But he and his wife would like to press you right to the edge."

Sandbar would not soon forgive the Murrays for forcing the dissolution of their business.

Over the next few years, Mary's plan to consolidate power in Monterey was aided by the deaths of several of her husband's cronies and a brother. Robert Tobin died in 1906, followed by John Maguire and Murray's brother Daniel ("Danny") in 1907, and finally by Silas King in 1908.[190] Murray made his way from Los Angeles to Butte to be at King's bedside while he lay on his deathbed. Murray also likely made the trip to start unraveling the investments he had placed in King's name. Complicating the process would be jilted partner Sandbar Brown. Brown had not forgotten how he was treated following Murray's stroke, and he was looking for opportunities to make Murray pay.

Brown wrote to one of King's relatives, a nephew named D. M. Watts, suggesting ways to thwart Murray's attempt to claw back properties held in King's name. First, however, he let Watts know what he was up against. "He will do anything and everything to give you fellows the worst of it, and he never sleeps," Brown wrote. Brown then proceeded to advise Watts that he should form a syndicate to bid on one of the properties that was planned for liquidation. Brown felt Murray could be bid up by the syndicate because, "He will not quit, he's not built that way." Failure to have a shill in the bidding, Brown warned, would result in Murray acquiring the property quietly, buying it for "merely nothing."[191] Brown's complicated scheme was likely beyond what King's relative could understand. Watts worked as a butcher and was not engaged in any of King's real estate schemes with Murray. Murray ended up negating any potential complications by going to the courts directly and pulling his mining properties out of the estate, presenting evidence that King was only on the titles as a custodian and held no actual interest.[192] Murray's victory over the King estate was Mary's victory, too. While Brown would have to look for revenge another day, Mary was one step closer to consolidating her husband's splintered estate and bringing it within reach of her legal team in Monterey.

Part III

End Games

1910—1921

12
Betting on San Diego

It seems to me you become very optimistic at times. Don't care to accuse you of drinking or anything of the kind, but like many others you have your ups and downs.

—James A. Murray to his San Diego partner[1]

Murray's interest in San Diego was piqued by the progress of the Panama Canal and the extensive rail network serving the coastal city. He surmised that the city, with a population in 1910 one-eighth the size of Seattle's, was destined to expand and become a great seaport.[2] To tap San Diego's potential, Murray had to find a local operative to scout opportunities and manage his future holdings.[3] A mutual acquaintance, E. Bartlett Webster, introduced Murray to a prime candidate named Ed Fletcher.[4] Fletcher was a good fit for Murray; he was hungry, personable, and knowledgeable about community politics.

Ed Fletcher, born and raised in Massachusetts, traveled to San Diego in 1888, when he was just fifteen years old, to live with his sister. His first job was working for a produce vendor. He traveled all over the county and came to know every inch of land surrounding the city. He knew when the streams ran dry and which land escaped the winter's frost. His optimism, persistence, and bravado—along with his local knowledge—allowed him to find work as a middleman on several important development and infrastructure projects in the region.

After their initial introduction in 1908, Fletcher wrote to Murray on a regular basis, pitching investment opportunities. Sometimes Fletcher included two or three proposals in one letter.[5] Every deal was a winner in Fletcher's eyes. Murray's responses to Fletcher's requests, throughout their partnership, ranged from surprise to dismay. On one occasion, after Fletcher wrote asking for one hundred dollars, Murray replied, "I'm surprised that a man of your age should refer the matter to me." Murray seemed incredulous that Fletcher, for all his great ideas, appeared helpless to act on even the smallest opportunity. Nevertheless, Murray never tired of Fletcher's suggestions, and Fletcher never tired of rejection. Eventually,

Murray funded two loans for Fletcher: one to purchase real estate in downtown San Diego, and another to build a trolley line serving the city's center.[6]

In 1910, Murray finally found a deal he liked for himself. One of Fletcher's letters included a suggestion that Murray acquire the bankrupt San Diego Flume Company, a private water company started in 1886 to serve portions of San Diego County.[7] The Flume Company was a perfect match for Murray. He was experienced at managing flumes and water utilities, and at orchestrating local politics to increase their revenues. In Pocatello, he had installed a nephew to watch his water company. At the same time, he started a newspaper, the *Pocatello Chronicle*, to promote his views, and he built a theater to generate goodwill in the community. He kept Idaho's fledgling State Utilities Commission at bay through various legal maneuvers. He did much the same in Livingston, Montana, where he also owned the local water system. The San Diego Flume Company served a much larger community, but the same dynamics were at play, and the price was just a fraction of the cost of the original owner's investment. After contemplating the opportunity for six weeks, Murray directed Fletcher to obtain the water contracts needed to assess the company's potential. He reviewed the terms of the contracts and decided that the Flume Company was worth his time and money. It would require a great deal of both.

The purchase price was $150,000. Murray paid $125,000 in cash for a five-sixths interest, and Fletcher borrowed $25,000 to secure a one-sixth interest.[8] They closed the acquisition on June 1, 1910, and renamed the company the Cuyamaca Water Company (CWC) after the mountain range that defined its watershed.[9] Shortly after the deal closed, Fletcher asked Murray for cash to hire consultants, pay himself a salary, and make repairs. Murray denied all three requests.[10] He expected Fletcher to donate his time and to focus on increasing revenues, not expenses. As a minority owner, Fletcher had no say in the financial decisions of the company. His primary role was to take orders from Murray.

Managing the system was not a simple task. The assets included a series of small dams, diverting structures, aqueducts, trestles, and flumes to move water fifty miles from the valleys of the Cuyamaca Mountains to reservoirs that served urban and rural customers. The system's thirty-six miles of trestles and flumes were a maintenance nightmare. The flumes leaked, and wind and wildfire constantly threatened the trestles.[11] Murray was in constant communication, sending Fletcher directives (some with detailed diagrams) while riding the rails to and from San Francisco, Seattle, Salt Lake City, and his resorts in Montana.

During the first few years of operations, Murray funded several improvements to serve new customers, and Fletcher managed contracts and worked on increasing rates.[12] At some point during CWC's early years, Fletcher's financial position must have weakened, for he sold half of his interest to San Francisco–based investor William Henshaw. Murray, knowing his partner's financial straits, provided Fletcher with an opportunity to make a fortune. In 1913, Murray granted Fletcher a three-month option to buy the company for $600,000.[13] If Fletcher could find a buyer within three months, he could purchase the company from Murray and sell it in one simultaneous transaction. Any proceeds above the option price would go to him as profit. Fletcher tried valiantly to get the city of San Diego to make an offer, but in the end the city felt it had enough water without buying the CWC.[14]

Fletcher returned to managing the company, with his prospects for a big payday dwindling as each month passed. Murray diminished Fletcher's initial ownership position significantly by using cash to improve and expand the system. As Murray poured more than $500,000 into the company for repairs and improvements, Fletcher was required to put in one-twelfth, or 8.3 percent, of all new funding to maintain his ownership percentage.[15] Fletcher had borrowed the money for his initial stake in the company and could not afford additional contributions. Murray responded by lending Fletcher $60,000 to keep his ownership position intact.[16] Without the loan, Fletcher would have seen his interest in the company shrink to less than 2 percent. With the loan, however, he was at Murray's mercy. Murray could demand that Fletcher repay the loan at any time, including just moments before the sale of the company. If Murray made such a move, Fletcher would not have been able to make the payment and would have lost his stake in the company.

In his memoir, Fletcher wrote that managing the water system was the biggest headache of his life, and it is easy to see why. Murray held Fletcher's fragile ownership position over his head, while giving him daily orders about everything, including the use of telegrams and postage stamps. On one occasion, after receiving a recommendation from Fletcher to spend more money on the system, Murray reminded Fletcher of his diminutive stature in their financial partnership, telling his front man that his share of the company "wouldn't buy a good breakfast for a poor woman." Murray chastised Fletcher twice for sending telegrams that cost sixty cents each when a two-cent postage stamp would have sufficed: "[E]very time you say 'stop' it costs me money, and I don't want any of these telegrams when 2 cents will answer the question."[17] When Fletcher stumbled on more substantial matters, Murray threatened to replace him as the project's manager. After receiving one request for repairs, Murray replied tersely,

> Enclosed you will find check for $15,000 for Cuyamaca expenses. Now I want this to be the last. If that thing don't pay fixed charges after this and running expenses, I will try and make a change and make it do so, as I am tired of working for twenty-five or thirty gentlemen looking at the sun to see when five o'clock comes.[18]

Recognizing that his performance did not always meet Murray's expectations, Fletcher once pleaded for Murray's "patience and good heartedness," and that Murray stick with him as the manager of the CWC.[19] Despite Murray's harsh criticisms, it is likely that he never intended to fire Fletcher. Another of Murray's partners, Sandbar Brown, also retained his letters from Murray, and they revealed similar treatment. Murray expressed disappointment often but always allowed his partners to continue, so long as they worked without pay and provided free advice on other projects. Perhaps Fletcher's only consolation was Murray's age. At seventy-four, how much longer could Murray possibly keep up his relentless pace? Fletcher's best hope was that Murray would die, and Fletcher could work out a more productive relationship with Mary and her son.

13
Trouble in Butte

There were scattered among the workers spies of every description—company gunmen, and Burns Detective Agency operatives.

—George R. Tompkins, IWW[20]

In 1914, the raucous mining town entered a new era of tension and violence, and Murray often found himself right in the middle of the conflict—sometimes by choice and other times by happenstance. The combatants were many and included the mammoth Anaconda Copper Mining Company ("the company"), private operators like Murray, union members, union leaders, local law enforcement, private security forces, state militia, US military, and politicians of every persuasion. The opening salvo came on June 13, 1914, when union members extracted a safe from their own union hall and later used a charge of dynamite to reveal its contents. The miners were frustrated with the ineffectiveness of their leadership and wanted to see if the safe contained information confirming their suspicion that company gunmen had infiltrated the leadership of their union. The miners found nothing of note in the safe but effectively ended their feud with labor leaders eleven days later, blowing up their own hall and shutting down the union for good.[21]

Murray owned a building directly across the street from the former union hall. His primary tenant was Larry Duggan, a fellow Irish Nationalist, and the city's best-known undertaker. (Duggan's name was etched into mining lore when prospectors began dubbing any potentially deadly rock perched inside a mine a "Duggan.") Murray's building suffered more than $500 in damage in the explosion at the union hall, mainly from broken windows. It was a minor event compared with what was to come. A few weeks after the union hall was reduced to a pile of rubble, an assassin's bullet on the other side of the Atlantic set events in motion that would raise Butte's copper mines to critical prominence as a source of materials for munitions in the First World War. State militia and US military started making regular trips to Butte, usually at the behest of the Anaconda Copper Mining Company, to ensure the mines remained open. The company supplemented the military presence with large, private security forces. Two of these company agents had Murray squarely in their sights.

Robert and Sadie Watson arrived in Butte on December 18, 1914. The husband and wife were undercover detectives with the Burns Agency. Hired by the Anaconda Copper Mining Company, their mission was twofold: rob Murray's private bank, and frame Harry Robinson for the crime. Both Murray and Robinson were thorns in the company's side. Murray was one of the last private operators in Butte, was a friend of labor, and allegedly (and probably) stole ore from the company's Speculator Mine.[22] Robinson was the recently elected vice president of a new union that vowed to take a hard line against the company's abusive employment practices. The Watsons' mission would send a message to Murray and place Robinson behind bars, where he could no longer organize employees.

Within days of their arrival, Robert and Sadie arranged a "chance" meeting with Robinson and his wife. They introduced themselves to the unsuspecting couple on Park Street while strolling through town. Over the next few weeks, the Watsons ingratiated themselves to the Robinsons, offering to rent rooms in their home and buying presents for their children.[23]

On January 21, 1915, while the Robinsons were at home taking care of their children, Robert Watson and two accomplices, Mark Foster and Fred Webster, headed over to Murray's bank. It was noon as they approached the front door. They could tell that several people were inside, so they dispersed and agreed to return in a few hours.

At 3 p.m., Watson, Foster, and Webster returned to the bank. Hearing no one inside, they entered. E. L. Chapman, Murray's lone employee at the bank, greeted the three men. One of the men mumbled something to Chapman. When Chapman asked the gentleman to repeat himself, the man pulled a gun and pressed it to Chapman's stomach. Instinctively Chapman's hands went up in the air. Chapman tried to reason with the men: "Really, there is no use for you fellows to rob this bank; there isn't anything here. All the money is kept in another bank."

The robbers pulled down the window shades and demanded Chapman open the safe. A nervous man, Chapman struggled to dial the combination. The burglars poked him in the ribs with their guns as he tried to concentrate. His first attempt failed. He tried once more with his hand visibly shaking. He failed again. The gunmen, growing impatient, placed two guns at his head and threatened to shoot him if he did not succeed on the next try. "You've monkeyed long enough," they said. Chapman stood up, stretched, and tried a final time. On the third turn of the dial, the tumblers fell into place and the safe opened. "Give us all the money in the safe," said one of the gunmen.

Chapman pulled out one box from the safe and handed it over. It contained just $100 in cash. One of the robbers then entered the safe and pulled out another box. It contained some of Murray's jewelry. After the robbers stuffed their pockets with cash and jewels, they pressed a gun against Chapman's back and forced him toward the safe. "For God's sake, don't lock me in there," Chapman pleaded. "I will die. There will be no one around this bank until 9 o'clock tomorrow morning."

"Get in there, you bastard. We don't care," the robbers replied. With Chapman inside the safe, the robbers locked the door, or at least so they thought. Chapman cleverly held a mechanism on the inside of the vault door to keep it from locking. He waited several minutes before opening the door and calling the police. A large crowd gathered around the bank as word of the robbery spread. Chapman locked the bank doors until the police arrived. He didn't know the names of the robbers, but he described two of them in detail. [24]

Upon receiving word of the robbery, Murray sent Chapman to Boulder Hot Springs to recuperate and posted a generous reward for the stolen jewelry—no questions asked. Witnesses to the bank heist identified Watson but not Foster and Webster. They named John Ryko (another Anaconda Copper Mining Company gunman) as one of the robbers. Both Watson and Ryko were taken into custody. When the county attorney, Michael Canning, traveled to Boulder to question Chapman, Judge Donlan released Watson and Ryko into the custody of the company's top gunman, D. G. Stivers. In the weeks that followed, witnesses affiliated with the company came forward to identify Harry Robinson as the robber.[25]

It took nearly a year for the county to bring Robinson to trial for the robbery charge. When it did, it was clear that officials had the wrong man. Chapman, asked on the witness stand if Robinson was the robber, said, "That is not the man. If he was, I would have told you." The jury acquitted Robinson of all charges. As for Murray's stolen jewelry, the reward money worked—some items were recovered in Butte, and some were found at a pawnshop 2,500 miles away in Washington, DC.[26] The company's mission failed on both counts. Murray continued to be a thorn in its side, and Robinson returned to organizing for the new union.

The next big shock to workers in Butte came on June 8, 1917, when a major fire in the Speculator Mine killed 163 men.[27] This was the catalyst that finally spurred employees to rally behind a union. Employees formed the Metal Mine Workers' Union on June 12, just four days after the disaster.[28] The company refused to recognize the fledgling union and started buying up newspapers around the state—a preemptive measure to stifle labor-friendly news coverage.[29]

In Butte, unions, including the radical Industrial Workers of the World (IWW) countered the company's media grab by starting a paper of its own: the *Butte Strike Bulletin*. William F. Dunne and R. B. Smith organized the startup and launched the paper as a weekly in December 1917. After several months of publishing as a weekly, they planned their move to a daily publication. Their biggest obstacle was raising funds for a larger printing press.[30] A new press cost $12,500, or $900,000 in today's dollars.[31] This expense was beyond the means of the unions that launched the weekly, and no conventional bank in town would consider extending a loan to the company's adversaries. So, Dunne and Smith turned to the only unconventional bank in town, the private bank of James A. Murray.

Murray agreed to fund the new printing press. Murray likely asked that his contribution be kept secret, as he did with most of his charity work, for no one disclosed the funding during his lifetime. Montana's Governor Samuel V. Stewart, a staunch opponent of the *Bulletin*, speculated that the funding had came from the IWW and other radical unions.[32] It wasn't until retired Senator Burton K. Wheeler revealed Murray's contribution nearly fifty years after the fact that it became public knowledge.[33] Murray helped keep the contribution a secret by taking a note, or mortgage,[34] on the printing press and then placing it in the name of his niece May Murray. There is no indication that either Murray or his niece attempted to collect payment on the note.[35]

Wheeler recalled, incorrectly, that Murray funded the startup of the *Butte Strike Bulletin* in December 1917,[36] leading one historian to suggest that the editorial staff adopted a radical agenda after the Bonanza King's financial commitment.[37] Neither is true. The date of Murray's note coincides with the purchase of the new printing press and the shift from a weekly to a daily. Murray fully understood the editorial direction of the paper because it had been in circulation for eight months prior to his involvement. He knew the paper espoused the views of the radical IWW, and he certainly knew, just eleven days before he funded the paper, that the state had banned new daily papers[38] in a direct attempt to scuttle the *Bulletin*'s expansion plans. Despite all of this, the wealthy capitalist funded the expansion of the radical paper.

No other Western millionaire would have given the slightest thought to such a contribution. W. A. Clark, commenting on demands levied by the union that sponsored the *Butte Daily Bulletin*, stated, "As far as I am concerned, and the Clark Mines, I will close them down, flood them, and not raise a pound of copper, before I will recognize the anarchist leaders of the Union."[39] Murray not only recognized the anarchists, but he gave them a powerful weapon—a direct means of communication with coal, oil, mining, and timber camps throughout the western United States. But Murray wasn't just arming labor. He had other interests that stood to gain from the *Bulletin*'s radical editorial content. Ireland was entering its final push for freedom, and its cause could benefit from an organ that reached Irish Nationalists throughout the western labor camps.

The new press launched the radical organ into daily production and a circulation of more than 17,000,[40] quickly making it the largest paper in the state. By contrast, the circulation of the next largest papers, the *Butte Miner* and the *Anaconda Standard*, averaged 16,000 and 11,728 daily, respectively.[41] A significant component of the *Bulletin*'s readership came from outside Butte, with between 10,000 and 12,000 copies delivered to labor centers throughout the West.

Federal, state, and Anaconda Copper Mining Company officials perceived the *Bulletin*'s expanded reach as an immediate threat to wartime copper production. The officials on the ground in Butte included US Justice Department Agent E. W. Byrn, who held responsibility to keep Butte's mines running at full capacity. He was supported by several military intelligence officers and infantry units. Lieutenant Will Germer led intelligence operations, and a new West Point graduate, Major Omar Bradley (who later become famous in World War II), commanded the local troops. In addition, Byrn wielded the power to arrest individuals for sedition under the newly amended Espionage Act.

The expanded *Bulletin* certainly reinforced the opinion of the army's Military Intelligence Division that Butte served as the tactical center for the IWW's national operations.[42] The intelligence division monitored editor Dunne's movements in and out of the state. Intelligence officers were on high alert during the trial of IWW leader, and former Butte labor boss, "Big Bill" Haywood in Chicago for espionage. The fear was that a conviction would trigger wide-scale strikes. They were right. When a Chicago judge sentenced Haywood to twenty years in prison on August 31, 1918,[43] the IWW organized a strike. Everyone in the *Bulletin*'s office went to work supporting the IWW, printing the *Bulletin*, posters, and handbills.

Germer's intelligence indicated that the strike was scheduled for September 12, 1918. The goal of the work stoppage was to break the supply of copper to the war effort and force the release of IWW officials held in prison. Germer asked his commander for permission to use Bradley's troops to round up the organizers and take them as military prisoners,[44] but his commanders denied the request, suggesting that Germer instead conduct a quiet investigation into the possible strike.

Undeterred, Germer found another way to engage Bradley's troops. One of his agents caught a man posting strike handbills in a local saloon. The man later agreed to show Germer where he had picked up the small posters. Germer then called on Major Bradley for backup. The informant led Major Bradley, along with a couple of his men and some company gunmen, to the pick-up spot, which turned out to be the office of the *Bulletin*. The offices were housed in a building known as Duggan's Church, named after the owner, Larry Duggan, a known socialist, Irish Nationalist, and friend of Murray. Bradley entered the building without authorization and personally searched for evidence linking the *Bulletin* to strike publications. Among the items he discovered was an IWW publication, printed in

German, promoting the end of capitalism. Bradley also found several pieces of potentially incriminating evidence linking the *Bulletin* to the strike handbills. He called in a local printer to verify his findings and, satisfied that he had found the source, closed the *Bulletin* offices and set up an illegal picket to block entry. Bradley then moved on the *Bulletin*'s editors, assisting with the arrest of Dunne and Smith that night. Initially, the men were charged with concealing weapons without a permit; later, both were charged with sedition.

The next morning, the Justice Department was furious that Bradley had overstepped his bounds and occupied the *Bulletin*'s offices. Agent Byrn attempted to survey damage to the paper's property but was turned away by Bradley's men. Later in the day, Byrn was able to reopen the offices, and the *Bulletin* continued operations uninterrupted, even while its owners went to trial. Bradley, whom some military leaders thought should be removed from Butte for his transgressions, remained in charge of the local forces.

Dunne and Smith found support throughout the Irish American community during their trial (another indicator of their paper's usefulness). Judge Jeremiah Lynch, a stalwart in the Irish community, issued a concealed-weapons permit to Dunne. Testifying at Smith's sedition trial, Murray's nephew James E. Murray "declared emphatically that the *Bulletin* never advocated revolution in the United States" and that the paper "consistently fought for correction of the wrongs to the working people of Butte and elsewhere."[45] The younger Murray also promoted Dunne's stature in the community by inviting him to sit at the head table during Eamon de Valera's first appearance in Butte.[46] De Valera, the only Irish commander who was not executed by the British following the Easter Rising in 1916, was making a highly publicized tour in America to raise funds for Ireland's fight for independence.

The *Bulletin* was targeted several more times during the war years. When a new commanding officer for the army units came to Butte in January 1919, local leaders provided a briefing on labor issues in Butte. Most advocated for martial law to deport foreign radicals. Mine superintendent and company man John Berkin added the *Bulletin* to the list of targets and urged the new commander to "Get to the *Butte Bulletin* and destroy it."[47] Lieutenant Germer also continued to focus on the *Bulletin*, citing the paper as a continuing source of problems.[48]

After the war ended, Governor Stewart continued to seek military intervention to shut down the paper or at least stop it from being circulated by the post office. He wrote an impassioned plea to Colonel Herman Hall:

> The one thing that has been more disturbing than anything else is the publication of the Butte Daily Bulletin. This paper was started as a handbill entitled "The Bulletin," handed around among the radicals during the

WITH THE UNITED PRESS SERVICE AND A COMPETENT STAFF OF WRITERS, WE WILL SERVE THE NEWS AS IT REALLY HAPPEN

TELEPHONES
Business Office 52
Editorial Rooms 292

The Butte Daily Bulletin

EIGHT PAGES
TODAY'S PRESS RUN
8,400

PRICE FIVE CENTS

LABOR WAR IN ENGLAND, IRELAND AND THE U. S.

Shipyards Workers' Strike in England and Ireland Spreads to Other Industries---The Workers and Demobilized Soldiers Are Co-Operating---Glasgow, Scotland, Workers Are Out---U. S. Threatens to Cancel Contracts.

(Special United Press Wire to The Bulletin.)

London, Jan. 28.—The industrial war which broke out in Britain and Ireland is beginning to fight in the interests of the demobilized soldiers, labor officials said. It is denied that the strikers are in any way connected with bolshevism. The strike situation, which resulted in paralyzing shipbuilding, and seriously affecting other industries, is unchanged. It is believed the trouble will be extended later through sympathetic walkouts. Nearly two hundred thousand are striking in various parts of the country.

(Special United Press Wire to The Bulletin.)

London, Jan. 28.—Nation-wide shipbuilding strikes are on in Britain and Ireland. Other industries are being rapidly tied up by sympathetic strikes. Belfast is practically paralyzed by a strike in sympathy with the walkout of 40,000 shipyard employes, who demanded a 44-hour week. Twelve thousand London shipbuilders struck today, asking for a wage increase.

A partial strike is also on in the Glasgow yards and threatening to become complete before night. Shipbuilders and engineers in the Leith and Edinburgh yards also quit work. A sympathetic strike of all allied trades is threatened unless demands are granted.

SPARTICANS CAPTURE BANKS

By Sudden Coup d'Etat Followers of Liebknecht Control Public Buildings in Wilhelmshaven.

Getting Down to Real Business

Seattle, Jan. 28.—The executive committeemen, representing 110 unions affiliated with the Seattle Central Labor Council, late yesterday voted to campaign for "mass action" and a general strike in February in support of the 25,000 metal trades workers who have been on strike here since last Tuesday for higher wages. This vote was reached after the committeemen rejected a resolution offered by H. F. Jones, president of the Building Trades council, asking that a general strike be deferred.

YANKEE SOLDIERS ON WARPATH OVER SEAS

Thirty-four Murders and 220 Assaults in One Month. Police Force Is Strengthened.

BIG FIVE IS BUSY IN PARIS

Discussing the German Possessions and "Broad" League of Nations Principle Is Being Considered.

"TALK UNITED STATES" DON'T GET FAR AT THE PEACE TABLE

(Special United Press Wire.)

Paris, Jan. 28.—Despite the solemn decision of the peace conference that English should be the official language at the sessions, American and British delegates and an eloquent, gestureful interpreter are the only ones complying. All others, including Chinese and Siamese, speak French.

W. F. DUNN FLAYS MONTANA OCTOPUS

Talks for Hour and a Half at Helena. Black Flag of Piracy of the A. C. M. Flaunted Before the Company Tools. Resolution Asking Millionaire Profiteers to Open Mines Gets No Second.

Helena, Jan. 28.—With the eyes of the Anaconda Mining company upon them and the murderous tyranny of the Montana octopus hanging over both legislators and audience; with the majority approving and yet afraid to applaud, W. F. Dunn, the only representative sent by the Silver Bow county electors to the sixteenth assembly whose seat has not been contested and his pay check withheld, yesterday introduced a working class resolution in the house and talked for an hour and 2

Murray funded the expansion of the radical Butte Daily Bulletin. *The paper was viewed as the communication arm of the IWW in the Northwest but also served as an Irish organ.*
—Library of Congress

strike times. Later it was issued weekly and grew into the proportions of a newspaper. During the war some sort of a combination was made with the IWW, Nonpartisan League and other radical societies, and the paper was launched as a daily. Ever since that time it has been so conducted. The paper is radical beyond expression and revolutionary without question of a doubt. Time and time again efforts have been made by State and Federal authorities, to suppress the publication of the organ, but always without success. In my opinion, the Butte Daily Bulletin is responsible for more of the trouble in Butte than any other one thing. Not only that, but I'm satisfied that radical propaganda is disseminated through the Bulletin to many parts of the United States.

In my opinion the Department of War should declare at least a limited degree of martial law sufficient to justify the closing of the Butte Bulletin and other seditious publications and sufficient to warrant the arrest of red radicals, whether alien or citizens.

> I challenge anyone to produce a more radical or revolutionary paper than the Butte Daily Bulletin. I know from two years of close observation that is has peddled poison, sedition, and revolution to the detriment of the good citizenship, patriotism, and loyalty to Government.[49]

Colonel Hall relayed the governor's request to his commanding officer, who denied it.[50] The Military Intelligence Division took up the governor's argument with the post office, requesting a halt on distribution of the newspaper through the mail, but this too was rejected.[51]

The *Bulletin* continued production for the remainder of Murray's life and beyond, providing a voice for labor throughout the West. And although the *Bulletin* never reversed the balance of power between capital and labor in Butte, it was hailed by the national Communist Party as a model for counteracting the publicity machines of the "plutes" and the "venom of the press" toward unions."[52] Locally, the *Bulletin* also served as an effective voice in local and state politics, eventually helping Larry Duggan, Murray's longtime friend and a leading voice in the IWW, win election to the office of sheriff for Silver Bow County. Duggan led the reform of the office by appointing his fellow radicals to nearly half of the deputy sheriff positions.[53] Finally, and perhaps most important to Murray, the *Bulletin* also served an important role in rallying financial and political support for Ireland's final push for freedom.

14
The Final Push to Free Ireland

The Butte Daily Bulletin . . . in the face of the powerful British influence in this country and in opposition to its crushing system of propaganda, has thrown open its news columns . . . on the subject of Ireland's right to independence, and has, in an able and fearless manner, espoused its cause editorially.

—Clan na Gael, Butte chapter[54]

Irish Nationalists in the United States shared a common problem with labor: company-funded newspapers. Corporations that used their papers as a weapon against labor[55] were also "cold, unsympathetic and in many quarters openly hostile"[56] to Ireland's quest for independence. The *Butte Bulletin*, in addition to being a voice for labor, also championed the cause of Ireland's freedom. Of the many historians who have reflected on the radical editorial bent of the *Bulletin*, only Dave Emmons noticed this important element. In *The Butte Irish*, he writes, "No involved Irishman . . . failed to associate the government's attempt to suppress the *Butte Bulletin* between 1918 and 1920 with the suppression of the *Gaelic American*, the official paper of the Clan-na-Gael, and the *Irish World*." All three, according to Emmons, were more interested in seeing an "Irish victory" in World War I than an American victory.[57] For some Irish Nationalists, a German victory over England seemed the clearest path to Ireland's independence.

Irish allegiances became apparent shortly after the assassination of Archduke Franz Ferdinand initiated the First World War. During Butte's St. Patrick's Day in 1915, the hopes of both Germans and Irish came together as thousands of Butte Irish parading through town were joined by hundreds of German and Austrian patriots carrying their own flags.[58] A month later, Jim Murray made it clear that he was also sympathetic to the German cause, making the largest single donation to a war relief fund organized by German and Austrian residents of Butte. His $500 contribution accounted for one-fifth of the money raised by Butte Teutons and was featured prominently in the local press.[59]

Not all Irish Nationalists agreed that an alliance with Germany was the right path to freedom. Some wanted Ireland's soldiers to join British

This political cartoon appeared in the Butte Bulletin *on November 24, 1920. The* Bulletin *offered competing views to those of corporate-owned newspapers on matters of labor and Irish Nationalism.The* Bulletin *was as staunch an advocate for Irish independence as the* Irish World *or* Gaelic American. —Library of Congress

forces, believing that aid to Britain would gain Ireland favor in future cessation talks. The Irish, as often was the case, could not agree on the best approach. Some Irish soldiers joined British troops, and some rebels conspired with German forces and Irish Americans to launch an attack on British forces stationed in Dublin. The goal was to divert British resources from the battle with Germany. The initial attack, known as the Easter Rising, took place during Easter week in 1916. British troops crushed the rebel attack decisively and then quickly tried and executed every leader of the Easter Rising, save American-born Eamon de Valera.

The hope for England's defeat ended with the surrender of Germany and the conclusion of the Great War on November 11, 1918. Nevertheless, the fight for Ireland's independence immediately resumed on two fronts. First, the Irish American community pressed President Woodrow Wilson to take up the cause of Ireland's sovereignty under the fifth point in Wilson's fourteen-point peace plan. This point called for "a free, open-minded, and absolutely impartial adjustment of all colonial claims, based upon a strict observance of the principle that in determining all such questions of sovereignty the interests of the populations concerned must have equal weight with the equitable claims of the government whose title is to be determined."[60] Second, rebels in Ireland moved to evict the 150,000 British guards who enforced colonial rule in their homeland.

Murray, now seventy-eight, tapped his nephew James to be his representative in both battles. Murray had forced James to handle many chores prior to this, most with little or no pay, straining the relationship between the two. However, this task James accepted with enthusiasm. Murray had previously transferred several income-producing properties to his nephew[61] and appointed James one of three officers in his company (the senior Murray and his office assistant being the other two). Murray likely allowed his nephew to use income from these properties for living expenses and to support Ireland's cause. This was a practice Murray permitted with at least one other relative, and it is doubtful that James, with six children at the time, could travel around the country for extended periods without this financial assistance.[62] With ready access to the senior Murray's deep pockets, and with relationships forged at Tammany Hall during his time at New York University, James wasted little time ascending to the national stage advocating one of his uncle's highest priorities.

With the *Butte Bulletin* providing positive coverage of his every move, James started his climb at the National Race Convention in Philadelphia. More than five thousand Irish and Irish Americans converged on February 22 and 23, 1919. Collectively, they adopted two resolutions: (1) calling for the upcoming postwar peace conference to apply the doctrine of national self-determination to Ireland, and (2) proclaiming a state of war between Ireland and England. The conventioneers also pledged $1.25 million to aid Ireland's cause. The chair of the convention, New York Supreme Court Justice Daniel Cohalan, appointed a retired colleague, Justice John Goff, to lead a committee of twenty-five convention delegates to Washington, DC, to deliver the resolutions to Congress and the president. James, previously selected to lead the fundraising effort in Montana, received an appointment to this important committee.

James was in impressive company on his trip to Washington. Goff had been a central figure in the famous rescue of six Fenian rebels in 1875 from a British penal colony in western Australia, and Cohalan had helped Irish rebels plan and fund the Easter Rising. Others on the committee included Frank Walsh, Wilson's appointee to lead the Industrial Relations Commission; Edward Dunne, the former governor of Illinois; and Michael Ryan, the past president of the United Irish League of America.

The House Rules Committee gave the committee a warm reception. A resolution supporting its request to have Ireland's independence included in postwar peace talks passed quickly and went to the full House for consideration. But the committee's reception at the White House was decidedly cooler. After waiting a week for a meeting, they received late notice that they could see President Wilson in New York after another commitment. Cohalan, Murray, and the rest of the committee packed their bags and headed north on the next train.[63] The meeting lasted all of twenty-eight minutes and was preceded by an ultimatum that almost scuttled the entire affair. At the last moment, Wilson refused to attend if Justice Cohalan was present. The president viewed Cohalan as a traitor for his pro-German activities during the war.[64] Despite the protests of his peers, Cohalan bowed out of the meeting for the greater good of the cause. The meeting proceeded with Justice Goff and Walsh providing the initial remarks. Wilson was unpersuaded and gave no commitment to raise Ireland's issues at the peace conference. After the meeting, Wilson shared with others that he really wanted to tell the delegation to "go to hell."[65]

Undeterred, the committee designated Walsh, Dunne, and Ryan to travel to Versailles to participate in the peace talks.[66] James returned to Montana to lead the fundraising effort in his home state and rally US support for Ireland's quest for independence. Murray's first action was to organize a meeting of Irish Americans in his hometown. Judge Jeremiah Lynch and others joined Murray in making Ireland's case for independence. At the end of the evening, the packed auditorium adopted resolutions calling for the president to advocate for Irish freedom at the Versailles Peace Conference and to oppose any League of Nations that did not include a free Ireland.

The *Butte Bulletin* covered Murray's inaugural meeting with a prominent story above the fold on the front page. The headline read "Irish Must Be Made Free, Such Is Purport of Masterly Addresses by the Hon. James E. Murray and Judge Jeremiah J. Lynch."[67] The editors paired the story with a large editorial cartoon depicting a working-class Irishman taming a cowering lion wearing a crown and a monocle.

Over the next several months, James traveled around the state raising awareness of the push for Irish independence. He hosted a number of Irish dignitaries who visited Butte on national fundraising tours (including Irish President Eamon de Valera on two occasions), and was selected the grand marshal of Butte's St. Patrick's Day parade in 1920.[68] The *Butte Bulletin* provided extensive advance publicity and coverage for all these events, and James's uncle was present for many.

James found a groundswell of support from the Irish in Montana and around the country as the British government's execution of the Easter Rising leaders created significant backlash against the empire's tightfisted colonial rule. Unfortunately, he and his colleagues could not win over the one person they most needed on their side. They were unable to convince President Wilson to take up Ireland's cause.

Having failed on the political front, James took a leadership position with the newly formed American Association for the Recognition of the

The Butte Bulletin *gave equal coverage to labor, socialism, and Irish independence.*
—Library of Congress

Irish Republic (AARIR), [69] a rival group to the Friends of Irish Freedom. The new group aligned itself with Eamon de Valera and sought to channel funds directly to Ireland. James started as the director of the Montana chapter at de Valera's request. [70] Within a year, he was vice president of the organization and chairing its national convention in Washington, DC.[71] Soon after, James was promoted to president of the sixty-thousand-member organization.

Jim Murray was certainly pleased with his nephew's spirited fight on behalf of Ireland. James's rhetoric was equal to Jim's own from the days of Charles Stewart Parnell, but his nephew's impact was much greater.[72] James was the perfect surrogate, but he probably heard little praise from his sponsor. Jim Murray didn't like to pay salaries or compliments. If James was to be recognized for his exceptional service, it would likely come after his uncle's passing.

15
Ring Down the Drop

There is only one great conqueror. Death is the sure winner, and few there are who care much about you or remember you for long after Death has conquered you.

—James A. Murray, 1900[73]

While the *Butte Bulletin* rallied opposition against the company, and his nephew worked as his powerful surrogate on the Irish question, Murray continued to crisscross the western United States by rail and assert his will on every aspect of his business empire. However, for the few employees he retained in Butte, it was clear a transition was underway. Murray started liquidating complex businesses in favor of loans with strong collateral and easily managed leases. It became apparent that a sizable portion of his portfolio was being positioned to provide a reliable income for his wife, Mary. The transition likely started in 1914 after Murray commissioned his final monument—this one destined for an abandoned mining camp close to where his empire began. Following the dedication ceremonies, however, the septuagenarian showed no indication that his estate planning would slow him down. He proceeded to bankrupt a nephew, torture two small towns, bail out an old-timer, and double down on San Diego's future.

Society of Montana Pioneers

Fifty years had passed since Murray and Sandbar Brown first set foot in the primitive mining camps along Henderson Gulch near Philipsburg. They revisited the site in the winter of 1914 to commemorate the founding of those camps and memorialize the pioneers who lost their lives in the earliest days of the territory. Murray and Brown had reconciled a few years earlier, and this commemoration was likely a debt Murray felt he owed his old friend. The centerpiece of the event was a tall granite shaft conceived by Brown and funded by Murray. Brown met Murray in Drummond, Montana, and together they drove twelve miles south by automobile to the site of the ceremony.[74]

Sandbar was the driving force behind the granite monument. He called for the marker in 1906—about the time his feud with Murray was at its peak—in a local-history article he penned for the *Anaconda Standard*. He wrote of the mountain that towered over the mining camp:

> It was a landmark for the prospectors and Indian as well, but not until the discoverer of the torn and mutilated gulch at its base found gold in bedded deposits did it become known to men by the name it bears today. And from the hour of that stormy evening in October 1864, when three prospectors out of the Boise basin unloaded their packs in the gulch and panned free gold from the gravel overshadowed by its frowning eastern front, Henderson Mountain has unconsciously honored a noble man.

Sandbar continued his article with a short history of the hallowed site:

> Big Joe Henderson along with two other prospectors discovered gold in the gulch. They were soon followed by many other hardy prospectors. A handful of small mining camps were established in the area, the largest being Emmetsburg. . . . The buildings were of logs and one story in height. The roofs were principally of dirt and hewed exteriors of mitered corners showed the handiwork of skilled axemen. Féinian hall was completed in the early 70s and the town had a place to gather and celebrate St. Patrick's Day and July 4th when blood, whiskey and oratory flowed in reckless abundance.
>
> The towns on Henderson Gulch disappeared as the streambeds were exhausted of their precious metals, but the land that surrounded the towns remained the final resting place for many of Montana's earliest pioneers. As the streams and hills were turned over in pursuit of every speck of gold, these important gravesites were lost and forgotten. . . . hardly a trace remains to indicate its once populous and busy existence, tottering piles of stone and the outlines of foundations alone show where its many log buildings stood. The long winding street, once the scene of active frontier life, where men fought to the death with knife and gun, is grass grown and deserted.

Brown concluded his article with a call for a monument dedicated to the pioneers that called Henderson Gulch their final resting place.[75]

Robert Anderson, E. S. Paxson, H. H. Barrett, and Father D. P. Meade joined Brown and Murray at the dedication. Anderson had panned gold in Henderson Gulch in 1865. Paxson frequented the camps in his early days and was an active supporter of the Society of Montana Pioneers. He was also John Maguire's set designer in the 1880s and had since gained fame as a Western artist. Barrett designed and guided the fabrication of the monument, a marble obelisk, which Father Meade of Philipsburg dedicated in a brief ceremony. Anderson then led the party on a tour of the ghost towns that remained and shared a few stories about life in the camp.

The obelisk, which still stands today, bears the names of seven miners beneath a pick and shovel crossed with a gold pan. The miners are Pat

McHenry, Thomas Roach, James Fletcher, James Grimes, William O'Hara, Ed Clusky, and Jimmie Jones. On one face, inscriptions penned by journalism student Percy Stone read, "To the known and unknown dead of Henderson Gulch this monument is dedicated," and on another, "God sent you here to make the wilderness a state. This done, He called you home but left your work for inspiration." [76]

Brown recapped the dedication for the membership of the Society of Montana Pioneers this way:

> The first Monument to be erected through the efforts of the Society was over the dead in the old and almost obliterated cemetery of Henderson Gulch, a one-time great and prosperous placer camp of Granite County, but of which nothing remains but the wreck of a single log cabin and the decaying remnants of long unused sluice boxes. This elegant testimonial to the memory of the dead of nearly half a century was given by Mr. James A. Murray of Butte, a onetime resident of the camp. The fourteen-foot shaft has inscribed upon its face the names of the men sleeping there, and may we not hope that during all of the years to come it will stand in solemn watch and ward over these brave, intrepid men who gave their young manhood and their lives to the development of the mining industry of the state."[77]

After the ceremony Murray returned to Butte, where he received word that George Winter had passed away in Pocatello.[78] Winter had been a loyal and trusted employee who enjoyed Murray's greatest confidence. Besides the loss of a friend, his death also meant that Murray's Pocatello water plant was now in the hands of his young nephew Alex. Operating a water plant and battling politicians were beyond Alex's capabilities. On his way to California, Murray stopped in Pocatello to meet the mayor and discuss the city's purchase of the plant. This would be the first of several moves by Murray to liquidate his businesses. The initial discussions were not productive, but the sale could wait a few months. Murray continued to Monterey to wait out the winter.

Bankrupting Alex

After winter passed, Murray returned to Pocatello to continue negotiations with the city.[79] He previously offered to sell the system to the city for $425,000. The mayor had declined, citing the Public Utilities Commission's valuation of the system at $230,000 to $290,000. [80] Murray and the city were $135,000 apart on price.

Murray had no interest in discounting his price. The water company netted him $60,000 a year. Under different circumstances, he would ask at least $600,000 for the plant. However, the city was poised to build its own system if Murray did not sell. The city received approval from the voters to issue $400,000 in bonds to either buy Murray's plant or build one of its own.[81] Murray had to close a deal or else sabotage the city's plans.

Murray, by reputation alone, put a hitch in the city's construction plans. Investors wanted a guaranteed revenue stream before purchasing city bonds, and it was not clear that Murray would allow the city to build and operate a new plant unencumbered by lawsuits. A bond investor's worst nightmare is a half-built plant, generating no income, tied up in court by a well-funded opponent. The city struggled to convince investors that their prospective bonds were a solid investment. [82]

Murray also actively worked to reduce citizen support for a new plant. He claimed his waterworks had been sold to a syndicate led by his nephew Alex,[83] and that the new ownership group would be more accommodating to city residents. The sale was quickly revealed as a fraud. When the city asked for relief from onerous water restrictions, Alex referred the matter back to his uncle.[84] Further investigation into the transaction by the Public Utilities Commission found there had never been a sale. Murray had simply transferred the company to Alex, along with $400,000 in notes and bonds—all held by Murray.[85]

As negotiations dragged into the spring and then summer, the city scored a victory that chipped away at Murray's advantage. The Idaho Supreme Court ruled in July that Murray did not hold an exclusive right to deliver water in Pocatello.[86] This removed a major concern of bond investors. Murray responded by putting two new negotiators in front of the city. Murray and Alex signed a sixty-day brokerage agreement with Ed Fletcher to sell the system to the city. If he was successful in completing the sale by December 1, 1915, Fletcher was promised a $5,000 commission.[87] The minimum purchase price acceptable to Murray was $400,000. Murray simultaneously asked his nephew James to negotiate the system's sale. For Murray, it was a win-win. If his nephew succeeded, Murray would not have to pay a commission to Fletcher, and if Fletcher negotiated a sale, Murray could deny Fletcher's demand for a commission and claim that his nephew had brokered the deal behind the scenes.

Fletcher hadn't been through the wringer yet with Murray, so he thought there was a real chance of hitting a nice payday. He made several trips to Pocatello to try to sway the city council. However, his window to close a deal came and went. The best he could do was get the city to consider a possible purchase at $350,000.[88] Murray was pleased with Fletcher's effort. Fletcher increased the city's offer by $60,000 at no cost to Murray.

As James E. Murray continued negotiations, the city received more good news from the state. Following the Idaho Supreme Court ruling that Murray did not have exclusive rights, the Public Utilities Commission deemed construction of a new city water system a necessity.[89] This was the last piece of security that investors needed. Murray, sensing the city was about to start construction, played his last card. He demanded that individual homeowners and businesses sign long-term water contracts to continue their service. If they did not sign, he would shut off their service. With the new city plant taking several months to complete, lack of service could cripple Pocatello's businesses.[90] If businesses agreed to Murray's terms, the city would lose the customer base necessary to pay off its bonds. With rumors swirling about Murray's latest maneuver, the city came to the table. On May 16, 1916, Murray's nephew James closed a deal with the city for $350,000 in cash and $52,000 in penalty waivers.[91]

With the sale closed, Murray moved quickly to tie up loose ends in town. He closed his newspaper, the *Pocatello Chronicle*,[92] and transferred the Auditorium Theater out of Alex's name and back to his own. This left Alex cut off from any income and still holding debts for the water company. Alex had no choice but to file for bankruptcy protection.[93] His court filing showed his home, worth $3,000, as his only significant asset. His liabilities totaled $58,000. He owed $40,000 to his uncle for the down payment on the sham purchase of the water company, $11,000 to a plumbing company for construction work contracted for the water company, $8,200 to several banks for personal expenses, and $1,300 to his father and two brothers.

The court designated local attorney H. E. Ray to represent Alex's creditors. Ray quickly focused on the recent transfer of the Auditorium Theater to his uncle, just four months prior to Alex's bankruptcy filing. Jim Murray claimed Alex was simply holding the property as a trustee, but Ray knew that Alex's ownership of the theater qualified him to be a rate commissioner for the elder Murray's water company. Ray filed with the courts to reclaim the property from Murray so it could be sold and used to satisfy Alex's debts.[94]

The trial to reclaim the Auditorium Theater property revealed Alex's struggles with the duplicity of his uncle's financial maneuvers. Several bankers testified that Alex had led them to believe the Auditorium Theater was his property. The bankers relied on this information when they decided to lend Alex more than $8,000. When asked if he knew about his nephew's use of the property, Murray replied, "No, and if I had, he would have reconveyed it right then." As the testimony continued, it became clear that Alex had violated his uncle's trust. Murray expected his trustees to hold his property for his exclusive benefit. In this case, the property transfer made Alex eligible, as the property owner, to set rates for Murray. It also kept the city from seizing the property after it won a court judgment against Murray. Murray denied any wrongdoing with the transaction. As for hiding the property from the court judgment, he stated that he didn't keep track of his litigation with the city. Murray testified, "I had so many lawsuits I didn't pay much attention to them."[95]

Ray won his case against Murray and reclaimed the theater property for Alex's creditors (Murray being the largest). Judge Frank Dietrich wrote in his verdict a clear response to Murray's expectation that his nephew would return his gift of the Auditorium Theater on demand: "To convert such a moral consideration into a legal one would be to transform a transaction of doubtful propriety into an odious fraud."[96]

On July 22, 1919, the Auditorium Theater property sold for $22,000.[97] With these funds, Ray paid Alex's creditors about thirty-eight cents on the dollar. Murray likely received about $15,000 as partial repayment for the phony loan he made to his nephew, but recovering a portion of the loan and dodging a portion of unpaid invoices was minor consolation. Murray wanted to hold on to his building, and Alex, by using the Auditorium Theater for collateral on personal loans, contributed to its loss. Alex received nothing from either the bankruptcy or his disappointed uncle and returned to Pennsylvania to live with his parents.

All of Murray's nephews and nieces must have taken note of Alex's fate. They had seen Murray abuse his partners and stiff his creditors, but this was the first time their uncle had crippled a blood relative with his tight-fisted business practices. Were they next?

Livingston, Montana

Murray also owned the waterworks in Livingston, Montana, just a few miles from his Hunter's Hot Springs resort. Murray had purchased the company in 1904 after its owner and founder passed away.[98] The waterworks was one of several investments Murray made in Livingston while he developed his nearby resort. As he had in Pocatello, Murray tested the patience of his customers and city officials in an effort to secure an inflated offer for his plant. Per the terms of the franchise agreement that came with his purchase, Murray was obligated to provide water for fire protection until 1910. The understanding was that when the agreement expired, the city would either purchase the plant and distribution facilities or renew the franchise agreement.

During Murray's tenure, city residents began to connect with his system for domestic purposes, despite the lack of any filtration system. Concurrent with this demand for residential service, the source of water, the Yellowstone River, became increasingly compromised. Upstream from Livingston, new communities and farming operations dumped raw sewage and animal carcasses into the river. One witness claimed to have seen fifty dead animals near the location where Murray drew water for his system. A mechanical treatment plant was desperately needed to make the water safe for household use. Safe drinking water, however, was of no concern to Murray. His interest was in liquidating his interest at the highest possible price. Maintaining control over a system that threatened the health of city residents was great leverage.

After the franchise agreement ended in 1910, the process to set a purchase price was simple. Murray was to appoint a representative to set a value, the city would do the same, and then the city and Murray would jointly select a third party to appraise the utility. A price would be negotiated based on the three valuations. Murray appointed himself to set the value on his waterworks, the city appointed its representative, and then Murray refused to agree on a third party. If the city hadn't already determined that Murray would be difficult to deal with, this certainly made it clear. Murray valued the plant in the range of $300,000 to $400,000. The city, taking into consideration the cost of building its own system, placed the value at about $200,000. Murray did not budge from his numbers, and the city proceeded to pursue voter approval for a bond measure in 1912 to build a system of its own. Murray wasn't about to let the city move on so easily.

Over the next seven years, Murray concocted a number of obstacles designed to prevent Livingston from building its own water system. He sued the city for back payments for service and promoted a competing special assessment to pave the city streets. Both actions stalled the city's progress and raised doubts as to whether city finances were solid enough to issue bonds for the new water plant. When the city finally sold its water bonds in 1917, Murray dropped his water rates by 20 percent, undercutting the city's ability to maintain revenues and pay off bond holders. Finally, after losing several of his nuisance suits in the state courts, Murray sold his water company to his primary holding company, the Monidah Trust. Since the Monidah Trust was incorporated in Delaware, Murray was able to initiate a new series of nuisance suits in the federal court system. Murray kept the federal suits in play until he took his last breath.

Tacoma, Washington

Moving on to Tacoma, Murray closed out his affairs in typical fashion: by destroying partners and employees through deft financial and legal maneuvers. Tacoma, located thirty miles south of Seattle at the southernmost portion of Puget Sound, was a side bet to his bigger investments in the Emerald City. Murray entered the Tacoma market in 1913 with his usual bluster. The *Tacoma Times* reported his enthusiasm on October 24, 1913, writing that "Tacoma looks like the best to him of anyplace he has seen for future development." Coming from a multimillionaire with holdings all across the West, his enthusiasm must have filled the city fathers with great pride. Murray followed his boast a few months later with a big splash, purchasing a controlling interest in Tacoma's Bankers Trust. He brought his traveling nephew banker, Marcus Murray, to town to watch over his stake.

Just twenty months later, however, Murray hedged his bet on Seattle's poor sister, lending money to W. R. Phillips, a banker from Seattle, to buy out his stake in the bank. Phillips was bullish on Tacoma. He thought the opening of the first railroads to Alaska portended a huge future for the port city. In 1915 Phillips purchased Murray's stake in the bank for $50,000 in cash and approximately $80,000 in personal notes. Murray's private loans typically held a term of one or two years, and it appears Phillips had only a year to make Murray whole. Phillips started his tenure as president full of pride, announcing his new role to the press and showcasing costly renovations to his bank. One year later, Phillips's reign ended in resignation. Murray, who let many of his personal loans run for years after their terms expired, found a buyer for the bank he didn't own, and all he had to do was call his loan to cut Phillips out of the equation.

It took nearly a year for Murray to clean out Phillips and clear the way for a sale. During the process he found another impediment to his payday. A lowly clerk had been embezzling money since the day Murray took over the bank in 1914. Edward J. MacDonald cleared $17,000 in checks to himself over four years. In preparing the books for the impending sale, Murray caught the cashier's misdeeds. MacDonald made a valiant effort to pay back Murray and the bank, returning all but $1,000 by the time Murray was ready to close his sale. Murray had no interest in holding up his big payday for the small restitution that remained. He sold his interest to the Scandinavian American Bank of Seattle and Tacoma on November 15, 1917, just twenty-five days after foreclosing on Phillips. Six days later, MacDonald was sentenced to prison after coming up short on his restitution to Murray.

San Diego, California

No one watched Murray's maneuverings in Pocatello, Livingston, and Tacoma more closely than his partner in the San Diego waterworks. Ed Fletcher, after donating his time to Murray for nearly a decade, was holding on to his interest in the project by a thread. To remove Fletcher from their partnership, all Murray had to do was call the loan between them. As with Phillips in Tacoma, or Alex in Pocatello, it would be a decisive blow and leave Fletcher with nothing. Murray, however, was in no rush to oust his San Diego project manager. The San Diego waterworks project was one of two he seemed to have little interest in winding down (the other was a silver mine in Arizona). In fact, in 1916, Murray handed Fletcher his biggest assignment of their eight years working together. Murray wrote a check to build the largest dam in Southern California—990 feet across and 117 feet high—and Fletcher was tasked with overseeing construction. Murray hired hydraulic engineer John Eastwood to design the structure, using a controversial but cost-effective multiple-arch design. The project replaced the La Mesa dam and increased the capacity of its reservoir sixfold.[99] The cost of the new dam was $119,000 ($32.9 million in today's currency).[100]

Murray Dam, now referred to as Murray Reservoir, is currently owned by the city of San Diego.
—Courtesy of Helix Water District

Murray Reservoir in 1924. —H. A. Erickson photo, courtesy of Helix Water District

Murray made the investment in order to capture thousands of new water customers moving into the region, and to replace an earthen dam that was vulnerable to erosion in violent storms. Fletcher, who liked to place his own name on roads and buildings, thought he was ingratiating himself to his partner when he named the new structure "Murray Dam." This, however, brought a strong written rebuke from Murray: "Naming dams after men is very poor policy, and I am superstitious about it. [You] Had no business to call that the Murray Dam; [you] should have called it La Mesa Dam and maybe we will change it to La Mesa after a while."[101]

After the Murray Dam was completed, Murray again assigned Fletcher the task to sell the improved water system to either the city of San Diego or the newly formed La Mesa, Lemon Grove, and Spring Valley Irrigation District that served rural San Diego County. Fletcher was confident he could get $1.5 million for the company.[102] If they succeeded in selling at that price, Murray and Fletcher would each be repaid their cash contributions and interest, and both men and fractional owner William Henshaw would earn a profit according to their ownership percentages (Murray's being 83.3 percent, Fletcher's 8.3 percent, and William Henshaw's 8.3 percent). After paying back his loans to Murray, Fletcher was in line to net about $40,000 for ten-plus years of work—that is, if Murray did not force him out before they closed the deal.

Kingman, Arizona

Even as Murray was liquidating his businesses in Idaho and Montana and positioning the San Diego waterworks for sale, he couldn't resist the chance at one more big strike. Murray owned several silver mines in Arizona and Mexico, and he visited them on a regular basis for inspection and to scout new prospects. On one of his visits he was approached by William B. Ridenour, owner of an established mine in Hackberry, just outside of Kingman, Arizona. Ridenour was an old-timer who once operated a freight wagon between Salt Lake City and Virginia City, Montana. He carried some of W. A. Clark's first shipments of supplies into Montana mining camps in the winter of 1864.[103] Ridenour moved south in the 1870s and landed in Arizona. He hoped Murray would purchase the special property, keeping it in the familiar hands of a fellow old-timer.[104] Murray sat down with Ridenour to learn about the history of the mine. Ridenour, like all miners from his generation, had a story to tell.

In 1872, Ridenour and his partner, Sam Crozier, were working in the mining camps of Chloride, Arizona. Before leaving Chloride, a mystic told Ridenour that he would make a trip into the desert, and that next to three trees he would find a mine with great riches. Ridenour and Crozier left the camp and headed east into the territory of the Havasupai Indians.

They traveled along the rim of Cataract Canyon, occasionally tying up their horses and exploring the face of the canyon for rock formations likely to yield precious metals. On one of the trips down into the canyon, they came across a small band of Havasupai. A fierce gun battle ensued, and the Havasupai forced the pair back up to the rim of the canyon. There, Ridenour and Crozier mounted their horses and sped away to safety. They rode until reaching the town of Peach Springs, where they made camp.

The night was clear as they went to sleep. Around midnight, Ridenour woke up to the sound of a prowling animal. He gazed out into the hills searching for the animal. Nowhere to be found, his eyes were drawn to three trees along the ridge of the Peacock Range. Was this the sign the mystic foretold? When he woke up that next morning he hiked up to the trees. They were lined up in a row, as if pointing to the mine of great riches. He followed their direction and located the Hackberry Mine.[105]

It was a good story, and an even better mine. Since that fateful day in 1872, the Hackberry Mine had provided Ridenour with a small fortune. Unfortunately, his other investments had not fared so well, and along the way he encumbered the lucky mine with financial obligations of one sort or another. He was about to lose it for good.

Murray saw little risk in continuing the development of the mine. Plenty of investors in New York were willing to pay for a chance to share in a silver bonanza.[106] He purchased Ridenour's mine and cleared all of its financial obligations. The sale allowed Ridenour to retire. W. A. Clark, speaking in Butte to the Society of Montana Pioneers about the state's mining history, mentioned the purchase in his remarks: "I was delighted to learn . . . that Jim Murray, our fellow townsman, had bought this mine from Ridenour, as it enabled the old man to spend the rest of his days in happiness; and, of course, the mine must have been a good one or Jim Murray would not have bought it."[107]

Murray set the value of the Hackberry mining company at $1 million.[108] He brought in Gus Holmes, his partner in Salt Lake City, to find investors and operate the mine. Like Ed Fletcher, Holmes had to borrow from Murray to buy shares in the company. He borrowed $300,000 using his Semloh Hotel in Salt Lake City as collateral.[109] Once the company was established, Holmes traveled to New York and spent two months selling shares on the unregulated Curb Market.[110]

Conflicting reports about the success of the mine followed Murray's investment. One contemporary report indicated that the mine generated $125,000 a month in revenue. Other articles in local newspapers told of Murray's investment in a mill, power plant, and camp buildings to support expansion of operations at the mine.[111] However, it is likely that Murray and Holmes boasted about production and expansion plans simply to encourage outside investors to buy shares. There is no evidence that expansion ever occurred, and production reports, verified by geologists, indicated a fraction of the success that was reported by the newspapers. Perhaps Murray's last mine gave him only the reward of using other people's money to help an old acquaintance retire.

A Final Butte Reunion

Five years after Murray reunited with Sandbar Brown and E. S. Paxson to memorialize some of the early pioneers in southwest Montana, he made one of his final trips to Butte. It had been more than ten years since John Maguire, Silas King, and William Penrose passed from the earth, but their memories still lingered. With his eightieth birthday approaching, Murray set out to visit a few close acquaintances who were still alive. First on his list of old-timers was Fat Jack.

Murray caught up with Jack in the lobby of the Thornton Hotel, where Teddy Roosevelt's wild ride had begun. It was the fall of 1919. Jack had retired from work as a cab driver in 1917 (he traded his horse-drawn carriage for an automobile in 1913, when Murray bought him a seven-passenger Packard). Now Jack spent most of his time in hotel lobbies catching up with old friends traveling through town. General Charles Warren[112] was there as well. When Warren spotted a local reporter looking for a story, he pulled the scribe aside to tell him about the two local celebrities sitting at the nearby table. Warren had known both Murray and Fat Jack for more than forty years. When Warren was sheriff of Deer Lodge in 1874, Murray was a regular at the court-ordered sales held at Silas King's saloon.[113] Warren proceeded to the tell the reporter about the biggest tip a hack driver ever received in Butte:

> Long before the days of the taxi-cab, Jack's team and hack were reaching the stage he describes as "passay." Jack concluded to stake himself to an entirely new outfit and after he had reconnoitered in the neighborhood of the Murray Bank for several days, he boldly presented his proposition. He would pay so much a month out of the earnings from the fashionable conveyance and would give his note for the amount which he estimated would not exceed $1,500. The bargain was closed.
>
> For the first few months Jack paid the interest and a small—a very small—portion of the principal. Months passed into years and Jack's sole relations with Murray were to meet him occasionally at the depot as he arrived from California and haul him up to the hotel, promptly and regularly collecting his fare, to wit: 50 cents in the coin of the republic.
>
> One stormy Christmas night, Jack waiting for the North Coast [train] sat in his high seat his head and beard buried in the collar of his old buffalo overcoat while the snowflakes settled all over him from the tip of his silk hat to the toes of his generous overshoes. The train hissed and groaned and with the last whine of the airbrakes, a familiar figure swung

down from the observation car. It was Jim Murray. He made a beeline for Jack's hack.

"Thornton, Mr. Murray?"

"Yes, Jack."

Jack toted the Murray suitcase into the hotel.

"Have a Christmas drink?" Murray asked.

The bar just glowed with Christmas cheer. Jack shook himself while the snow radiated from his fuzzy coat and fell in great flakes on the bright tiled floor.

"Tom and Jerry?"[114] said the bartender, hardly waiting for a reply.

Jack's dark eyes fairly twinkled as he glanced around at the knots of convivial merrymakers who were doing justice to the "Tom and Jerry." He was proud to be seen with Jim Murray—taking a Christmas drink with one of the richest men in the West.

"Cigar, Jack?" asked Murray.

Jack lit the perfecto and blew concentric rings at an imaginary point with the ease and grace of a connoisseur. This was the life.

"How much do I owe you, Jack?"

It was evident the tête-à-tête was about to be brought to an abrupt end.

"Just the same Mr. Murray, 50 cents."

Murray fumbled in his vest pocket. Then he reached deep into the recesses of his inside coat pocket. From it, he drew a heterogeneous collection of letters, cards and memoranda. From them he selected a small multifolded slip of paper, which he opened with studied deliberation. It was Fat Jack's note, renewed and augmented because of delinquent interest. It stipulated in seven different legal phrases that John Jones, alias "Fat Jack," some ten years earlier promised to pay James A. Murray, the sum of $1,500 in gold coin, the same to be paid in the City of Butte.

It was Christmas night and Jack, like Murray, was an old-timer. Murray spread the note on the bar so that Jack could see what it was. A smile half mischief, half kindness, stole over the face of the millionaire.

"Fifty cents" he mused. "Christmas night! Take this instead," he added quietly, as he handed him the note instead of the 50 cents."

Jack hesitated long enough to blow a great cloud of smoke from the perfecto. "If it's all the same to you Mr. Murray, I'd rather have the 50 cents."

After finishing the story, Warren introduced the reporter to Murray and Fat Jack. Murray verified Warren's account of that Christmas night and then turned to Fat Jack, asking him if he remembered the time he left Murray half-shaven. Fat Jack said he would never forget it. Murray then proceeded to tell the reporter about the time Fat Jack had left him in his barber's chair for a game of faro.[115]

This was the last time Jim and Fat Jack saw each other in Butte. In 1920, under doctor's orders, Fat Jack moved to Southern California and a climate more kind to his ailments.[116] He first moved to a veteran's facility in Los Angeles County,[117] but he quickly realized he needed different accommodations. The Soldiers Home required patients to wear the same military-style beret. Fat Jack only cared to wear his signature stovepipe hat. Murray's home in Monterey was too cold in the winter, so Jack found a friend in Los Angeles, where W. A. Clark Jr. offered Fat Jack two rooms in his mansion and access to a car. Junior and his brother Charlie had both been benefactors of Jack's late-night service and discretion during their rowdy days in Butte.[118] Fat Jack lived in luxury for a year before finally passing at the age of seventy-six.[119]

Before leaving Butte, Murray disposed of his interest in the Blue Bird Mine. He sold his share, earned in a notorious lawsuit[120] thirty years prior, to a group from New York.[121] News of the sale brought back stories of Murray's nemesis in the case, Ferdinand Van Zandt, and his suicide in London, just days after the courts handed Murray a stunning victory over the celebrity mine owner. The sale was another move by Murray to clean up the loose ends of his estate.

Murray ended his regular tours of the Northwest the following September. On his final stop, in Spokane, Washington, he caught up with former business associate Charles A. Cummings. Their last deal had ended in acrimony,[122] but time had erased any bad feelings, and the two enjoyed a candid conversation. Murray spoke freely to Cummings about his estate planning but also mixed in a few good stories from his earlier, wilder days. Murray shared stories about his first marriage and subsequent divorce, and the time a lover had shredded his clothes. He then turned to current affairs and confided in Cummings his thoughts about his estate. He shared that he was moving income property into the name of his wife, Mary, and stepson, Stuart Haldorn. He liked Stuart because he addressed him as Mr. Murray, never asked for anything, and never took advantage of his relationship.[123] Murray's conversation with Cummings confirmed what others likely had observed. Murray was getting ready for the day he no longer could step on the iron horse.

Stuart's Good Show

Murray's comments about Stuart were likely a product of Mary's careful coaching. She knew first-hand the deference Murray required. If the nephews and niece who worked for Murray had eavesdropped on his comments they likely would have been infuriated. They, for the most part, experienced a wild ride as Murray wound down his affairs. Alex was wiped out financially and sent packing to Pennsylvania. Marcus had just been moved from Tacoma to Butte and was experiencing life in the wild mining town for the first time. Just prior to the forced move, he lost one of his children during an operation. James traveled across Montana and the country raising funds for the Irish rebellion. May was swamped with managing a good share of her uncle's loans and bank accounts. Freeman House, Murray's former stepson, was tracked down in Utah and sued for using the Murray surname (Murray's intent with the lawsuit appears to have been a preemptive strike to prevent any claim on his estate). The only youngster spared the tumult of Murray's final years was Stuart, who was carefully guarded by his cunning mother.

Stuart, after attending the School of Mines in Butte in 1908, settled in San Francisco and went into business as a real estate broker of sorts, under the close eye of his mother. Mary had a clear plan for her only son. She wanted him to become entrenched in the power elite of the city and marry a socialite from a well-connected family. This meant purchasing a box at the San Francisco Opera and a golf membership at the Olympic Club, and pushing Stuart to attend tea and dance parties at the St. Francis Hotel and the Cliff House. Stuart's life was far removed from the saloon brawls and smelter stacks his half-cousins experienced in Butte.

It probably helped Stuart Haldorn that he had a different name than his stepfather, for just as the young man was working his way into the San Francisco Blue Book, Murray's name was splattered across the San Francisco papers. Jim Murray was a frequent visitor to San Francisco but was relatively unknown until he started a one-man crusade to send a young banker, Frederick Signor, to prison. The episode occurred between 1908 and 1909 after Murray found himself the victim of what one paper dubbed "One of the Most Remarkable Stories in the Criminal History of the State."

Signor had forged Murray's signature, first on drafts and then on notes totaling $450,000. He also forged a power of attorney making himself Murray's agent. Signor presented the falsified drafts to William and Tyler Henshaw for the purchase, on Murray's behalf, of their cement factory in Southern California. The checks bounced, and Signor substituted falsified notes instead. The Henshaws, feeling something was amiss, decided to bypass Signor and contact Murray directly regarding the financial documents. As they came close to pinning down Murray's whereabouts, Signor confessed the forgeries. No money was ever embezzled from Murray's accounts, and the local district attorney initially declined to press charges over the harmless scheme. Murray would have none of that and made it his personal mission to see Signor thrown in jail. He succeeded in short order, dragging the respected Henshaw name through the mud in the process, accusing the brothers of being coconspirators. The Henshaws were exonerated, and San Francisco was introduced to the fiery litigant who Mary hoped would be some debutante's new father-in-law.

Stuart's search for a bride reached its final stage in 1913 when he started appearing in the society pages of the city's newspapers. His attendance at several events was noted, as was his companion, the popular Enid Gregg, daughter of Wellington and Leonie Gregg. Wellington was the vice president of Wells Fargo Bank and a member of every prestigious club in the city. He owned a ranch and quarry in the Monterey area near the Murray hacienda. (Gregg's quarry provided stone for Murray's renovation project at the Carmel Mission.) Enid, twenty years old when her courtship with Stuart began, debuted on the city's social scene in 1908, when she was

Enid Gregg appearing in the New York Times*'s feature "Girl of the Day" on December 7, 1913.* —Photographed by Arnold Genthe, Library of Congress, Serial and Government Publications Division

sixteen. Over the next four years she became a fixture of the society pages, with her photograph appearing four to six times a year, and rarely a week passing without some notice of her weekend activities. Her relentless social schedule included the children of the city's wealthiest patrons: de Young, Sutro, Tobin, and Crocker.

Enid cultivated a reputation as stellar dancer and fashion icon in just a few short years. Her image was carefully managed, with regular portrait sessions with some of the nation's most renowned photographers and painters. She sat for annual portraits with photographer Arnold Genthe and sat for a painting by Walter Cox and a photograph by Francis Bruguière when she turned twenty-one. She was also sure to stay at the forefront of every fashion trend, a penchant duly noted in the press: "Miss Gregg is wholly Parisian in style of dressing and if anything new comes out one will be sure to see it on her. She represents an almost oriental type of beauty and the large round hoop earrings she is now wearing enhance the resemblances."[124]

When Enid traveled to Europe with her friends, Elyse Schultz and Kathleen de Young, reporters knew they would be in for a treat on their return, noting that the trio "in all probability will return with many wonderful creations with attractive accessories, as they have been spending many weeks in Paris and ordering their clothes from some of the biggest establishments." The writers went on to note that "Miss Gregg without doubt will appear in something daring and extreme on her return, but as she has the style of the French women, she will soon cultivate the provincial taste of her critics."[125] Enid did not disappoint.

On her return from her Parisian shopping spree, the press caught up with her at the tearoom of the St. Francis Hotel and reported, "Miss Gregg wore the mummy skirt yesterday in the tearoom of the St. Francis and the hobble skirts were eclipsed. There were exclamations of 'Oh!' and 'Ah!' from the group of younger girls who greeted Miss Gregg and subdued remarks of 'Perfectly stunning' and 'Too stylish for anything.' There were sighs of chagrin too, for the hobble skirts that were forgotten in the new craze over the mummy skirt." A photograph of Enid in her latest fashion statement accompanied the article.[126]

Stuart and Enid's first appearance together was at a masquerade ball on October 27, 1913. The press noted that "Gregg was the most striking at the ball." She wore a fandango costume of flame-colored chiffon "enwrapped in a rare and beautiful old Spanish shawl with a jaunty sombrero."[127] For the remainder of the winter the couple was inseparable, and in the spring of 1914 they were wed in a small ceremony. After a brief honeymoon in Hawaii, Stuart and Enid returned to San Francisco and remained active in the social scene, both in San Francisco and in Monterey, where they could stay in the guest quarters of the Murray hacienda.

Last Will and Testament

After the fall of 1920, Murray spent considerable time in Monterey tending to the final details of his estate. The Monterey mansion was already in his wife's name. He had transferred it to her after his stroke in 1905. He transferred a ground lease in Seattle to her name, along with several large mortgages. In all, he arranged for his wife to collect $2,000 a month in income after he died, an income greater than 99 percent of Americans at the time. He made all of these moves outside his last will and testament to avoid inheritance taxes. For everything else in his empire, he executed a simple will, drafted by W. S. K. Brown of Mill Valley. It left the ultimate disposition of his estate a mystery, except for what might be distributed to anyone presenting a paternity claim.

> This is my last will,
>
> I revoke all former wills.
>
> I declare that heretofore and at various times I have transferred and conveyed unto the Monidah Trust, a corporation organized under the laws of the State of Delaware, all or nearly all of my property, and that I am the owner of all the issued shares of the capital stock of that corporation; that I have caused to be executed in certain certificates in the names of various persons whom I desire to be owners thereof, evidencing various amounts of said shares, which said certificates will be found duly executed and contained in an envelope marked "Monidah Trust Stock Certificates" either on my person or in one of my safe deposit boxes; and I hereby give and bequeath unto the said various persons whose names so appear upon the faces of said certificates, so contained in said envelope, the said executed certificates evidencing the number of shares of the capital stock of said corporation represented by the certificate executed in his or her name as aforesaid.
>
> I declare that I have no children, and in the event that any person or persons should present himself, herself, or themselves claiming to be a legal child or children of mine, and should prove his, her, or their lineage and right of inheritance in a court of competent jurisdiction, then I give to each of such persons the sum of Ten ($10.00) Dollars.
>
> All of the rest and residue of my estate, together with any legacy which shall fail for want of a taker, or which shall fail for any reason whatsoever; I give, devise, and bequeath unto my wife Mary H. Murray.[128]

Murray called on Brown, and local businessmen R. A. Crocker and Will T. Jacks, to meet at his home on January 26, 1921. Brown presented the will, Murray acknowledged that it was correct and then asked Jacks, Crocker, and Brown to sign it. Murray signed last.[129] Neither his wife nor stepson were present.

None of the witnesses viewed the stock certificates mentioned in the will. Murray held all of them in his name in a secure location. He endorsed each certificate to his chosen benefactor. Murray's plan afforded him complete flexibility. He could make a change on the certificate with a simple stroke of the pen and never have to revise his will.

His wife and nephew James, despite not seeing the will, knew Murray was actively organizing his affairs. James, as an officer of the Monidah Trust, saw the transfer of income properties and mortgages into Mary's name. They both knew this accounted for only about twenty percent of the estate. Neither knew where the rest was going, and it certainly wore on them. James and Mary put up with Murray's hot and cold personality for more than twenty years, and each felt strongly that they deserved a big reward. Alex's fate, however, was a reminder that Murray's rewards were often elusive.

A Roaring Life Ends

Three months after Murray executed his will, he started to feel listless. He requested his physician, Dr. William Lillie, to make a house call to see what was wrong. Dr. Lillie came to Murray's home on April 28, 1921.[130] Lillie was well known in the community, having twice served as Monterey's mayor. He was not looking so well himself that day. He had a nagging cough that he muffled with a handkerchief.[131] He checked Murray's vital signs and drew blood to run tests. Lillie likely suspected the cause of Murray's declining health, but he waited for the results to be sure. When the results come back, Lillie's suspicions were confirmed. Murray was dying of kidney failure.[132]

On April 30, Dr. Lillie returned to provide Jim with the results from the blood work. It was a message best delivered in person. Murray's time on earth was growing short. Lillie probably offered Jim some comfort regarding his predicament. If Lillie and his colleagues could choose a way to die, kidney failure would be their choice. One loses energy slowly and one's appetite subsides. Pain medication can easily manage any discomfort. It was an unexpected outcome for someone who had faced so many dangers in life, but there he lay, in the care of several servants, with a beautiful view of Monterey Bay. Soon there would be a peaceful ending to a roaring life.

As the calendar turned to May, Murray's affairs were all in order. The only business matter that he still attended to was the sale of the San Diego waterworks. He scratched out handwritten letters and dictated others, giving Ed Fletcher instructions on how to close his final deal. All other matters were settled. His will was in place,[133] and he had a plot in the cemetery where his best friend, John Maguire, had been laid to rest.[134] His mind was free to wonder about the other side of life. Perhaps he thought of seeing

Maguire, Penrose, and Fat Jack. Perhaps Silas King had a saloon where they all could meet.

On the morning of May 11, 1921, Jim lay motionless in bed, his breathing fast and shallow. Dr. Lillie stopped by to check on his patient. His visit was very short. He checked the texture of Jim's skin, the temperature of his body, and his respiration. He let Murray know that his time was near, and that it was time for last rites. Mrs. Murray could not have been too far away. Perhaps she paced in the salon with her advisers and son. She had waited patiently for this moment, and it was nearly upon her.

By 2:30 in the afternoon, Jim's body was cold to the touch. Old Jim Murray had passed quietly in his eighty-first year—a faint shadow of the pioneering young man who built a fortune in the Wild West. Dr. Lillie returned to the estate, checked for signs of life, and, finding none, recorded the time of death as 3 p.m.[135]

16
Dead Man's Chest

Let your plans be dark and impenetrable as night, and when you move, fall like a thunderbolt.
—Sun Tzu, *The Art of War*

Murray's death marked the beginning of a high-stakes battle for his immense fortune. Murray left behind an estate worth as much as $15 million—an impressive sum in 1921, and the equivalent of $3 billion in today's dollars, placing him between contemporary billionaires Oprah Winfrey ($2.8 B) and Mark Cuban ($3.2 B).

Mary knew that finding and recapturing all of her husband's wealth was a significant challenge. She held title to the hacienda and several income-producing properties in Seattle. She would fight to the end to keep those in her name. She knew many others held Murray's property in their names, and they too would fight to keep it that way. Despite the challenges, Mary's goal was clear: she wanted it all. In her perfect world, she would find only her name on the Monidah stock certificates, and then her only task—a daunting one—would be to find and recapture all of her husband's holdings. If her husband had split the shares among several people, her work would be doubled—she would have to fight off Monidah shareholders and find all of the dispersed assets.

All indications suggest that Mary and Stuart were the first to find the envelope that held the shareholder documents. It was located in the family safe. When they leafed through the eleven certificates, totaling 10,000 shares in all, they found that the first certificate, for 500 shares, was assigned to Murray's nephew James E. Murray. James certainly was deserving of a portion of the estate, having provided legal services (probably with little pay) to his uncle for many years.

The second certificate, also for 500 shares, was signed over to another nephew, Marcus Murray. Marcus also was deserving, having faithfully worked for his uncle's banks in Seattle, Tacoma, and finally Butte.

The third certificate was for Jim's brother, Thomas J. Murray, in the amount of 500 shares. Thomas, who had passed away nine months earlier, was the father of Alex, the nephew Murray had bankrupted in Pocatello.

The fourth and fifth certificates allocated 1,000 shares to Murray's niece May. She was working at Murray's bank in Seattle when he passed, and she held more than $350,000 in notes and bank accounts as Jim's trustee.

The sixth and seventh certificates, dated from 1904, were assigned to Murray's brother Daniel. Each transferred 1,000 shares to a brother who may never have set foot outside of the Canadian province where the Murray boys were raised. Daniel, who passed away in 1907, never sent any of his eight children out west to serve his wealthy brother.

Murray endorsed the eighth certificate to Eliza Murray Poole. She was a niece (a daughter of Daniel) from Detroit and received 500 shares. Eliza had dutifully taken care of the gravesites of Jim's brothers back east.

After seeing the first eight certificates, and with just three remaining in the stack, Mary and Stuart must have had large knots in their stomachs. Fifty percent of the shares had already been allocated, and neither had yet to read their name. Mary and Stuart pressed on.

The ninth certificate was endorsed to James E. for 12 shares.

The tenth certificate, for 988 shares, was blank. Finally, the eleventh certificate, the grand prize of 4,000 shares, was signed over to James E., the dutiful attorney and national leader in the Irish American community. It seems Jim Murray really did appreciate his nephew's service to his most important cause.

Blood relatives with a Murray surname were the only ones named on the certificates. James E. Murray received 4,512 shares, Daniel Murray 2,000, Marcus 500, May 1,000, Thomas Murray 500, and Eliza Murray Poole 500.[136]

It was small consolation to Mary, having been named in the will as the beneficiary of anything unassigned, that she could lay claim to the blank certificate for 988 shares. Fighting the distribution would be a nightmare for Mary and Stuart. They wanted it all, and now they faced an impossible task of fending off a large pack of Murrays from all over the country. In addition, they had little ground to stand on as not one of the certificates was endorsed with their names.

Their first salvo in the fight for Murray's millions came almost immediate. Mary and Stuart carefully changed the middle initial on James's 4,000-share certificate from an "E" to an "A."[137] Their story would be that Jim made a certificate out to himself, James A. Murray, and not to his nephew James E. Murray. Just as with the blank certificate, those 4,000 shares would then go to Mary. They placed the altered certificate along with the others into an envelope and typed Stuart's name on the front. With these changes, they hoped to make a case that the presence of Stuart Haldorn's name on the envelope implied that all of the stock certificates were de facto endorsed to him. They would be assisted by the legal team that Mary had solidified during her time in California. They placed the certificates back in the safe for Brown to discover upon his arrival.

Stuart sent telegrams to inform friends and family of Jim's passing. One went to James E. Murray in Butte, several went to local papers, and the most important went to Ed Fletcher in San Diego. The telegram to Ed likely included a note that Mary wished to speak with him as soon as possible.

When morning broke on Thursday, May 12, the day after Jim's passing, papers from San Diego to Seattle carried the news. The West had lost one of its great pioneers. One headline read, "Prominent in the Development of the Entire West." Another: "James A. Murray Dies at Monterey: Prominent Montana Millionaire with Rich Holdings in the West Passes Suddenly."[138] The editors of the *Anaconda Standard* carefully penned an editorial that captured all of the unique aspects of a full life. It read, in part,

> Wealth never spoiled Jim Murray. He preferred the companionship of men who had been comrades and friends in the days of his beginnings to that of many who liked to see his name on their board of directors. To those who knew him intimately he was an entertaining raconteur, a keen, unerring analyst of human nature, a loyal friend and a delightful companion. He was as intense in his animosities as in his attachments. He held that he who never made an enemy was not worth having as a friend.

Jim's death certainly stirred a wide range of emotions among his family and friends. Family members and associates who helped Murray hide pieces of his fortune wondered what was in store for them. May Murray held several notes and bank accounts. Murray's nephews James and Marcus held property as well. So too did R. B. Lelande, Murray's secretary. Several friends had borrowed substantial sums from Jim and enjoyed generous repayment terms. Gus Holmes, Murray's partner in the Arizona silver mines, owed Murray $300,000 for his stake in their mining company. Josephine Kline had borrowed $70,000 to expand her hotel in Livingston, Montana. Charlie Clark, W. A. Clark's son, had borrowed more than $20,000. And Ed Fletcher, Jim's partner in the San Diego waterworks, owed nearly $80,000. These were just a few of the trustees and borrowers who were anxious to find out what would come next.[139]

James was anxious to travel to Monterey and defend his stake in the inheritance, but he had to delay his trip for a day to transfer a valuable property into his name. His uncle had set up all the paperwork to transfer the Boulder Hot Springs and Resort to James as the first step in a transaction that would eventually pass the property to an orphanage. Prior to his uncle's death, the transaction had been of little interest to James, but now he was in a position to take the property for his own personal gain. James completed the transfer and proceeded to Monterey the following day.

Services for Murray were held on the Saturday following his death, with a high mass at the Carmel Mission he had helped to restore. James E. and May arrived in time for the service but were primarily interested in seeing Mary's first move. Dr. T. J. Murray came from Butte, but he simply wanted to remember a friend who had helped him build that city's first hospital. After the service, Murray's body was not laid to rest next to John Maguire but instead was held in a vault pending Mary's decision on a final burial location.

On the Monday following the service, W. S. K. Brown traveled to the Murray hacienda to view the stock certificates. Brown reviewed the contents with Mary and Stuart present. Shortly after they reviewed the altered documents together, James E. arrived. He noted right away that a certificate bearing his name had been altered. Mary made no conciliation, and the war was on. With only a brief break that Wednesday to bury Murray at a Catholic cemetery eighty miles to the north in Colma, Mary and James each moved to set aside the will and control the selection of the estate's executor. Both believed they were entitled to the majority of the estate. Detectives on both sides worked long hours to dig up dirt on each camp. James claimed that Mary's marriage was a fraud. Mary found evidence that James was not the biological son of Jim's brother. Lawsuits were filed blocking any distribution of assets to either. The fight played out in newspapers across the country and captured front-page headlines six times in the *San Francisco Chronicle*.[140]

Caught in the middle was Ed Fletcher. The San Diego water company represented Jim's single most valuable holding at the time of his death. James wrote passionately to Fletcher begging for his assistance. James expressed that he and Mary deserved most of the money because they had suffered the brunt of Murray's difficult personality over the years. (Ed was certainly able to relate.) James finished his letter with a request that Fletcher destroy the letter after reading it.[141] Unbeknownst to James, Fletcher had already chosen sides and was firmly in Mary's camp. She had offered to forgive all his loans in exchange for his cooperation in blocking James's attempts to gain a portion of the inheritance (a move that Mary later admitted was illegal).[142] Fletcher did not destroy Murray's letter. Instead, he turned it over as evidence in the probate proceedings. James, perhaps with an eye toward a political career, downplayed his role as the fight escalated, while castigating the uncle who left behind the fortune. He told the press, "I believe my uncle's money was the cause of his failing to get his full share of happiness out of life. I have been 'immensely wealthy' for years. I have six children and each one is worth in excess of one billion dollars."[143]

It took four months of mudslinging before Mary and James realized they had a bigger problem than their fight with each other. Twenty-six relatives swarmed the courts in Monterey, Butte, and Seattle—all trying to make a claim. The two reconciled just as Mary was about to be forced to testify under oath about the tampered-with certificate. They joined forces and proceeded to bully and settle with the blood relatives, most of whom were James's cousins. James and Stuart went east to confront the would-be heirs. They demanded immediate cash from the claimants to settle the inheritance tax claims against the estate, and they indicated that actual distributions would take years to make it to their bank accounts. If the heirs did not have the cash, they were offered a fraction of their interest as a settlement.[144] To any relative living in the United States without being naturalized, they threatened deportation if their offer was not accepted.[145]

It took approximately six years to tie down all the agreements with the would-be-heirs. In the end, 6,000 shares were used to divide the estate. Mary received 3,100 shares. James, May, and Marcus split 1,500 shares. Thomas J. Murray's family received 500 shares. And the rest of the relatives split 900 shares.[146] There were plenty of assets that fell outside the settlement, so it is difficult to determine the dollar value that each received. The only sanctioned side deal that was made public was for May Murray to retain the assets she had held for her uncle.[147] The executor of Murray's estate filed his final accounting in 1930—nine years after Murray's passing.[148] His report included only items that had been publicly disclosed. All of the side deals remained secret.

Epilogue

> *Don't get it into your head that things would not go along without your presence. Things will go along all right if we are both dead.*
>
> —James A. Murray, writing to Ed Fletcher

Murray's vast fortune, the equivalent of $3 billion in today's currency, splintered and dissipated over the many decades that followed his death. Not one of the legatees, legitimate or otherwise, could replicate Murray's business success, but they had no problems spending his wealth. Mary and Stuart lived the good life in Monterey, James used his status to join the millionaires' club in the US Senate, Ed Fletcher fumbled away his fortune, and Alex, the bankrupted nephew, opened an art school.

Mary's Spoils

Mary Haldorn's third marriage was a charm. She invested more time in this marriage than she probably expected. It was nearly twenty-five years before she could bury Murray. When she finally did, she found the experience so pleasurable that she did it twice—once after he died and a second time when the hard-fought inheritance made it to her bank accounts. Seven years after Murray passed, Mary exhumed him from his earthen grave and moved him to a simple public crypt, where only the faint engraving of his name records his existence on this earth.

The spigot on Mary's great fortune opened in earnest in 1928 when all claims on the Murray estate were settled. She moved to a new home in Monterey and transferred title to the seaside mansion to Stuart. She donated several pieces of her art collection to local institutions. The Léon Trousset painting of Serra's first mass went to the Carmel Mission. A painting of Toledo, Spain, by Francis McComas ended up in the city library, and another McComas work made its way to city hall. She reconnected with her daughter, Marie, from her marriage to Frederick Smith. Marie had also married into wealth and was living in Paris near the Notre Dame cathedral on the Île de la Cité. Mary led a quiet life in Monterey, with three well-paid servants and few reports of charitable works. She died sixteen years after Murray's passing, at seventy-one years of age, on December 14, 1940.

Mary's home, valued at $35,000 in the 1940 census, was sold, along with most of her belongings, to a Monterey couple. The inventory of her home included a bearskin rug and several works by famous California artists. Her cars—a brand-new Lincoln-Zephyr coupe and a ten-year-old Ford coupe, reflected a modest lifestyle. She left a couple thousand dollars to two of her servants, $25,000 to her daughter, Marie, and $300 per month to her sister in Panama City, Panama. The remainder of the estate, generating more than $3,000 per month in income, remained with Stuart. During the seven-year wait for the final settlement, Stuart pulled more than $150,000 in cash from his mother's bank accounts to support the lavish lifestyle that he and his wife enjoyed.

Stuart's Easy Life

Stuart Haldorn squandered a good portion of his windfalls on prestigious country clubs, a large waitstaff, and several yachts. While he waited for his first payday from Jim Murray's estate, he spent considerable time on the links. His practice paid off in 1923 when he won the Washington's birthday tournament at the Pebble Beach golf course. When the first wave of cash landed in his lap in 1928, he took a break from golfing and dredged Stillwater Cove, which borders the fourth, fifth, and sixth holes at Pebble Beach. He anchored his own boat there and became yachting's biggest promoter on the West Coast. He purchased six starter boats to introduce his fellow layabouts to the popular blue-blood hobby. Over the next twenty years, Haldorn purchased and raced boats of every length. His fleet of sailing vessels included the *Ay Ay Ay*, which he sailed to victory in the Pacific Regatta in 1930.

As the canning industry expanded around the Murray hacienda during the 1940s, Stuart and Enid decided to leave the seaside estate for less industrialized quarters. In 1945, they commissioned Frank Lloyd Wright to design a home for an oceanfront parcel at the intersection of Ocean View Avenue and Scenic Road in neighboring Carmel. Wright, who steadfastly refused to pick his favorite project, admitted that the Haldorns' prospective home "was one of the best houses I ever designed." Wright's design featured a tunnel under Scenic Road to connect the rocky shoreline with subterranean elements of the house. The home was never built, probably due to the unique and costly design, but Wright used similar design elements in future works—notably the nearby Walker House. A sketch of the Haldorn design graces the the introduction to a recent compendium of Wright's works.[1] After scuttling the project, the Haldorns opted to move away from the ocean to a ranch in Carmel Valley.

As Haldorn grew older, he hung up his skipper's hat and returned to the links, this time at the Cypress Point Golf Club. He made his mark there lifting crackers from the dining room and feeding the pigeons. One day in 1948 his foursome included Bing Crosby. Haldorn played only a few holes with the crooner before retiring to the clubhouse. There he spied Crosby knocking down a hole in one on the iconic sixteenth hole. Crosby remembered the moment vividly. It was only the second hole in one at the seaside hole, which required a 220-yard shot over an ocean inlet. Crosby told the press, "I was shooting into the sun, so I just stood up and smacked one blind." Haldorn immediately rang up every member he could reach and had a large crowd gathered at the bar to greet Crosby at the end of his round. Crosby spent about $700 that day quenching the thirst of the club's membership, but it was well worth it.[2]

In 1948, Stuart commissioned another high-profile talent, Salvador Dali, to paint a portrait of his wife. Enid was fifty-six years old at the time. In the portrait she sits with her left side to the artist on a small section of crumbling adobe bricks on a vast sandy beach with just one twisted, barren tree. She is dressed in a flowing gown and sandals as a stiff wind blows her salt-and-pepper hair and thin scarf. Her left arm hangs down as her hand releases a few seashells to the sand below. In the distance, nine characters wander the shoreline. An angel holding the hand of a small girl offers a handout to a beggar. A woman walks alone, passing a solitary man sitting by the shore. The man she passes appears to be sitting aboard a small, invisible sailboat. A man in a religious robe stands facing the same direction as Enid, leaning slightly into the wind. A woman and a small child hold hands where land and sea meet. Finally, there is a woman who appears to be dancing, just as Enid had at charity events during her debutante days in the city. The sky is shared by wispy white clouds, a dark, imposing thunderhead, and a sliver of the moon. The sun's rays break through the puffy dark clouds, casting long shadows from each of the characters in Enid's gallery.

It is no easy task interpreting the symbolism of a surrealist image. But there are some things we know about the subject that are reflected in Dali's work. Mary and her husband lived for many years in a seaside mansion in Monterey with their own small, private beach. Their Monterey community cherished adobe structures. Aside from the crouching man and the girl dancing on the beach, it is difficult to pin down the meaning of the other characters. Enid lived a fairly private life in Monterey after her marriage to Stuart.[3] The dark clouds certainly could represent the suffering she experienced early in life. She lost her mother when she was just twenty-two,[4] only a year after her marriage to Stuart.[5] Just a few years later she experienced a severe mental breakdown.[6] Then, in 1923, she lost her father.[7] The rays of light could represent that she never wanted for money.

Despite the challenge of interpreting the complex painting, it is fitting that the former debutante, who started her adult life with artists capturing the beauty of her youth, should have her life bookended with the work of another celebrated artist. Enid died two years after the sitting, at fifty-nine years of age. On his passing, Stuart bequeathed the painting to San Francisco's de Young art museum.

Stuart died alone in 1973 at age eighty-seven, having spent the last twenty-two years of his life a widower. He left behind $2.6 million in assets and investments generating $140,000 a year. He borrowed a provision from his stepfather's will, claiming no children but offering $10 to anyone who could prove paternity. He left the bulk of his estate to his wife's sister and her oldest son. The rest, about $300,000, was split fifty ways. He left three half-sisters $20,000 each. His doctor, ranch hand, and gardener were each gifted $10,000. Fourteen friends, including the artist Francis McComas, split $82,000. Fifteen golf caddies and three groundskeepers each received $500. Three yacht clubs split $25,000, and twelve charities were gifted a combined $80,000, the largest donation going to the community hospital in Carmel in the amount of $20,000.[8]

Senator James E. Murray

James's fight for his uncle's bequest must have been particularly frustrating because it coincided with his increasing responsibilities within the American Association for the Recognition of the Irish Republic (AARIR). In the year following his uncle's death, and shortly after England and Ireland signed the Anglo-Irish Treaty, he was selected to the presidency of the sixty-thousand-member organization.[9] James's presidency was short-lived however, because he could not bear to preside over an organization deeply split by the contested treaty. Although he sided with de Valera's view that the treaty—which gave Ireland many freedoms but required it to remain under the crown—was unacceptable, he could not support a civil war in Ireland to settle the differences between pro- and anti-treaty forces. After Ireland's first free election, in June 1922, selected a pro-treaty parliament, he publicly lashed out at members of the majority faction, labeling them "Irish tools of England,"[10] before privately submitting his resignation as president of AARIR.[11] His time with AARIR, despite ending on a bitter note, helped the organization raise $5.8 million to aid Ireland's revolution,[12] solidified his political base in Montana, and demonstrated his ability to manage political issues at the national and international level.

James never acknowledged the great wealth he inherited. When speaking in public about the windfall, he said it was not an inheritance but simply payment for a lifetime of service to his uncle. Murray went on to say that it was "dumb luck" that had led his uncle to his fortunes. After the stock market crash of 1929, Murray turned to politics and, at the request of Franklin Delano Roosevelt, ran for and won a seat in the US Senate.[13]

Senator James E. Murray was a close ally with FDR in executing the New Deal. Right to left, Senator Murray, Eleanor Roosevelt, and President Roosevelt. —Archives and Special Collections, Mansfield Library, University of Montana

Murray found great success in the Senate, proving he was as adept at writing bills, editorials, and speeches as his uncle had been at making money. James's political agenda, which was remarkably similar to that of his uncle, developed through his observation of labor relations in Butte and his reading of the works of economists and socialists. He served in the Senate for twenty-six years (1934–1961) and sponsored groundbreaking legislation to benefit working men and women throughout his career. His most important accomplishment was authoring Senate Bill 380, the basis for the Employment Act of 1946. Historian Stephen Bailey credits Murray with providing the "spark of will" that transformed ideas and discussions into this landmark legislation.[14] Writing to support passage of the final bill, the American Federation of Labor, Congress of Industrial Organizations (CIO), and National Farmers Union signed a joint letter stating that the legislation, if properly executed, could "mark the beginning of an American crusade for economic security, stability, and justice, and consequently a contribution of enormous significance to the cause of international peace."[15] Twenty years after passage of the bill, economist John Kenneth Galbraith opined that it appeared to be "the most important single piece of economic legislation of the postwar years."[16] Murray was also instrumental in passage of the Fair Labor Standards Act, and coauthored the Wagner-Murray-Dingell Bill, the nation's first proposal for comprehensive national health insurance.

Senator Murray's achievements were recognized in 1951 with the CIO's Philip Murray Award (no relation). Congratulations came from politicians and labor leaders across the country. President Harry S. Truman, who had served beside Murray in the Senate, said the award was "richly deserved and symbolizes his enduring concern for the health and welfare of all Americans."[17] Former Senator Claude Pepper wrote, "No man in my knowledge of the Senate has written a more glorious record for the health, the welfare, and the progress and security of our country than he."[18] Senator Hubert Humphrey called Murray the "staunchest advocate of social legislation in the United States Senate" and ranked his battles for medical care and full

Senators Truman (left) and Murray (right) were part of the same freshman class in 1934. —ACME

employment among the top historic contributions in social legislation.[19] From the podium of the award ceremony, Philip Murray remarked that the senator was "a pillar of the CIO" and "knows that we must have a strong labor movement in America if we are to achieve the economic and social progress to which all men of good will aspire."

Senator Murray's recognition by the CIO highlighted the peak of his productive years in the Senate. He spent nine more years in the upper chamber, stymied for eight of them by a Republican president opposed to his polices. During his last Senate campaign, President Dwight D. Eisenhower and Vice President Richard Nixon campaigned hard for Murray's Republican opponent, Wesley D'Ewart, who employed campaign literature casting Murray as a communist. Murray survived the attacks and won reelection with campaign support from Senators Al Gore Sr. and Lyndon B. Johnson. Murray retired from the Senate on January 3, 1961, and passed away shortly thereafter, less than three months after completing his fourth full term. Murray's death on March 23, 1961, ended the Murray family's unique seventy-eight-year span of radical politics.

Senator Murray's final accolades came posthumously in 1965, as President Lyndon B. Johnson recognized Murray for his work on the Wagner-Murray-Dingle legislation, which laid the groundwork for adoption of the Medicare Amendment to the Social Security Act. At the signing of the Medicare Amendment, President Johnson remarked that the legislation had been made possible by "the long-enduring, and often thankless, efforts of earlier presidents and earlier congressmen. This is their victory too. It is the victory of Harry Truman and of great congressmen like . . . James Murray."[20]

Fletcher's Fumble

Mary's original plan had been to compensate Fletcher for his service by forgiving all of his personal loans from her late husband, totaling $80,000. At some point, Mary's legal team advised her that it was illegal to forgive loans in exchange for Fletcher's work conspiring against Murray's heirs.[21] As an alternative, Mary became Fletcher's financial angel, optioning the Murray interest in the Cuyamaca Water Company (CWC) to him for a discounted price of $650,000.[22] Fletcher paid $5,000 in October 1922 to hold this extremely favorable option in place until June 1, 1923. This provided Fletcher with a little more than seven months to buy and sell the system in a single transaction, or to find a financial partner to advance the down payment of $145,000. The terms and conditions that Fletcher secured from Mary were remarkable and gave him an opportunity to seize a significant windfall. If he had purchased and sold Murray's interest on his own he could have realized over $600,000 in profit from the transaction.

Unfortunately, Fletcher lacked the cash or business acumen to capitalize on the opportunity and had to turn to others for help. Fletcher asked Charles F. Stern, a Los Angeles banker, to advance the $145,000 down payment in exchange for half of the Murray estate's interest.[23] Subsequent exchanges between the two were remarkably similar to those between Murray and Fletcher during their partnership. Fletcher proposed to acquire the Murray interest through a complicated partnership with a rival water company. Stern advised against the complex venture and eventually had to explain to Fletcher in detail why the deal was not in their best interests.[24] Fletcher acquiesced, and the two entered into a simple partnership and successfully renegotiated the terms of the option agreement to delay the $145,000 down payment by one year, to June 1, 1924. They signed the agreement on June 1, 1923.[25]

While they were negotiating and documenting their purchase agreement with the Murray estate, Fletcher and Stern tried to sell the system to the city of San Diego but came up short, leaving them with two options: sell to the La Mesa, Lemon Grove, and Spring Valley Irrigation District, or raise funds through a stock offering to purchase the system with shareholder funding. They worked on both tracks, securing Public Utilities Commission approval to issue bonds while negotiating a sales price of $1.1 million, for a portion of the system, to the district. The district was clearly the easiest path to a quick payday, so Fletcher focused his effort on closing the deal. Unfortunately, they were not able to close the sale before their first significant payment came due, so Stern had to pay $145,000 to the Murray estate to maintain control of the CWC. Eighteen months later, on January 4, 1926, they completed the sale to the district. Two years later, they sold the balance of the system for $400,000 to the city of San Diego.[26] Old Jim Murray must have rolled over in his grave when Fletcher and Stern earned more than $600,000 in profit on their $150,000 investment.[27] After repaying his debts, Fletcher, likely cleared $350,000 in the deal.

Ed Fletcher's suspicious windfall may have escaped public scrutiny if not for Mary's strident efforts to collect every dollar owed to her husband's estate. In the year prior to the CWC sale, her attorneys had filed suit in San Diego to recover $5,000 her husband had lent to Joseph and Anna Sauer.[28] Records do not reveal the original purpose of the loan, but the fact that the Sauer's son Abraham was the publisher of the *San Diego Herald* may hold part of the explanation. The collection effort certainly heightened the younger Sauer's interest in other matters relating to the Murray estate. When the CWC sale concluded, Sauer took note of the significant discrepancy between the purchase and sale prices but mistakenly accused Fletcher of fleecing Mary when, in fact, he was her accomplice. Murray's widow came to Fletcher's aid in a libel suit against the publisher.[29] The jury could not agree on the charges against Sauer, who later apologized publicly for his accusation, never realizing that the fraud he'd spotted was committed against Murray's heirs.

Fletcher later claimed in his memoir that he had netted only $78,000 for the sale of the CWC, contradicting testimony in the libel case indicating that he had split $500,000 with Stern.[30] If Fletcher cleared only $78,000, then Murray had been right: Fletcher was a "damn poor trader."[31] Another explanation, however, is that Fletcher parsed his words carefully in his memoir and referred only to the terms of his original partnership with James A. Murray, excluding the compensation Mary provided for helping to conspire against the legatees of the Murray estate.[32] Fletcher's account of the CWC sale in his memoir concluded with the comment that he had been treated splendidly by Murray's widow, and that "everything was adjusted financially satisfactory to all parties concerned."[33]

Fletcher authored a chapter on water development in Carl Heilbron's *History of San Diego County* in 1936 and wrote himself into a leading role, implying that he had been an equal partner with Murray. Sixteen years later, when writing his memoirs, he embellished further, changing his role to that of a visionary owner.[34] Local historians, starting with Heilbron, accepted Fletcher's version of San Diego's development without question. Heilbron wrote of Fletcher, "[His] wisdom and foresight together with his fine connections with men of wealth made possible the development of the majority of our county water system."[35] In 1978, local historian Claire Crane characterized Fletcher as one of twelve people who shaped San Diego, listing him alongside Portuguese explorer Juan Rodríguez Cabrillo, Father Junípero Serra, and real estate mogul John D. Spreckels.[36] Donald C. Jackson, writing about John Eastwood's dam projects in San Diego, cited Fletcher's memoir as his primary source. He cast the developer as a potential rival to Spreckels's empire, and attributed the success of Murray's projects to Fletcher's managerial and political skills.[37] Historian Leland Fetzer, meanwhile, suggested that local elites supported Fletcher's projects "because they recognized his integrity, his business acumen, his record of success, and his ability to manage the endless details of his project indefatigably day and night."[38]

Collectively, these historians accepted Fletcher's autobiography at face value and conferred upon him a significant role in the history of San Diego. They bestowed upon Fletcher the vision to conceive a water system to serve a vast population, and the skill to develop and deliver this system by orchestrating the complex elements of design, financing, permitting, construction, and rate making. It was a far different Fletcher than the one who suffered through Murray's tortuous micromanagement and insults.

May Murray

After Jim Murray's passing, the courts allowed May Murray to keep the $84,000 in cash, $240,000 in notes, and a judgment for $29,000 that she had held for her uncle. She likely pooled her bounty with her brothers in coming to a final settlement with Mary Murray and Stuart Haldorn. The largest note, for $90,000, was secured by the Kline Hotel in Livingston, Montana. May moved to Livingston to take over the hotel when the owner, Josephine Kline, ran afoul of several contractors. May bought the hotel at a sheriff's auction to protect the note. She renamed the hotel "The Murray" and managed its operations for a short time until her untimely death, in 1925, at just forty-two years of age. The Murray remains open today under the coownership of Dan and Kathleen Paul. Celebrity chef and travel expert Anthony Bourdain places the Murray among his ten favorite hotels in the world.[39]

Alex's Art School

Alex Murray, the nephew Murray bankrupted to save a few dollars, received a portion of the inheritance that came to his father. The bequest allowed Alex to pursue a career in art. He first attended several fine art institutes and completed a master's degree at Columbia University. He then served as an instructor in the Wilkes-Barre, Pennsylvania, school system and started two art schools—one in Wilkes-Barre and one in Scranton. He also operated an art supply store in Scranton. Alex published two instructional books on drawing and contributed articles to national and local publications.

Butte Copper Kings

Murray happily built and operated his empire in the shadow of three notorious Copper Kings. Murray had little interest in gathering attention from the public at large. In this respect, he was much different than Augustus Heinze, Marcus Daly, and W. A. Clark. Perhaps his penchant for staying out of the newspapers enabled him to work with each of these men, all of whom had large egos and fought among themselves. In the end, Murray outlived Heinze and Daly, and he held on to a greater fortune than Heinze.

Heinze, a Brooklyn native, returned to New York in 1902 with $12 million from his sale of Butte copper mines to the Anaconda Copper Mining Company. He parlayed his profits into a series of banking relationships and stock positions in partnership with his brothers. In 1907, with markets still reeling from the devastation of the 1906 earthquake in San Francisco, Heinze's brother Otto made a colossal failure of a "big short" and sparked widespread panic similar in scale to the 2008 mortgage meltdown. Heinze, by association, became inextricably linked to the "Panic of 1907." His brother's reckless abandon is credited in part with the creation of the Federal Reserve banking system in 1913, and with Heinze's personal demise. Murray's former nemesis and partner died with just a fraction of his former wealth, a broken marriage, and a ravaged liver in 1914. He was forty-four years old.

Marcus Daly frequented the East Coast in the early days of his wealth to race his stable of horses in the nation's richest stakes races. In 1897, his Scottish Chieftain won New York's famous Belmont Stakes. Two years later, when his company was sold to parties associated with the Standard Oil Company, he leased William Waldorf Astor's mansion on Fifth Avenue to be closer to his new employer. Exchanging his sprawling estate in Montana's Bitterroot Valley for congested city streets did not sit well with the successful executive and horse breeder. He lasted only one year in his Central Park mansion, passing away in 1900 at age fifty-eight. All the while, his rival W. A. Clark was rooting for his demise. After Daly's death, his wife, Margaret, returned to Montana, where she managed his sizable estate, some of which was tied up in partnerships with Murray.

W. A. Clark came to New York, not with fake pearls to mock the nouveau riche, but to use his mountain of cash to break away from the hinterland millionaires and join society's highest circles. Clark's mansion on Fifth Avenue was centered on Millionaires' Row between the smaller abodes of Vanderbilt, Astor, and Carnegie. The 121-room mansion featured twenty-six bedrooms, thirty-one bathrooms, and five art galleries. The opulence of this and other Clark estates is featured in the 2014 book *Empty Mansions* by Bill Dedman and the late Paul Clark Newell Jr. Clark outlived all of his fellow Copper Kings, passing away in 1925 at eighty-six years of age. His fortune was one of the largest ever built on American soil.

Dr. William Lillie

Less than two months after he pronounced Jim Murray dead, Dr. Lillie committed suicide. Initial reports of his death pointed to his coughing fits, raising speculation that he had contracted tuberculosis. Other reports noted that Lillie had invested heavily in overheated automobile and Mexican oil stocks, and both suffered tremendous losses. Whatever pressure he may have been under, he decided at age fifty-five to take his own life. The papers recounted his last moments in gripping detail. According to the coroner's inquest, Lillie woke up at 3 a.m. on June 21, 1921, picked up his shotgun, and headed down to his garage. There he "placed the nozzle of the gun into his mouth, struck the trigger with his right hand, the charge plowing through his head completely blowing off the top of his head."[40]

Murray's Monuments and Memory

After Jim Murray's death, stories of his colorful life continued to appear in Montana newspapers until 1933, when the memory of his remarkable life completely faded from the printed media. No city contemplated a permanent monument to his goodwill. City officials in Butte, Livingston, Pocatello, and San Diego were likely relieved that he would never sue them again. Memories of Murray's life remain in the monuments he built for others: the pioneers of Henderson Gulch, Junípero Serra, and good friend John Maguire. His memory also remains in the projects that bear his name: Murray Reservoir in San Diego and the Murray Hotel in Livingston. The former is now surrounded by the millions of residents in the nation's eighth-largest city. Other reminders include the still-standing Boulder Hotel and Hot Springs, now operating under a partnership headed by author Anne Wilson Schaef, and a large plaque that marks the location of the Murray hacienda in Monterey. The Clark chateau in Butte, which Murray acquired through foreclosure in the 1910s, served as Senator James E. Murray's home for several years, and today it operates as a cultural arts center. Finally, his private bank at the corner of Copper and Main in Butte still stands today.

True to his own words, there were few who cared or remembered much about James A. Murray after death dealt him a final blow. It was not because he was ruthless and cruel in business. Virtually everyone in his income bracket was no different. History, however, tends to forget those with superstitions about self-promotion. It is not difficult to imagine that, with the right publicist, Murray's story could have been painted in a much different light and gained some measure of notoriety. Drop the brutal business battles, focus on Murray's man-of-the-people lifestyle, promote every good deed he kept secret, and Murray might have entered history as a popular business leader, revered for generations. Murray's unvarnished story, however, tells us much more about the beginnings of our industrialized economy. We can thank him, and his humility, for allowing an unfiltered glimpse of our untidy past.

Appendix

The Passing of an Oak

By Mary Sullivan Spence

FOREWORD

Close to the Monterey sea-shore, on the high road between Monterey & Pacific Grove, a little weather-beaten oak stood for a century & a half; renowned in California's history as the tree under which father Junípero Serra landed and said mass. As it was attacked by the engraving-beetle, its decay necessitated its removal three years ago. A stone shaft, erected by Mr. James A. Murray of Montana & also of Monterey, marks the spot where it once stood.

It was but a wistful thing,
It was but a little tree,
Sad with much remembering,
Old and wind-bent near the sea;
In a sheltering hollow set,
Out of touch with worldly fret
And the stress of years to be;
Gulls wheel near the lone retreat—
Near-by breezes seaward urge
White sails of the fishing fleet—
Not a stone's throw from the verge,
Barrack's-road and village meet,
Where the guarding sentry's gun
Glints beneath the moon and sun,
At the foot of road which winds
To the hill o'erhead, and finds
Monterey's Presidio spread,
Listening to the bold Bay's tread.

Years agone the dust soared high
When flashed by the steed of Don,
Or Vaquero galloped by,
And the ox-cart rumbled on—
These the gray Oak gazed upon:
Gobernadores sought the shade,

Riding by it now and then;
Commandantes there delayed,
And the dust wreaths floated when
They spurred past it with their men;
Dust that laid on Serra's tree,
In its robe of sea-mist pale,
The gray crown of history
And the queenship of the vale.

Queenship of the dying, laid
On that vanishing sweet shade,
While its shell stood, frail and old,
Did the human tide that rolled
Past it, with indifferent gaze
Of these cruel latter days,
Reck that underneath that Oak—
Once a meek Franciscan's fane—
Western empire's spirit woke
In the name of God and Spain.

Many moons have silver poured,
Many surfs have ebbed and roared,
Myriad changes have set seal;
Countless hopes have sunk and soared
Since the sand felt Serra's keel;
Spanish bugles sang and died—
Mexic conquest flowered—to fade—
Where a younger martial pride
Hears the Eagle's anthem played.
And the gnarled tree sadly heard
Knell of change, from breeze and bird;
So its faithful heart of oak
Slowly—sadly—surely—broke.
Time had breathed the fatal word.

Fading like the rose-touched past
And its genesis—it failed,
Craving pity, at the last,
For the death-stroke that it hailed;
And borne thence that it might rest,
In conservative kind shade,
By the Mission church walls made,
Where Life slumbers on Death's breast.

Lonely wraith, some see it yet,
Like the past's earth-bound regret,
Sunset gun and clear taps gave
Honors of a soldier's grave,
To a sentinel who wooed
Winds that battled—storms that brewed;
While its hardier brother-train
Flourishes as vernal still,—
Curious eyes may search in vain
For that Oak beside the hill,

Vacancy—where once it rose
Centuries beneath the sky;
'Til came *one** who saw, and chose
That a memory should not die,
And a white shaft guards the fame
Of a little oak at rest—
Cenotaph that yet shall claim
Kinship with the old world's best;
But for this there would not be
(In a world which can forget),
Aught a memory of that tree;

Thus one rare link of romance,
Golden chain the young world wore,
Slipped past ken of careless glance;
Still—beside the fairest shore:
Measuredly the sentries pace—
Past the old time-haunted space;
Changes steal across Time's face,
The old order is no more;
Round the dream-environed place
Fuller life more quickly streams,—
Ah! old leisure, dying grace,
Must decay touch *all* our dreams?

*Mr. James A. Murray

Of this poem, "The Passing of an Oak," by Mary Sullivan Spence, twelve copies were done for Mrs. James A. Murray, for private distribution, by Paul Elder and Company. Printed by the Tomoye Press, San Francisco, under the direction of J. H. Nash, during the month of December, Nineteen Hundred and Nine.

Why the Humming Birds Nest at Monterey

By John Maguire[1]

When St. Patrick preached in the Emerald Isle
The fairies that haunted the green,
And their revels had held in olden time,
Were filled with envy and spleen.

So they went where the water lilies float,
On the edge of the shallow bay,
And they chose themselves each a little boat
To carry them far away.

Merrily now that little fleet
Bounds o'er the waters blue;
Boldly the fairies have taken their seat
Each in her light canoe.

They gave their queen the largest flower,
Their perilous course to guide,
And after her, like a tiny shower,
The tiny vessels glide.

The eddying ripples, that bore them along.
A murmuring melody played,
And the fairies who knew the words of its song
A whispering answer made.

The waters are hurrying away to the South
And bear them on with their tide
Till safely they reach the river's mouth
And float on the ocean tide.

Through many a day and night they sailed,
Warmly the sunshine fell,
For the might of the winds and waves was stayed
By the power of their magic spell.

That magic spell has banished the night
While the westward course they take,
For a glorious trail of burnished light,
Is following in their wake.

The fairies have reached the silv'ry strand.
And left the lily flowers,
And fly away in a merry band
To the pleasant citron bowers.

Tho' centuries old, long since have passed,
And exiles yet were they,
Till an Irish home they found at last
In an Eden at Monterey.

And the humming birds seen in this sunny clime,
Sparkling with rainbow hues,
Are the fairies who left the Emerald Isle
In their lily white canoes.

Pioneer Tributes (Murray, Maguire, Fat Jack)

Politicians and editorial staffs recognized many of Montana's early pioneers with thoughtful tributes that captured romanticized views of their notable lives. Presented here are tributes to Jim Murray, John Maguire, and John "Fat Jack" Jones.

James A. Murray—Tribute Paid by Senator Mantle

Senator Lee Mantle when informed last evening of the death of Mr. Murray, paid the pioneer business man, banker and miner of Butte an eloquent tribute.

> "I had known Mr. Murray for more than 40 years," he said. "He was one of Montana's most remarkable and successful citizens. As a business man, shrewd, calm, calculating and always ready to take a chance, if in his judgment a chance should be taken, he was without a peer in the early development of the Butte Camp. He was a man of kindly disposition and while extremely independent and determined in his own judgment, he had a host of friends. Men who transacted business with him banked on the word of Jim Murray. It was as good as his bond.
>
> "Mr. Murray was a self-made man. He came from humble beginnings, but by his perseverance, his indomitable will and indefatigable energy, he became interested in many lines of business and amassed a great fortune. He was one of Montana's wealthiest men.
>
> "While he was stern and relentless in business affairs, Mr. Murray was a man of a kindly disposition. He never made public his benefactions, but it is known of him that he never failed to assist those who were less fortunate than himself. Mr. Murray had a particular affection for many of Montana's pioneers and he was the benefactor of many of these upon whom fortune failed to smile.
>
> "My long acquaintance with Mr. Murray was always pleasant. I appreciated his wonderful business acumen. Years ago he suffered a physical break that caused him much trouble and suffering. He was an incessant traveler, always going from one place to another to inspect his enterprises. His infirmities must have been a tremendous handicap to him during recent years, but with his wonderful will power he overcame all such obstacles.
>
> "There are many in Butte who will be shocked and saddened to learn of Mr. Murray's death." [2]

James A. Murray, by the Editors of the Anaconda Standard

Another of old Montana's famous men passed away yesterday in California. Like so many of the state's pioneers, James A. Murray was as picturesque as he was unique. He was not a type as types are understood today, for like many who early cast their lot in the new West and exercised a large influence in its development, he was a type unto himself. It was his accentuated individuality which made him immediately interesting even to a stranger. In many respects "Jim" Murray was a paradox. Meticulously insistent upon the terms of a business obligation, he frequently considered sentiment rather than expediency. He matched wits with others in the game of life and was relentless in his pursuit of those who, by artifice or chicanery, endeavored to get the better of him. At the same time he was a man innately kind and sympathetic, lavish in his benefactions, yet extremely secretive in the exercise of his bounty. The extent of his charity will never be known, for one of the first conditions he imposed upon his beneficiaries was absolute secrecy. He amassed during the period of a long life an immense fortune, yet he preferred the role of a person of modest means.

His mining enterprises extended over a large territory and there is hardly a mining camp from British Columbia to old Mexico in which, at some time or another, he did not have an interest or an investment. Of late years he devoted his attention to the business of banking and was known as a successful banker in California, Washington, Idaho and Utah, as well as in Montana. He was as well known in business circles in San Francisco, Los Angeles, Portland, Seattle, and Salt Lake as he was in Deer Lodge or Livingston.

In the palmy days of horse racing Mr. Murray was an owner who liked to ride and drive himself, and nothing delighted him more than to gather around with some of his old cronies and swap stories of the turf.

Wealth never spoiled Jim Murray. He preferred the companionship of men who he had been comrades and friends in the days of his beginnings to that of the many who liked to see his name on their board of directors. To those who knew him intimately he was an entertaining raconteur, a keen, unerring analyst of human nature, a loyal friend and a delightful companion. He was as intense in his animosities as in his attachments. He held that he who never made an enemy was not worth having as a friend. His familiar figure will be missed in Butte and many hearts will be saddened at the news of his passing.[3]

John Maguire, by Judge C. C. Goodwin

John the kindly, John the generous, John the genial, John the gifted—the avant courier of Northwestern theatricals, has been called home. He built theatres and was his own star performer; he organized theatrical companies and supported them; most of his time for 40 years he faced misfortune, but was never cast down, played with McCullough and Barrett in California, played with his own company in Nevada, organized theatre companies in Oregon and Washington; was the very father of the profession in Montana, where the last twenty-five years of his life had been passed; at home in every role; comedy on the stage, almost a tragedy on every payday. Alas, how much he suffered, how much he enjoyed. He was the friend and companion of the very highest in his profession, a gentleman, a genius everywhere, the very soul of honor; the friend of the lowly, but the full equal of the lordliest Hamlet that ever walked the boards—he would have filled the day with delight for Apollo, and such a night as he would have made with Bacchus.

So for forty years he struggled on; forty years between hope and fear, between poverty and affluence; his upper chambers filled with songs of birds, the shadow of the gaunt wolf of want under his window. But he always turned a smiling face to the world and never sought to make the world share his sorrows. In his way he was a teacher of people. He tried to give them the highest art that could be obtained and he abhorred anything low and unclean. The whole northwest is his debtor, for he wore out his life there and gave the people the best that was in him.

He was here about a year ago and stated that he had retired from active work; that his friend, Murray, of Butte, had made it possible for him to live and be comfortable all his life, without great exertion and absolutely without those cares that had beat upon his life for two score years. Poor John, he should have lived longer. It was another case of an old war-horse turned into a rich pasture. He could not bear the rest and the peace. May they both have come to him now.[4]

John "Fat Jack" Jones, by the editors of the Anaconda Standard

"FAT JACK"

As celebrated a character in real life as ever was Yuba Bill, the stage coach driver immortalized by Bret Harte in fiction, was Fat Jack, Butte's quaint, whimsical, picturesque old hack driver. On alighting in the city, strangers from the East, to whose ears his fame had reached, but who were ignorant of his personal appearance, were struck by the exquisite drollery, the delicious irony of his sobriquet. It was a masterly touch of true Western humor. Instead of a man of monstrous obesity, a waddling puffing monument of human flesh, they beheld a shape that rivaled Abraham Lincoln's in all essential peculiarities, a figure whose remarkable height and tenuity were still further set off and emphasized by as altitudinous a plug hat as ever head of mortal donned.

It is not enough to say that Fat Jack stood at the top of the old hack-driving profession in the West, exemplifying in his own person the very peak of it. He towered head and shoulders above all the hack drivers of his period. Mounting to the driver's seat of an old-fashioned hack, he literally rose to eminence. Lincoln they tell us, was a bit awkward and ungainly but Fat Jack, especially when he was engaged in the transportation of a distinguished visitor, was grace and dignity personified.

When a notable came to town the reception committee would as soon have thought of hamstringing him as they would of letting anybody but Fat Jack take him to and fro between railroad station and hotel. But his glory did not attain its full height, did not blossom into full magnificence, until he conducted his notable in a procession of citizens. What pomp and pride and pleasure, what honor and renown were his when he drove such illustrious guests as William J. Bryan, William Howard Taft, Theodore Roosevelt, Sarah Bernhardt, James J. Jeffries, Richmond P. Hobson, John L. Sullivan and Mark Twain! For a fact, he towered over every one of them. Yet at the end of the journey never did he fail to dismount, relax and unbend and with fine suavity mix and hobnob with his famous passenger. They all knew him, jollied him, respected him, felt a sincere affection for him. Was he not a famous character himself, a genuine, concrete representative of Western hospitality and Western humor? Was he not entitled to meet them on terms of equality? Certainly overtures so far from ever being resented were always cordially welcomed, appraised and appreciated in their true and gracious spirit

A good and kindly soul was Fat Jack; a rugged character in some ways, perhaps, but a child in others; a genial, gentle, sympathetic man, of swift intelligence and fine, imaginative sensitiveness and frank and friendly charm.[5]

Private Loans Uncollected by James A. Murray

	Amount	Made	Due	Notes
P. D. Delmas	$50	1912		
J. W. Wilson	$85	1904		Chicago
C. A. Fries	$100	1914		San Diego
John Kelsey and George C. Thomson	$200			
John Kelsey	$200			
Grant Milligan	$500	1920	1921	Livingston, MT
Harry C. Cotter	$500			
John and Edith Dickenson	$700	1920	1921	
David Marks	$700			
Ralph Babitt	$1,000	1917	1917	Livingston [MT] Publishing
Cary Boyd and Robert Shorthill	$1,200	1921	1924	
S. P. Hogan and James G. Keefe	$1,500	1920	1920	Montana Press, Butte
M. L. Megladerry	$1,500	1913		Monterey
Bud Doble	$1,610	1908		horse trainer, Monterey
E. B. Webster	$1,835	1912		San Diego
Butte and Corbin	$2,000	1910		Butte, MT
P. R. Nye	$2,500		1921	bank cashier, Livingston, MT
Charles Bruckert	$2,500	1920	1923	
A. G. and Emma Straszer	$2,500	1920	1923	
Richard Brown	$2,500	1920	1923	
Thomas Buggy	$2,500			
Eulalie Jones	$2,600	1920	1925	
Elmer Lee	$3,000	1920		
Paul Bickell and I. B. Perrine	$3,067	1911		Pocatello and Twin Falls, ID
Lester P. Work	$3,250	1920	1921	Livingston, MT
Daniel Dwyer	$3,600			
James F. O'Conner	$5,000	1920		Livingston, MT
Joseph Sauer	$5,000			mortgage, father of San Diego
C. T. Henshall	$5,000	1908		New York
McLeur	$5,000			
Larry and Mary Duggan	$5,000			Irish radicals

	Amount	Made	Due	Notes
W. W. Merk via A. Pincus	$5,728	1918		mine operator
A. Steinberg	$6,000			
George Waggoner	$6,250		1919	labor representative
George A. Davidson	$6,500	1920	1921	San Diego
Portneuf Lodge, F. A. Masons	$10,000			Butte, MT, real estate mortgage
George McCann	$10,000			Hunter's Hot Springs operator
W. Hruza and O'Conner	$12,500	1920	1921	Livingston, MT
Butte Bulletin	$12,500	1918	1919	printing press
A. and Mary C. Laurens	$12,500	1918		
Rea and O'Conner	$13,000	1920		Livingston, MT
Frederick Cutter	$13,000	1909		Butte, MT (doctor at Hunter's Hot Springs)
A. G. Metz	$24,521			for Longfellow Quartz Mine, CA
Charles Clark	$27,596	1920	1921	wealthy son of W. A. Clark
Hackberry Mine	$35,000	1919	1920	
James Breen	$35,000	1920	1922	a millionaire
Oliver Ebert	$40,000	1918	1923	wealthy sheep rancher in Park Co., Montana
Silver Bow Club	$50,000			Butte, MT, real estate mortgage
Josephine Kline	$90,000	1920		Livingston, MT, hotel (now Murray Hotel)
Ed Fletcher	$92,680	1910–21		San Diego, Cuyamaca Water Co.
Cuyamaca Water Co	$160,200	1912		a note to himself
Gus Holmes	$345,000	1919	1922	secured by Semloh Hotel, Salt Lake City
TOTAL	$1,083,680			

Comparing Wealth and Economic Power

Understanding the economic power of historic figures requires us to convert their wealth into a unit of measure that can be compared with that of like individuals from another period. Michael Klepper and Robert Gunther, in *The Wealthy 100*, accomplished this by using a ratio of reputed net worth to the gross national product (GNP).[6] Lawrence H. Officer and Samuel H. Williamson developed several methods to compare wages, cost of living, commodity pricing, construction costs, economic prestige, and economic power across time. Officer and Williamson used a similar approach to Klepper and Gunther, except Officer and Williamson used a ratio of gross domestic product (GDP).[7] Williamson's website, www.measuringworth.com, does an excellent job of explaining the utility of a wealth/GDP ratio, versus other methods, to compare the relative economic power of individuals in different time periods.

To illustrate some of Williamson's points, consider the relative wealth of W. A. Clark. When Clark passed away in 1925, his fortune, estimated at $150 to $250 million, made him the second-richest man in America next to John D. Rockefeller. Clark's fortune has been a subject of two recent books about his daughter, Huguette Clark. Both state that W. A. Clark's fortune, adjusted for cost of living, would amount to approximately $3.4 billion in today's dollars.[8] This valuation would place Clark 190th on *Forbes* magazine's 2016 list of the wealthiest individuals in America. He is in fine company, just ahead of Mark Cuban and Oprah Winfrey, though far removed from Bill Gates (1st) and Warren Buffett (2nd). How did he fall so far from number two in his day? The answer lies in the methodology applied by Huguette's biographers.

The books' authors used the Consumer Price Index (CPI) to estimate Clark's wealth in current dollars. The CPI is a tool traditionally used to compare the cost of a set of goods from one year to another. The CPI, prepared by the US Bureau of Labor Statistics, includes groceries, housing, apparel, transportation, medical care, recreation, and education. The index is the ratio of these costs in any one year to the CPI's baseline year of 1982. However, determining comparative net worth based on increases in the cost of living for an average family omits several factors important to evaluating the wealth of tycoons. Simple consumer price comparisons do not capture labor rates, construction costs, lending rates, and investments.

Klepper and Gunther, using a ratio of net worth to GNP, place Clark at 43rd among the wealthiest Americans of all time.[9] On their list, Clark is just behind Gates (31st) and Buffett (39th). Gates and Buffett possess wealth estimated at $81 billion and $67 billion, respectively, according to

Forbes's 2016 ranking. Estimating Clark's wealth at $3.4 billion in today's dollars does not do the empire builder justice. Clark's wealth to GDP ratio (Willianson's method), using an estate estimated at $150 million, put the pioneer's economic power in contemporary dollars at $27.5 billion. Using the high-end estimate of Clark's wealth, $250 million, produces an estimate of $45.8 billion. This range, $27.5 to $45.8 billion, compares favorably with the net worth of modern-day tycoons.

Jim Murray's economic power, calculated using a wealth to GDP ratio, would be approximately $3 billion in today's dollars. This places him 222nd on the *Forbes* list, ahead of Oprah Winfrey (239th, $2.8 B) and just behind David Rockefeller, Sr. (214th, $3.1 B) and Mark Cuban (204th, $3.2 B). Footnotes in the this book indicate the method, from Willianson's website, used to estimate current dollars amounts for individual expenditures (real estate, equipment, construction projects, and so forth).

The Family of James A. Murray

❖ Beneficiaries named in Murray's will (6)

♦ Litigants who challenged the execution of Murray's estate (26)

♣ Born in Ireland (7)

Father
Michael Murray ♣
(abt. 1820–aft. 1848)

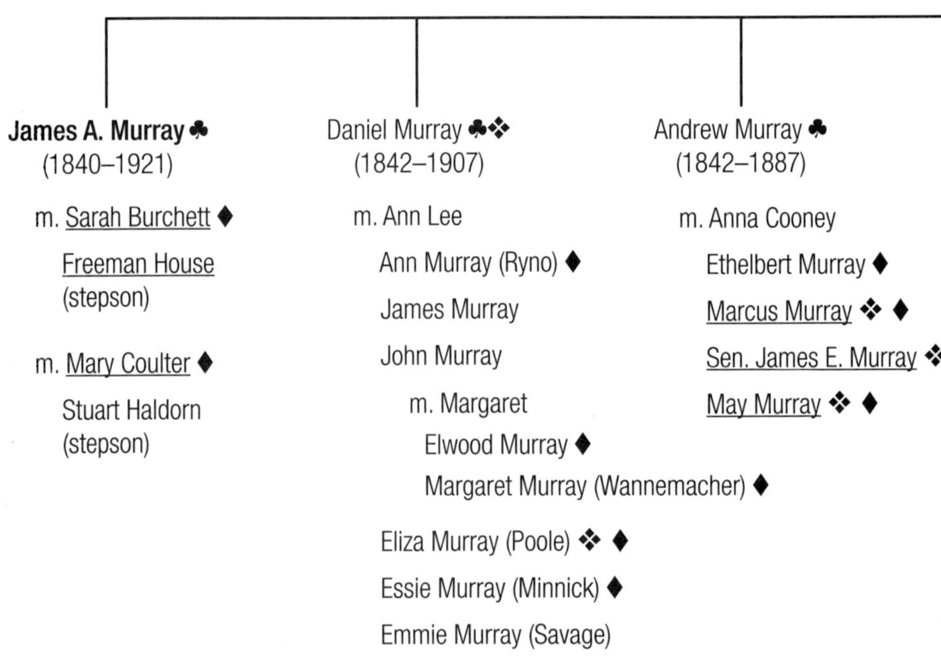

Notes:

Names underlined were prominent in Murray's business operations.

Includes only nieces and nephews who were involved in Murray's business or estate litigation.

Conflicting information exists on birth dates.

Married names in parenthesis.

An "m." indicates marriage, with children listed below.

William S. Murray, son of Daniel, is the author's great-grandfather. William challenged (and lost) the settlement of the estate up to the US Supreme Court.

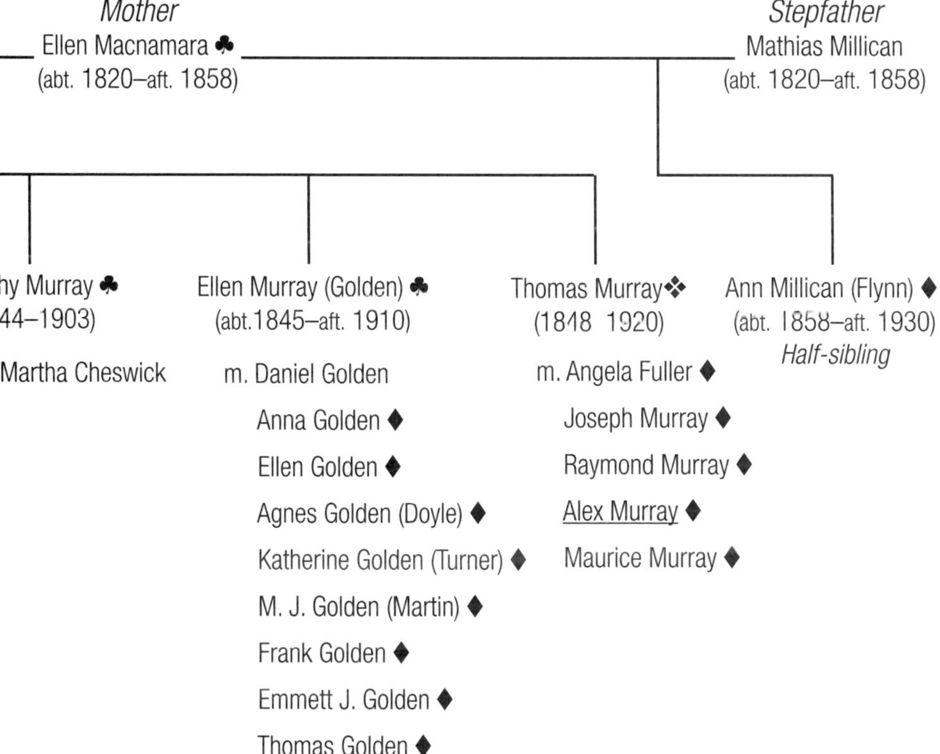

Mother
Ellen Macnamara ♣
(abt. 1820–aft. 1858)
Stepfather
Mathias Millican
(abt. 1820–aft. 1858)
hy Murray ♣
44–1903)
Martha Cheswick
Ellen Murray (Golden) ♣
(abt.1845–aft. 1910)
m. Daniel Golden
Anna Golden ♦
Ellen Golden ♦
Agnes Golden (Doyle) ♦
Katherine Golden (Turner) ♦
M. J. Golden (Martin) ♦
Frank Golden ♦
Emmett J. Golden ♦
Thomas Golden ♦
Thomas Murray❖
(1848 1920)
m. Angela Fuller ♦
Joseph Murray ♦
Raymond Murray ♦
Alex Murray ♦
Maurice Murray ♦
Ann Millican (Flynn) ♦
(abt. 1858–aft. 1930)
Half-sibling

Endnotes

PART I: THE MAKING OF A BONANZA KING

1 Margaret Gleason, "Margaret Gleason to Jim Farley," Letter (January 30, 1993). Margaret is a granddaughter of Daniel Murray, grandniece of Jim Murray, and my father's aunt. Accounts from Cecil Woodham Smith's classic *The Great Hunger* are used to provide details of the Murray's life in County Clare. Robert Whyte's 1847 *Famine Ship Diary* provides details on the suffering Irish immigrants endured during the voyage to North America (presumed to be no better or worse than a prison ship): lack of food, cramped quarters, little daylight, and burials at sea for those who did not survive. The brutal conditions on these ships earned them the moniker "coffin ships" from their passengers.

2 "Convict Transportation Registers 1788–1868," 1868, The National Archives.

3 Elizabeth Gurley Flynn, *The Rebel Girl: My First Life (1906–1926)* (International Publishers, 1979), 23.

4 Census records, birth dates, and places point to the Murrays' arrival in Canada in 1848. This year produced one of the highest totals of Irish immigrants escaping the Great Hunger in Ireland. One account from Andrew Murray's children holds that the family landed first in New York and, not finding work there, migrated to Canada, but no records exist to substantiate an initial landing in the United States.

5 H. C. Pentland, "The Development of a Capitalistic Labour Market in Canada," *The Canadian Journal of Economics and Political Science* 25, no. 5 (November 1959): 450–61.

6 "Fortune Is Left to Local Family by Copper King," *Wilkes-Barre Times-Leader*, June 30, 1921.

7 Edwin Purple, *Perilous Passage: A Narrative of the Montana Gold Rush, 1862–1863* (Montana Historical Society Press, 1995), 100.

8 "Prominent in Development of the Entire West," *Anaconda Standard*, May 12, 1921; "Fortune Is Left to Local Family by Copper King." These articles include independent references to Murray working passage on a steamship, and traveling to California by way of Cape Horn. It is presumed that both stories, told secondhand, are related, and that Murray worked for his passage from Canada to California, and that he did so on a one-way steamship.

9 James P. Delgado, *To California by Sea* (University of South Carolina Press, 1990), 18–46. Murray's experience on a steamship traveling around Cape Horn is presumed to mirror accounts from this book.

10 Throughout Murray's life, he favored mining districts that were off the beaten path of other prospectors, partnerships, or corporations.

11 Purple, *Perilous Passage*, 17–95. Murray's travels from Salt Lake City to the Montana Territory are presumed to mirror the firsthand accounts in this book. Purple traveled the same route one year prior to Murray.

12 "Those Were the Days of Real H. C. of L. in the Territory," *Anaconda Standard*, August 30, 1919.

13 Murray appears in newspaper reports in 1870 in Pioneer, Yamhill, and Deer Lodge with substantial business interests. It is presumed that he established his enterprises in this mining district upon entering the Montana Territory. One of his obituaries mentions that he had worked Alder Gulch for a period, but no records were found to substantiate this claim.

14 Muriel Sibell Wolle, *Montana Pay Dirt* (Swallow Press,1963), 211. La Barge City was next to the future city of Deer Lodge.

15 Ibid., 24. Description of Mining Camp Court and Laws.

16 P. A. O'Farrell, *Butte: Its Copper Mines and Copper Kings* (Printing House of J. A. Rogers, 1899). O'Farrell writing about Murray. O'Farrell was the editor of Copper King Augustus Heinze's newspaper in Butte.

17 "Another Montana Millionaire: James A. Murray Planning to Give New York a Surprise," *St. Paul Globe*, June 10, 1900.

18 Wolle, *Montana Pay Dirt*, 220; Granville Stuart, *Forty Years on the Frontier*, ed. Paul C. Phillips (Arthur H. Clark Company, 1925). Granville Stuart's diaries indicated his party also left the Gold Creek area in 1862.

19 Wolle, *Montana Pay Dirt*, 211; Captain John Mullan, *Miner and Travelers' Guide to Oregon, Washington, Idaho, Montana, Wyoming, and Colorado* (Wm. M. Frankling, 1865), 19.

20 Wolle, *Montana Pay Dirt*, 25–26.

21 Mullan, *Miner and Travelers' Guide to Oregon, Washington, Idaho, Montana, Wyoming, and Colorado*, 14.

22 "Another Montana Millionaire: James A. Murray Planning to Give New York a Surprise." *St. Paul Globe*, June 10, 1900.

23 "Testimony All in in Alex Scott Suit," *Anaconda Standard*, March 4, 1910.

24 "Notice of Dissolution," *The New North-West*, March 19, 1875. Dissolving J. A. Murray & Company in Yamhill, Deer Lodge County. James Murphy to continue operating business.

25 "Notice of Dissolution," *The New North-West*, June 28, 1873. James Talbot and James Murray dissolve partnership in Murray & Talbot Saloon.

26 "Local Brevities: The famous Tradewater Bar Flume at Yamhill owned by James A. Murray." *The New North-West*, April 30, 1875.

27 "The Pilgrim Bar Country," *The New North-West*, May 31, 1873.

28 "Late James A. Murray Was Second Richest Citizen of Montana; Dies in His 84th Year," *Redstone (Montana News Association Inserts)*, May 25, 1921.

29 During the course of his life, Murray operated banks in Deer Lodge, Butte, Salt Lake City, Seattle, Tacoma, Livingston, and Pocatello.

30 "Another Montana Millionaire: James A. Murray Planning to Give New York a Surprise." *St. Paul Globe*, June 10, 1900.

31 "May Be Arbitrated: Early Settlement of the Opera House Trouble's Probable," *Anaconda Standard*, December 4, 1896.

32 "Another Montana Millionaire: James A. Murray Planning to Give New York a Surprise." *St. Paul Globe*, June 10, 1900.

33 "Delegation Selected," *The Daily Independent*, July 8, 1874.

34 Bryon Cooney, "Millionaire Jim Murray Was Fond of Cinch Bets; Used to Frame Them," *Montana News Association Inserts*, September 4, 1933.

35 "Pilgrim Bar & Running Race," *The New North-West*, April 25, 1874. Modern horses run the mile in approximately 1:45.

36 "Local Brevities: 7 Up Pete Racing in Blackfoot" *The New North-West*, October 3, 1874.

37 "The Territorial Fair," *Rocky Mountain Husbandman*, October 9, 1879.

38 "Is It the Horse?" *The New North-West*, October 24, 1879.

39 Sam Aaron, "An American Pioneer: Memoirs of Sam Aaron," ed. Jacob R. Marcus, *American Jewish Archives* 10, no. 2 (October 1958): 95–120. The author's father left the territory in disgust after Murray refused to repay the money that Aaron had staked Murray for a poker game.

40 "Wine with a History: Twelve Precious Bottles That Once Came across the Atlantic," *Evening News*, December 11, 1886. (The *Evening News* was published in San Jose, California.)

41 "Tangled Up in the Law," *Anaconda Standard*, December 16, 1900.

42 "He's John Maguire of Montana," *Anaconda Standard*, June 14, 1903.

43 Frank Brown, "When Days Were Young In Emmetsburg," *Anaconda Standard*, May 13, 1906.

44 "Autographed Letter from Late General Custer Treasured by Maguire," *Anaconda Standard*, June 29, 1902.

45 "Maguire's Entertainment," *The New North-West*, October 8, 1875.

46 "John Maguire," *Helena Weekly Herald*, September 9, 1875.

47 "Local Brevities," *The New North-West*, October 15, 1875. (Review of Maguire's performance.)

48 "John Maguire," *Bozeman Avant Courier*, November 19, 1875.

49 Archie L. Clark, "John Maguire Butte's 'Belasco,'" *The Montana Magazine of History*, January 1952.

50 "Fort Union Receipt for Purchase of Grubstake," Receipt (February 22, 1865), Frank D. Brown Family Papers 1865–1950, Box 3, Folder 21, Mansfield Library, University of Montana, Missoula.

51 Bryon Cooney, "'Sandbar' Brown Got His Nickname When He Killed Two Piegan Indians in '72," *Cut Bank Pioneer Press*, August 20, 1928.

52 "Court," *Philipsburg Mail*, March 3, 1899; Frank Brown, "Frank Brown to James A. Murray, Butte, Montana," Letter (February 8, 1899), Frank D. Brown Family Papers 1865–1950, Mansfield Library, University of Montana, Missoula. Frank's letter of February 8 responds to Murray's question about getting the woman out of jail. Brown offers to put up bond if Murray supplies the money. On March 3, High-Card Jennie is released on bail.

53 "Civil War Pension File for John C. Jones (1897 to 1920)," n.d., Union Pension Records, National Archives and Records Administration.

54 "He's Supporting Deadwood 'Fat Jack' Is Wearing a Badge," *Anaconda Standard*, September 1, 1902.

55 Ibid.; "Civil War Pension File for John C. Jones (1897 to 1920)." There is no record of Jones at Bull Run, but he did participate in several smaller battles.

56 "Fat Jack Takes the Cash A Tale of High Finance," *Anaconda Standard*, September 14, 1919.

57 "An Old Fat Jack Story: But It's a Good One," *Anaconda Standard*, December 14, 1913.

58 Stuart, *Forty Years on the Frontier*, 213.

59 "First Execution on Montana Soil," *Anaconda Standard*, January 7, 1906. Henry Plummer used his position as sheriff to gain the trust of unsuspecting travelers. He led a gang of highwaymen who used the information he collected to rob and kill travelers with valuable luggage.

60 "United States Federal Census, 1870, Montana Territory," 1870.

61 Rufus Thayer, "Rufus Thayer to Bruce Kremer," Letter (August 20, 1921), Probate Case File #3274, County of Monterey Superior Court.

62 "Personal," *Butte Miner*, February 19, 1878. Identifies Murray and wife as residents of Pioneer.

63 C. B. Glasscock, *The War of the Copper Kings* (Grosset & Dunlap, 1935).

64 Ellen Baumler, "Devil's Perch: Prostitution from Suite to Cellar in Butte, Montana," *Montana: The Magazine of Western History*, Autumn 1988, 4–21.

65 "The Mining Metropolis in the Days of Its Infancy," *Anaconda Standard*, August 14, 1919.

66 Tunnels perpendicular to the shafts.

67 Otis E. Young Jr., *Western Mining* (University of Oklahoma Press, 1970). Provides details on various mining techniques.

68 "Like Old Days," *Anaconda Standard*, April 2, 1913. Working in pairs, prospectors could excavate exploratory shafts using a hoist and buckets to remove dirt.

69 "Murray Loses Claim for Mine—Set Precedent. Tried to Claim Mine Not Worked." *The New North-West*, May 21, 1880; "Then, Now, and Thereafter: Nuggets Found in a Pan of Butte Placer Gold," *The New North-West*, August 19, 1881.

70 *Patent* and *claim* are used interchangeably. Miners had to first stake a claim and then confirm or patent their claim with the courts. During the early day of placer mining, each camp set up its own courts to approve claims.

71 "Murray Sued for Trespassing Underground," *The New North-West*, May 28, 1880.

72 Alva Josiah Noyes, *The Story of Ajax: Life in the Big Hole Basin* (State Publishing Company, 1914), 91.

73 "New Mining Incorporation," *Helena Weekly Herald*, May 5, 1881.

74 The capitalized amount refers to the total value of stock that was offered for sale. If every share of stock was sold, the funding covered acquisition, development, and initial operating expenses. If all shares were not sold, the lead investors had to either

cancel the venture, buy shares themselves, or squander the money on some other venture and hope the East Coast investors did not want to cross Indian country to recover their investment.

75 Successful mines paid significant taxes, and neither the Talbot nor Daly partnerships were found in tax reports (published in newspapers) from that era.

76 Richard E. Lingenfelter, *Bonanzas & Borrascas: Copper Kings and Stock Frenzies, 1885–1918* (University of Oklahoma Press, 2012).

77 "Murray Purchases 25% Interest Smokehouse Lode," *The New North-West*, May 7, 1880. It is presumed he acquired the balance of the mine because court actions in later years listed him only as plaintiff or defendant.

78 "For Sale and Partition," *Anaconda Standard*, August 19, 1899. Gives original date of Arctic patent as March 15, 1883. Murray patented this under the name of his first wife.

79 "Another Montana Millionaire: James A. Murray Planning to Give New York a Surprise"; "Passing Throng," *Ogden Standard*, November 22, 1892. Implied surface rent income of $35,000 per month ($420,000 annually).

80 "Local Hits," *Butte Semi-Weekly Miner*, February 10, 1886.

81 Territory v. Murray and another, 15 The Pacific Reporter 145 (Supreme Court of Montana 1887).

82 "For Ways That Are Dark," *Butte Semi-Weekly Miner*, October 19, 1887.

83 "Smokehouse Executions," *Butte Semi-Weekly Miner*, June 8, 1887.

84 "The Smokehouse Lode Case Settled," *Philipsburg Mail*, September 6, 1888; "The Smokehouse Settlement," *Butte Semi-Weekly Miner*, November 17, 1888.

85 "Bluebird Suit," *Helena Independent*, December 2, 1889.

86 "City Streets as Private Property," *Anaconda Standard*, July 5, 1901.

87 "A Gold-Region, Story. The Adventures and Romance of Mr. Ferdinand Van Zandt," *Elevator*, September 8, 1888; "Van Zandt to Be Buried Abroad," *The Sun*, March 7, 1892.

88 "Blue Bird Mill," *Butte Semi-Weekly Miner*, December 1, 1886.

89 "Montana's Mines," *Helena Weekly Herald*, December 9, 1886.

90 "The Bluebird Resumes," *Daily Independent*, March 9, 1891.

91 "Blue Bird," *Butte Daily Miner*, May 7, 1888.

92 "Bluebird Suit," *Helena Independent*, December 2, 1889.

93 "Suicide of Ferdinand Van Zandt," *Salt Lake Herald*, March 6, 1892.

94 "The Bluebird Resumes," *Daily Independent*, March 9, 1891; "A Truce Is Declared: The Troubles of J. A. Murray and the Blue Bird Company Settled," *Helena Independent*, March 6, 1891.

95 "Seized the Bluebird," *Helena Independent*, March 1, 1892.

96 "Blue Bird Sale To-Day," *Helena Independent*, May 9, 1892.

97 "The Blue Bird Mine: Arrangements Making for Reopening of the Valuable Property," *Anaconda Standard*, November 11, 1892.

98 O'Farrell, *Butte: Its Copper Mines and Copper Kings*, 31.

99 John Maguire, "How Heinze and His Parasite Bilked a Canadian Legislature: John Maguire Throws the White Light upon the Deals of These Two Friends of Labor—O'Farrell a Coward Who Needs Only Courage to Be an Assassin," *Anaconda Standard*, November 3, 1900.

100 "Schmidt's Story," *Butte Daily Miner*, July 6, 1882.

101 "First Mail Brought to Butte," *Anaconda Standard*, June 20, 1920.

102 "Application for Patent," *The New North-West*, January 17, 1879. Murray and King patented a mine on Pikes Peak.

103 "The Mining Metropolis in the Days of Its Infancy," *Anaconda Standard*, August 14, 1919

104 "History Time Line," 2013, http://www.buttecvb.com/history/; Great Northern in 1887, accessed: November 29, 2013. Writers Project of Montana, *Copper Camp: The Lusty Story of Butte, Montana, the Richest Hill on Earth* (Riverbend Publishing, 2002), 298. Utah Northern in 1881, Northern Pacific in 1883.

105 "Sues for Division of Bank Stock," *Salt Lake Telegram*, May 6, 1913.

106 "Butte Millionaire Visits Friend Here," *Salt Lake Telegram*, March 29, 1918.

107 "American Bank Control Sought," *Seattle Daily Times*, August 20, 1914.

108 "Property of Flume Company Deeded to New Owners," *San Diego Union*, June 2, 1910.

109 "Can't Attack Divorce Decree after 35 Years," *Anaconda Standard*, January 6, 1922. Divorce date: March 29, 1884, San Miguel County, New Mexico.

110 Thayer, "Rufus Thayer to Bruce Kremer." Thayer indicated Sallie's new husband's last name was White, but family history records from Burchett's ancestors indicate the husband's name was Hugh Wright.

111 J. M. Bistline, "Mayor J. M. Bistline to Dr. Minnie Howard," Letter (1946), https://familysearch.org/photos/stories/1354574.

112 "Ending of Automobile Show Was Like the Big Night of a Very Gay Carnival," *Salt Lake Telegram*, February 28, 1910.

113 "Some Inside History," *Seattle Daily Times*, February 18, 1902.

114 "Seattle Public Building Tied Up," *Seattle Post-Intelligencer*, July 26, 1899.

115 "First Avenue Lot Is Sold for $65,000," *Seattle Daily Times*, April 16, 1906 (Article refers to Third and Union); "American Savings Bank," *Seattle Daily Times*, May 24, 1908 (Madison and Second); "A Deed Was Filed," *Seattle Daily Times*, June 26, 1903. (Third and James)

116 "The Federal Building Will Stand at the Southeast Corner of Third and Union," *Seattle Star*, August 20, 1901.

117 "American Savings Bank." *Seattle Daily Times*, May 24, 1908.

118 "New Building to Go on Third Avenue," *Seattle Daily Times*, January 17, 1909.

119 "Four Shacks Condemned by City: Unsanitary Frame Building Owned by Millionaire James A. Murray at Third and Union to Be Closed," *Seattle Daily Times*, September 21, 1909.

120 "American Bank Control Sought." *Seattle Daily Times*, August 20, 1914.

121 Jack Jungmeyer, "Millionaires Cowmen and Women of a Sort Jumbled in the Golden Cocktail," *Evening News*, February 9, 1917.

122 Writers Project of Montana, *Copper Camp: The Lusty Story of Butte, Montana, the Richest Hill on Earth*, 1.

123 "Overrun with Crooks: Butte Citizens Will Organize Vigilante Committees to Deal with Them," *Aberdeen Daily News*, June 27, 1892.

124a "Tangled Up in the Law," *Anaconda Standard*, December 16, 1900.

124b "James A. Murray Made One Million Eating a Two Bit Meal," *Butte Inter Mountain*, May 9, 1901.

125 "When the Saloon Door No Longer Swings To and Fro," *Anaconda Standard*, January 14, 1917.

126 "Butte Pioneer, James McGovern Aged 79, Is Dead 'McGovern's Place,' North Main, Known for Atmosphere," *Anaconda Standard*, October 20, 1920.

127 Cooney, "Millionaire Jim Murray Was Fond of Cinch Bets; Used to Frame Them." Montana News Association Inserts, September 4, 1933.

128 "Accused of Claim Jumping: Prospector Tries to Kill a Butte Banker," *Oregonian*, September 13, 1901.

129 "Two Marriages: J. A. Murray and Mrs. Haldorn—Mr. Haldorn and Mrs. Hubert-Jones," *Anaconda Standard*, June 5, 1896.

130 "Personal Mentions," *Morning Oregonian*, August 20, 1892.

131 "Murray's Wardrobe: He Fails to Prove That Madame Wallace Mangled His Clothes," *Butte Daily Miner*, April 4, 1886.

132 "Butte Department: Murray-Haldorn Case," *Anaconda Standard*, August 17, 1896.

133 "James A. Murray's Suit Against Attorney George Haldorn: Counter Charges Made," *Anaconda Standard*, October 14, 1897; "Charges of Fraud Made: A Sensational Suit Brought against James A. Murray," *Anaconda Standard*, May 22, 1898.

134 "He Was a Character. Death of Poor Doc Larkin at Warm Springs Asylum," *Anaconda Standard*, August 6, 1898.

135 "Watson Made Guardian. He Will Sue the B. & M. in the Name of James Larkin," *Anaconda Standard*, May 14, 1898.

136 "Larkin Case Is Ended," *Anaconda Standard*, July 22, 1899.

137 "Humorous Vein: Was the Testimony of J. A. Murray in Larkin Case," *Anaconda Standard*, May 7, 1899.

138 "Was Treated Like a Prince: Butte's Hospitality Extended to Governor Roosevelt," *Anaconda Standard*, September 19, 1900.

139 Also known as a buggy whip.

140 "When Fat Jack Drove Teddy," *Anaconda Standard*, December 12, 1909.

141 "President Roosevelt Arrives To-Day. Distinguished Guests of the Great Mining Camp Will Be Greeted by Thousands," *Anaconda Standard*, May 27, 1903.

142 Theodore Roosevelt, "President Theodore Roosevelt to John Hay," Letter (August 9, 1903), Theodore Roosevelt Collection, MS Am 1785.2 (104), Houghton Library, Harvard University.

143 Jack Willis, *Roosevelt in the Rough*, ed. Horace Smith (Ives Washington, 1931), 159.

144 Ibid., 165.

145 Ibid., 165–66; "When Fat Jack Drove Teddy," *Anaconda Standard*, December 12, 1909.

146 "When Fat Jack Drove Teddy."

PART II: WEALTH AND LEISURE

1 Parker Morell, *Diamond Jim: The Life and Times of James Buchanan Brady* (Garden City Publishing Company Inc., 1934), 157.

2 "American Millionaires, How Big Fortunes Are Made," *New York Tribune*, June 1892.

3 David John Farmer, "Dogs of War: Fighting Back," *Administrative Theory and Praxis* 37, no. 4 (2015): 252–67.

4 Richard H. Peterson, *The Bonanza Kings: The Social Origins and Business Behavior of Western Mining Entrepreneurs, 1870–1900* (University of Nebraska Press, 1971).

5 Richard H. Peterson, *Bonanza Rich: Lifestyles of the Western Mining Entrepreneurs* (University of Idaho Press, 1991).

6 Byron Cooney, "Millionaire Jim Murray Was Fond of Cinch Bets; Used to Frame Them," *Montana News Association Inserts*, September 1, 1933.

7 Murray collected pearls before they were cultured on a mass scale, starting in 1916.

8 "Like Old Days," *Anaconda Standard*, April 2, 1913.

9 Ed Fletcher, *Memoirs of Ed Fletcher* (Ed Fletcher, Pioneer Printers, 1952).

10 "Inventory and Appraisement," December 15, 1922, Probate Case File #3274, County of Monterey Superior Court.

11 John Morrison and Catherine Morrison, *Mavericks: The Lives and Battles of Montana's Political Legends* (Montana Historical Society Press, 2003).

12 Drew Pearson, "Washington Merry-Go-Round," *Aberdeen Daily News*, May 8, 1960.

13 Editorial Staff, "James A. Murray," *Anaconda Standard*, May 12, 1921.

14 "Rowdy Wins Race," *Daily Independent*, May 10, 1874.

15 "Horse News," *Daily Independent*, April 6, 1884.

16 "Montana Rancher Buys Valley Land," *San Diego Union*, February 1, 1910; "J. A. Murray Turfman: Butte Capitalist Considering Plans of Entering Field," *Anaconda Standard*, May 23, 1902.

17 "Collector Jessup Starts Winning First Time Out," *San Francisco Call*, March 17, 1905.

18 Bill Dedman and Paul Clark Newell Jr., *Empty Mansions: The Mysterious Life of Huguette Clark and the Spending of a Great American Fortune* (Ballantine Books, 2013)

19 "For Mrs. Thornton," *Butte Inter Mountain*, August 31, 1901.

20 "Another Montana Millionaire: James A. Murray Planning to Give New York a Surprise."

21 Ibid.; "Is to Put up a New Hotel," *Butte Inter Mountain*, September 12, 1903.

22 "Purchases Picturesque Tevis Villa," *Riverside Independent*, August 30, 1904.

23 "Canneries Were Neighbors of the 'Queen of the Monterey Bay Waterfront,'" *Coasting*, March 27, 1985.

24 "Valuable Picture by Trousset Found in Golconda, Nev. Hotel," *Idaho Statesman*, August 29, 1906; "Probate Records for Mary Murray," December 15, 1952, File #6962, Monterey County Superior Court.

25 "James A. Murray Is Back: World Diminishing in Size," *Anaconda Standard*, March 27, 1903.

26 "Returned from Abroad: James A. Murray Saw Europe and Its Attractions," *Anaconda Standard*, October 27, 1900.

27 Lamar Cecil, personal communication, January 14, 2015; Lamar Cecil, *Wilhelm II, Prince and Emperor, 1859–1900*, vol. 1, 2 vols. (University of North Carolina Press, 1989).

28 "Butte," *Intermountain Catholic*, August 14, 1900.

29 Morrison and Morrison, *Mavericks: The Lives and Battles of Montana's Political Legends*.

30 Donald E. Spritzer, *Senator James E. Murray and the Limits of Post-War Liberalism* (Garland Publishing, 1985).

31 "In Pre-Cannery Days, Giant Mansion Ruled Waterfront," *Monterey Peninsula Herald*, ca 1969, Landmarks Folder, California Room, Monterey Public Library.

32 Betty Hoag McGlynn, "Casa De Las Olas Part II: The Murray Saga," *Noticas Del Puerto de Monterey* 26, no. 3 (September 1985): 1–11.

33 "Memories of Murray Hospital," *Montana Standard*, January 23, 1977.

34 "James Murray Pioneer Miner of Butte Dies," *Great Falls Tribune*, May 12, 1921.

35 "Burial Probably in Rochester, NY: James Murray Had Expressed Wish to Lie beside His Mother," *Anaconda Standard*, May 13, 1921.

36 David M. Emmons, *The Butte Irish: Class and Ethnicity in an American Mining Town, 1875–1925* (University of Illinois Press, 1989), 8.

37 Bill Farley, "Rocky Mountain Radicals: Copper King James A. Murray, Senator James E. Murray, and Seventy-Eight Years of Montana Politics, 1883–1961," *Montana: The Magazine of Western History* 66, no. 1 (2016): 39–58.

38 "The Sand Lot: Kearney Denounces the Irish Relief Subscription Fund," *The New North-West*, February 27, 1880. For a thoroughly Irish perspective on events, Murray could turn to Patrick Ford's *Irish World*, published in New York and distributed across the country.

39 On Charles Stewart Parnell's 1880 tour of the United States, see Ely Janis, *A Greater Ireland: The Land League and Transatlantic Nationalism in Gilded Age America* (University of Wisconsin Press, Madison, 2015). Butte, lacking rail access, and still in the infancy of its growing wealth, was not on either's tour stops.

40 "Territorial Exchange Items," *The Benton Record*, February 23, 1882. The Butte Chapter of the Land League reported donations of more than $4,000 during 1881 and the early part of 1882.

41 Emmons, *The Butte Irish: Class and Ethnicity in an American Mining Town, 1875–1925*, 104.

42 Ibid., 108.

43 Niall Whelehan, *The Dynamiters: Irish Nationalism and Political Violence in the Wider World, 1867–1900* (Cambridge University Press, 2012), 136.

44 Emmons, *The Butte Irish*, 108; "Membership Records," ca- 1890 1880, World Mining Museum, Ancient Order of Hibernians Collection, Butte–Silver Bow Public Archives.

45 James G. Maguire, *Ireland and the Pope: A Brief History of Papal Intrigues against Irish Liberty from Adrian IV to Leo XIII* (James H. Barry, 1888), 80. In January of 1883, Pope Leo sent a rescript to the Irish clergy commanding them to use their power to suppress certain classes of societies—including Irish political leagues. On May 11, 1883, he issued specific instructions forbidding subscriptions to Parnell's testimonial fund.

46 "The Parnell Meeting," *Butte Daily Miner*, June 17, 1883.

47 "The Parnell Fund," *Butte Daily Miner*, June 23, 1883. In today's terms, their donations were $6,000 each, with the total contribution being $60,000.

48 "Fo Old Ireland," *Butte Semi-Weekly Miner*, July 3, 1886.

49 "A Leading Irish Patriot," *Butte Semi-Weekly Miner*, October 20, 1886.

50 "The Peoples Party of Silver Bow," *The New North-West*, October 17, 1884.

51 W. Bourke Cockran et al., *Great Political Issues and Leaders of the Campaign of 1900* (W. B. Conkey Company, 1900), 163, http://babel.hathitrust.org.

52 "The People's Party," *Butte Daily Miner*, October 12, 1884. Beyond his participation in the People's Party, Murray made no effort to hide his concerns regarding the future of capitalism. On one occasion, he met with a reporter while reading Edward Bellamy's *Looking Backward*, a futuristic novel in which the United States is transformed into a socialist utopia. See "Gathered from Hotels: Mr. J. A. Murray on the Political Situation in Montana," *Kansas City Times*, December 9, 1889.

53 H. Minar Shoebotham, *Anaconda: Life of Marcus Daly, the Copper King* (The Stackpole Company, 1956), 68–80.

54 Michael P. Malone, *The Battle for Butte: Mining and Politics on the Northern Frontier, 1864–1906* (University of Washington Press, 2006), 22.

55 "James A. Murray," *Anaconda Standard*, May 12, 1921.

56 "To Abolish the Smoke," *Anaconda Standard*, November 16, 1890.

57 Ibid.; "Jim Murray Was Puzzled," *Anaconda Standard*, July 2, 1890.

58 "Newspaper Man Badly Beaten," *Sacramento Daily Record-Union*, October 24, 1881

59 "Sons of St. George," *Anaconda Standard*, August 18, 1901.

60 "Ashes to Ashes: The Grave Receives Its Precious Prize. Thousands Pay Their Last Respects to W. J. Penrose," *Anaconda Standard*, June 13, 1891.

61 "The Rotten Borough," *Helena Daily Herald*, October 15, 1889.

62 "The Butte Elections. The Democratic Dollars Make a Clean Sweep," *Idaho Statesman*, April 17, 1890; "Senator Clark," *Semi-Weekly Tribune*, April 19, 1890.

63 "Assassinated in the Street: W. J. Penrose, a Prominent Citizen of Butte, Mysteriously Murdered," *Chicago Herald*, June 11, 1891.

64 "Ashes to Ashes: The Grave Receives Its Precious Prize. Thousands Pay Their Last Respects to W. J. Penrose"; "Cowardly Murderer," *Helena Independent*, June 11, 1891.

65 "Ashes to Ashes: The Grave Receives Its Precious Prize. Thousands Pay Their Last Respects to W. J. Penrose"; "Assassins Not Known," *Helena Independent*, June 25,

1891; "Topics of the Town—A Firm Friend of Penrose," *Anaconda Standard*, July 2, 1891.

66 "Out of Court," *Anaconda Standard*, December 8, 1895.

67 "For Free Coinage," *Philipsburg Mail*, July 13, 1893.

68 "Silver Convention in Iowa," *Philipsburg Mail*, March 15, 1894; "Montana's Governor Selects a Delegation to the July Gold Convention," *Rocky Mountain News*, May 18, 1897.

69 "The Kansans' Day," *Seattle Post-Intelligencer*, April 26, 1893.

70 Michael Kazin, *A Godly Hero: The Life of William Jennings Bryan* (Alfred A. Knopf, 2006), 45–79.

71 Kenneth Whyte, *The Uncrowned King: The Sensational Rise of William Randolph Hearst* (Random House of Canada, 2009), 185.

72 "Combines, Trusts and Monopolies," *Kansas City Daily Journal*, November 1, 1896.

73 "Murray on Miner Wages," *Tombstone Daily Prospector*, December 9, 1896.

74 "May Be Arbitrated: Early Settlement of the Opera House Trouble's Probable," *Anaconda Standard*, December 4, 1896.

75 Nephew James E. claimed that workers at his uncle's mines had never once gone on strike. See Dorothy M. Thayer, "New Faces in the Senate-Montana's Young Jim Murray," *Washington Post*, November 23, 1934.

76 "John Maguire Appoints Jim Murray," *Helena Independent*, April 18, 1900.

77 "Montana's Latest Senatorial Suggestion," *Denver Post*, April 17, 1900.

78 "Jim Murray Is Undecided," *Helena Independent*, April 28, 1900.

79 Malone, *The Battle for Butte*, 128.

80 Melvyn Dubofsky, "The Origins of Western Working Class Radicalism, 1890–1905," *Labor History*, March 1, 1966, 131–55; Martin J. Sklar, *The Corporate Reconstruction of American Capitalism* (Cambridge University Press, 1988), 3.

81 "Splendid Monument to Maguire," *Salt Lake Herald*, July 18, 1909.

82 Shoebotham, *Anaconda: Life of Marcus Daly, the Copper King.*

83 Dedman and Clark Newell Jr., *Empty Mansions: The Mysterious Life of Huguette Clark and the Spending of a Great American Fortune.*

84 M. B. Leavitt, *Fifty Years in Theatrical Management* (Broadway Publishing Co., 1912), https://goo.gl/YPCVvE. Maguire may have been the only thespian in the West with a patron.

85 "How Trouble Began," *Anaconda Standard*, May 14, 1902; "No Agreement Yet: The Destroyers of the Opera House Cease Work for Awhile," *Anaconda Standard*, October 2, 1895, morning edition.

86 Doris Kearns Goodwin, *Team of Rivals* (Simon and Schuster, Inc., 2005), 33.

87 E. Anthony Rotundo, *American Manhood* (Basic Books, 1993), 76.

88 John Maguire, "Camping on the Trail: Reminiscences of Pioche," *Daily Nevada State Journal*, October 4, 1905.

89 William Edgar Paxson, *E. S. Paxson: Frontier Artist* (Pruett Publishing Company, 1984).

90 "Sopranos and Six Guns: The Frontier Opera House as a Cultural Symbol," *The American West* VII, no. 6 (November 1970).

91 "Jumping Off Place: J. A. Murray Says He'll Begin to Tear Down the Opera House Today," *Anaconda Standard*, September 28, 1896.

92 "Stockholder's Meeting," *Butte Daily Miner*, May 6, 1885.

93 "Montana Mentions (1)," *Daily Yellowstone Journal*, July 15, 1885.

94 "Personal," *Butte Semi-Weekly Miner*, December 27, 1884.

95 "Grand Opera House Seats," *Butte Daily Miner*, June 10, 1885.

96 "Manager Maguire," *Salt Lake Tribune*, September 19, 1884.

97 "Montana Mentions (1)." *Daily Yellowstone Journal*, July 15, 1885.

98 "The Butte Opera House," *Helena Weekly Herald*, July 30, 1885.

99 "How Trouble Began." *Anaconda Standard*, May 14, 1902.

100 Paxson, *E. S. Paxson: Frontier Artist*.

101 "Millionaire Moses," *Saturday Evening Post*, December 8, 1945.

102 "Enlarged the Capital Stock," *Butte Semi-Weekly Miner*, August 24, 1887.

103 "Jumping Off Place: J. A. Murray Says He'll Begin to Tear Down the Opera House Today."

104 "Big Blaze at Butte: Complete Destruction of the Grand Opera House and the I.O.O.F. Building," *Philipsburg Mail*, July 26, 1888.

105 "An Interesting Relic," *Butte Semi-Weekly Miner*, September 12, 1888.

106 "He's John Maguire of Montana," *Anaconda Standard*, June 14, 1903.

107 "Topics of the Town: How John Maguire Proposes to Get Rid of That Mortgage," *Anaconda Standard*, October 13, 1890.

108 "Jumping Off Place: J. A. Murray Says He'll Begin to Tear Down the Opera House Today."

109 Ibid.

110 Ibid.

111 "Still Maguire's: James A. Murray and Others Rescue the Opera House for Him," *Anaconda Standard*, November 19, 1890.

112 "In Maguire's Hands: The Opera House People Will Do Business with the Manager: Mr. Murray Is Out of It," *Anaconda Standard*, October 3, 1896.

113 "Woes of a Manager Mr. McFarland Has Troubles Enough for a Bonfire," *Anaconda Standard*, February 4, 1900.

114 "In Maguire's Hands: The Opera House People Will Do Business with the Manager: Mr. Murray Is out of It."

115 Archie L. Clark, "John Maguire Butte's 'Belasco,'" *The Montana Magazine of History*, January 1952; Roger DeBourg, "A History of Theater in Butte, Montana," Thesis, University of Montana, 1963.

116 "Montana Comment: Justice Has Been Done (Opera House)," *Anaconda Standard*, June 2, 1897.

117 James A. Murray, "James A. Murray to Ed Fletcher," Letter (February 17, 1920), Ed Fletcher Papers, Special Collections & Archives, University of California at San Diego.

118 "John Maguire Recall Memories from the Stage," *Los Angeles Herald*, April 17, 1904.

119 "John Maguire's Benefit: It Will Be an Event of More than Usual Interest," *Anaconda Standard*, November 20, 1898.

120 Frederick Warde, *Fifty Years of Make-Believe* International Press Syndicate, 1920).

121 Leavitt, *Fifty Years in Theatrical Management,* 253–54.

122 "Another Montana Millionaire: James A. Murray Planning to Give New York a Surprise." *St. Paul Globe*, June 10, 1900.

123 "Made an Offer," *Anaconda Standard*, April 5, 1901; "John Maguire in Harness Again," *Anaconda Standard*, September 22, 1901.

124 "Gift of Maguire to Historical Society," *Anaconda Standard*, October 1, 1903.

125 "Maguire in Bronze," *Evening World*, ca 1890, File Folders, Montana Historical Society.

126 Olin D. Wheeler, *Wonderland 1902* (Northern Pacific Railway, 1902).

127 James A. Murray, "James Murray to Frank Brown, Hot Springs, Arkansas," Letter (ca 1901), Frank D. Brown Family Papers 1865–1950, Mansfield Library, University of Montana, Missoula.

128 Joshua Scott Johns, "Empire Building, 1873–1885," *The Parks in Railroad Advertising*, August 1, 1996, http://xroads.virginia.edu/~MA96/RAILROAD/adverts1.html.

129 *Hunter's Hot Springs* (Northern Pacific Railway, 1920).

130 "Dr. A. J. Hunter Developed Hot Springs in Park County; Old Historical Site Destroyed by Fire Three Years Ago," *Philipsburg Mail*, June 14, 1935.

131 "Butte Current Notes," *Anaconda Standard*, May 30, 1897.

132 "Murray's New Hotel," *Anaconda Standard*, March 3, 1897; "Premature Rumor, J. A. Murray Has Not Built That Hotel at Hunter's Hot Springs," *Anaconda Standard*, April 11, 1897.

133 "Bought by J. A. Murray," *Butte Daily Miner*, June 2, 1899.

134 "Where the Press Gang Met," *Yellowstone Monitor*, September 9, 1909.

135 "Murray Visits Wrestler," *Anaconda Standard*, November 7, 1902; Ken Zimmerman, Jr., *William Muldoon: The Solid Man Conquers Wrestling and Physical Culture* (Ken Zimmerman Jr. Enterprises, 2014).

136 James A. Murray, "James A. Murray to Ed Fletcher (2)," Letter (June 6, 1914), Ed Fletcher Papers, Special Collections & Archives, University of California, San Diego.

137 "Millionaire Murray Said to Be Dying," *Monterey New Era*, January 11, 1905; "Cummings Loses Out in Murray Suit," *Anaconda Standard*, May 12, 1906.

138 Ethel Mintzer Lichtman, "The Zest for Learning," *Journal of San Diego History* 39, no. 3 (1993); George S. Gould Jr., "Report of Inheritance Tax Appraiser," November 1, 1922, Probate Case File #3274, County of Monterey Superior Court.

139 *Hunter's Hot Springs* (Northern Pacific Railway, 1920).

140 "Mrs. Murray Entertains," *Butte Inter Mountain*, September 4, 1902; "In Butte," *Anaconda Standard*, August 31, 1902.

141 "Buys Boulder Hot Springs," *Anaconda Standard*, April 20, 1909; *Boulder Hot Springs*, Photograph, 1920, Montana Historical Society; "Contractors Sue, Balance Asked for Work Done on Boulder Hot Springs," *Anaconda Standard*, November 21, 1918.

142 "Tennis Players at Hunter's Hot Springs," *Anaconda Standard*, August 22, 1909; "Butte Players Will Contest at Hunter's," *Anaconda Standard*, August 14, 1914; "Tennis Champion Invited to Play in Montana Cup," *Anaconda Standard*, April 18, 1920; "James A. Murray May Buy It," September 24, 1904; "Fine New Hotel for the City of Livingston," *Anaconda Standard*, January 4, 1920.

143 "Hot Springs Are Murray's Hobby," *Ronan Pioneer*, May 18, 1917.

144 Richard Astro, "John Steinbeck," in *A Literary History of the American West*, Western Literary Association (Texas Christian University Press, 1987), 438.

145 Neal Hotelling, *Pebble Beach: The Official Golf History* (Triumph Books, 2009); Michael Hemp, *Cannery Row* (The History Company, 1984).

146 William Issel, *Church and State in the City, Catholics and Politics in Twentieth-Century San Francisco* (Temple University Press, 2013).

147 McGlynn, "Casa De Las Olas Part II: The Murray Saga"; "Canneries Were Neighbors of the 'Queen of the Monterey Bay Waterfront.'" *Coasting*, March 27, 1985.

148 Mildred Albronda, *Douglas Tilden: The Man and His Legacy* (Emerald Point Press, 1994); "Serra Landing, (Sculpture)" *Art Inventories Catalog* (Smithsonian American Art Museum, 1994), http://siris-artinventories.si.edu/ipac20/ipac.jsp?uri=full=3100001~!341717!0.

149 Martin J. Morgado, *Junípero Serra's Legacy* (California: Mount Carmel, 1987).

150 "Monument for Serra's Landing Place," *Monterey New Era*, August 30, 1905; "Marks Place of Serra's Landing," *San Francisco Call*, November 19, 1906.

151 "Millionaire Murray Dying at St. Francis," *San Francisco Call*, January 9, 1905; "Millionaire Murray Said to Be Dying."

152 "At the Murray Home Down Near Monterey," *Anaconda Standard*, August 3, 1905.

153 John Maguire, "James A. Murray's Home at Monterey," *Salt Lake Herald*, September 17, 1905.

154 "Serra Landing, (Sculpture)." Indicated site was donated to city in December 1905 and monument was placed on March 20, 1908.

155 "Monument for Serra's Landing Place." *Monterey New Era*, August 30, 1905

156 "Concrete Work Complete," *Monterey New Era*, September 20, 1905.

157 "People Met in the Hotel Lobbies," *Washington Post*, April 30, 1906.

158 "Should Be Biggest Thing That Ever Happened," *Anaconda Standard*, May 14, 1906.

159 "Greatest Concert," *Inter-Mountain Republican*, April 23, 1906.

160 Monidah Trust vs. Chas. Rollo Peters, Civil/Criminal Index: Defendants: 1890–1925 (Superior Court of Monterey County, State of California 1912); Monidah Trust vs. Chas. Rollo Peters, Civil/Criminal Index: Defendants: 1890–1925 (Superior Court of Monterey County, State of California 1913).

161 Betty Lochrie Hoag, "The Gifted Peters Family," Colton Hall Exhibition, 1968 (Monterey Public Library, California History Room, 1986), Clippings File: Art-

ists; Rollo Peters, "My Father: Memoir of His Life and Times," *Monterey Peninsula Herald*, October 29, 1960.

162 Gail Sheridan and Mary Pat McCormick, *Art from the Carmel Mission* (Carmel Mission, 2011).

163 Scott Shields, *Artists at Continent's End: The Monterey Peninsula Art Colony, 1875–1907* (University of California Press and Crocker Art Museum, 2006).

164 Louie Gilot, "Border Painter's Life a Mystery," *El Paso Times*, January 11, 2006,

165 "Valuable Picture by Trousset Found in Golconda, Nev. Hotel."

166 "Salt Laker Gets Old Painting," *Salt Lake Herald*, September 16, 1906.

167 "Marks Place of Serra's Landing," *San Francisco Call*, November 19, 1906.

168 Albronda, *Douglas Tilden: The Man and His Legacy*, 95–96.

169 J. K. Oliver, *Views and Legends of Monterey and Surroundings* (The Murdock Press, 1907); J. K. Oliver, *Views and Legends of Monterey and Surroundings* (The Murdock Press, 1913).

170 "Social and Personal," *Intermountain Catholic*, January 5, 1907.

171 "Genial John Maguire Laid to Final Rest: Venerable Actor Passes Away Surrounded by Material Comforts of Life," *Salt Lake Tribune*, March 28, 1907.

172 "Funeral of John Maguire," *Monterey Daily Cypress*, March 26, 1907.

173 "Splendid Monument to Maguire," *Salt Lake Herald*, July 18, 1909; Gould Jr., "Report of Inheritance Tax Appraiser."

174 "Restoring of Church Floor," *Monterey Daily Cypress*, March 29, 1908.

175 "Former Mayor Is Dead in Stockton," *San Francisco Call*, October 15, 1909, http://chroniclingamerica.loc.gov/lccn/sn85066387/1909-10-15/ed-1/seq-5/.

176 "Butte's Pioneer Copper Miner," *Daily Inter Mountain*, November 21, 1900, http://chroniclingamerica.loc.gov/lccn/sn85053057/1900-11-21/ed-1/seq-3/.

177 "Monument Has Arrived," *Monterey Daily Cypress*, March 24, 1908.

178 Derek Bryce, *Symbolism of the Celtic Cross* (Red Wheel, 1995).

179 *1908–16 Sinn Féin Propaganda Labels*, 2015, Wolf Irish Stamps, Notre Dame University Special Collections, http://www.rarebooks.nd.edu/digital/stamps/irish/set4L/set4L.html.

180 Mary Sullivan Spence, *The Passing of an Oak* (Paul Elder and Company & Tomoye Press, 1909).

181 "Millionaire Clubman Will Rebuild Mission," *San Jose Mercury News*, May 10, 1910.

182 Peters, "My Father: Memoir of His Life and Times."

183 Monidah Trust vs. Chas. Rollo Peters, Civil/Criminal Index: Defendants: 1890–1925 (Superior Court of Monterey County, State of California 1913).

184 "For Mrs. Thornton." *Butte Inter Mountain*, August 31, 1901.

185 Michael J. Makley, *John Mackay: Silver King in the Gilded Age* (University of Nevada Press, 2009); Shoebotham, *Anaconda: Life of Marcus Daly, the Copper King*; Dedman

and Clark Newell Jr., *Empty Mansions: The Mysterious Life of Huguette Clark and the Spending of a Great American Fortune*.

186 The scandalous drama appears front and center in James Adams's *Urban Reform and Sexual Vice in Progressive-Era Philadelphia*, published in 2015. Adam retells Mary and Frederick's story in his first chapter, titled "American Maidens and Fallen Women."

187 "Philadelphia Pickings," *Patriot*, February 17, 1880; "Both Want a Divorce," *Evening Star*, February 18, 1880; "Pennsylvania Divorces," *The Sun*, December 6, 1880; "Married His Client," *Reading Times*, September 13, 1881.

188 "Property Sale of Monterey Home from James A. Murray to Mary H. Murray," Legal document, March 6, 1905, Salinas, California.

189 Frank Brown, "E. L. Chapman, Butte, Montana," April 5, 1905, Frank D. Brown Family Papers 1865–1950, Mansfield Library, University of Montana, Missoula; E. L. Chapman, "E. L. Chapman to Frank D. Brown," Letter (January 17, 1905), Frank D. Brown Family Papers 1865–1950, Mansfield Library, University of Montana, Missoula; E. L. Chapman, "E. L. Chapman to Frank D. Brown," Letter (April 18, 1905), Frank D. Brown Family Papers 1865–1950, Mansfield Library, University of Montana, Missoula.

190 "Robert J. Tobin Answers the Call of the Angel of Death," *San Francisco Call*, September 19, 1906; "Photo: Grave Marker of Daniel Murray," 1907, Box 1, Folder D, William Farley's Papers; "Silas King Led a Useful Life," *Anaconda Standard*, February 10, 1908.

191 Frank Brown, "Frank Brown to D. M. Watt, Butte, Montana," Letter (December 19, 1908), Frank D. Brown Family Papers 1865–1950, Mansfield Library, University of Montana, Missoula.

192 "New Order Made in King Estate," *Anaconda Standard*, January 29, 1909.

PART III: END GAMES

1 James A. Murray, "James A. Murray to Ed Fletcher," Letter, November 1, 1911, Ed Fletcher Papers, Special Collections & Archives, University of California, San Diego (UCSD).

2 *Fourteenth Census of the United States*, vol. 1 (United States Bureau of the Census, 1921), 86, 184; "Gets Lake and 1400 Acres," *Monterey Daily Cypress*, June 5, 1910.

3 Murray deployed nephews, a niece, in-laws, and lifelong friends in Butte, Salt Lake City, Tacoma, Seattle, and Arizona to watch over his affairs. He was out of cronies and family to manage any new businesses in Southern California.

4 Fletcher, *Memoirs of Ed Fletcher* (Ed Fletcher, Pioneer Printers, 1952), 179.

5 James A. Murray, "James A. Murray to Ed Fletcher," Letters (April 9, 1909; March 1, 21; 1910), Ed Fletcher Papers, Special Collections & Archives, (UCSD)

6 Fletcher, *Memoirs of Ed Fletcher*, 179.

7 "James A. Murray to Ed Fletcher," Letter (March 21, 1910), Ed Fletcher Papers, Special Collections & Archives, UCSD.

8 Fletcher, *Memoirs of Ed Fletcher*, 165.

9 "Property of Flume Company Deeded to New Owners," *San Diego Union*, June 2, 1910.

10 James A. Murray, "James A. Murray to Ed Fletcher," (July 27, 1910), Ed Fletcher Papers, Special Collections & Archives, UCSD.

11 Leland Fetzer, *The Cuyamacas* (Sunbelt Publications, 2009), 157. Wind blew down a portion of the trestles in 1919.

12 "Huge Dam to Be Built on Cuyamaca System," *San Diego Union*, February 15, 1912; Theodore Strathman, "Land, Water, and Real Estate," *Journal of San Diego History* 50, no. 3 & 4 (2004): 124–44.

13 James A. Murray and Ed Fletcher, "Option to Purchase," August 25, 1913, Ed Fletcher Papers, Special Collections & Archives, UCSD.

14 "Manney Ridicules Cuyamaca Plant as Asset for City," *Evening Tribune*, November 24, 1913.

15 "Cuyamaca Water Company Financial Statement (1922)," Financial Statement, December 31, 1922, San Diego, California: Cuyamaca Water Company, Charles Frank Stern Papers, 1880–1960, University of California, Los Angeles (UCLA) Library Special Collections.

16 "Accounting of Estate," 1923, Probate Case File #3274, County of Monterey Superior Court; Fletcher, *Memoirs of Ed Fletcher*, 180. The Murray estate documents indicate personal loans to Fletcher in excess of $60,000, but these additional amounts may have been for other properties.

17 James A. Murray, "James A. Murray to Ed Fletcher," Letters (July 23, 1919; February 17, 1920), Ed Fletcher Papers, Special Collections & Archives, UCSD.

18 James A. Murray, "James A. Murray to Ed Fletcher," Letter (March 21, 1914), Ed Fletcher Papers, Special Collections & Archives, UCSD.

19 Ed Fletcher, "Ed Fletcher to James A. Murray," Letter (November 23, 1915), Ed Fletcher Papers, Special Collections & Archives, UCSD.

20 George R. Tompkins, *The Truth About Butte*, 2nd ed. (Century Printing Company, 1917), 25.

21 "Famous Old Building Shattered by Blasts Nine Charges of Dynamite Explode under Walls of Union Hall," *Anaconda Standard*, June 24, 1914.

22 "Charged with Stealing Ore," *Garland Globe*, August 2, 1910.

23 "Minute Details of the Robbery," *Anaconda Standard*, April 6, 1916.

24 "Robbers of Bank Elude the Posse Officers on Trail of Bandits," *Anaconda Standard*, January 22, 1915.

25 Tompkins, *The Truth About Butte*, 24–26.

26 "Butte Millionaire Visits Friend Here," *Salt Lake Telegram*, March 29, 1918.

27 Michael Punke, *Fire and Brimstone: The North Butte Mining Disaster of 1917* (Hyperion, 2006), 10. This still ranks as the largest underground mine disaster in the United States.

28 "Attempt Being Made to Cause Strike of Miners," *Anaconda Standard*, June 13, 1917.

29 Tompkins, *The Truth About Butte*.

30 "The Bulletin Publishing Company (Investment Prospectus)," Investment Prospectus (Butte, Montana, 1921), William F. Dunne Papers, *Butte Bulletin*, New York University, Tamiment Library, Robert F. Wagner Labor Archives.

31 The present value of the printing press loan was determined using economic status value, as defined by: Samuel H. Williamson, "Seven Ways to Compute the Relative Value of a US Dollar Amount, 1774 to Present," *Measuring Worth*, 2015, www.measuringworth.com.

32 S. V. Stewart, "Governor S. V. Stewart to Colonel Herman Hall, Commanding US Troops in Butte," Letter (April 25, 1920), Record Group 60: Records Relating to the Study of the Use of Force in Internal Disturbances by the Federal Government ("Glasser Files"), Box 3, National Archives and Records Administration.

33 Guy Halverson and William E. Ames, "The Butte Bulletin: Beginnings of a Labor Daily," *Journalism & Mass Communication Quarterly* 46, no. 2 (Summer 1969): 266.

34 George S. Gould Jr., "Report of Inheritance Tax Appraiser," November 1, 1922, Probate Case File #3274, County of Monterey Superior Court; "The Bulletin Publishing Company (Investment Prospectus)." The Gould report identifies a $12,500 note with the owners of the *Bulletin*. The *Bulletin*'s financial statements indicate a $12,500 mortgage on the printing press used for daily production. It is presumed that Murray's funding was for the press. No other loans of this size show up in the *Bulletin*'s financials.

35 The $12,500 note carried a two-year term but remained in May's possession four years after it was originally executed. The notes held by May were generally associated with friends of Murray. Murray also provided Duggan $5,000 in a separate loan.

36 Punke, *Fire and Brimstone: The North Butte Mining Disaster of 1917*; Halverson and Ames, "The Butte Bulletin: Beginnings of a Labor Daily"; "The Butte Daily Bulletin," 1917, http://chroniclingamerica.loc.gov/lccn/sn83045085/. These and other sources incorrectly associate Murray's investment in the *Bulletin* with the startup of the paper.

37 Kurt Wetzel, "The Making of an American Radical: Bill Dunne in Butte" (Dissertation, University of Montana, 1970).

38 Jerry W. Calvert, *The Gibraltar: Socialism and Labor in Butte, Montana, 1895–1920* (Montana Historical Society Press, 1988), 128.

39 Arnon Gutfeld, "The Speculator Disaster in 1917: Labor Resurgence at Butte, Montana," *Arizona and the West* 11, no. 1 (Spring 1969): 27–38.

40 "The Bulletin Publishing Company (Investment Prospectus)."

41 *Nelson Chesman & Co.'s Newspaper Rate Book* (Nelson Chesman & Company, 1921).

42 Roy Talbert, *Negative Intelligence* (University Press of Mississippi, 1991), 101.

43 "Big Bill Haywood Gets Twenty Years for Plot to Obstruct US War Work," *Denver Post*, August 31, 1918.

44 G. Aertsen, "Captain G. Aertsen, Jr. to File (I.W.W. Strike Conditions in Butte, Mont.)," Memorandum (October 10, 1918), Military Intelligence Division Record Group 165, File 10110-903, National Archives and Records Administration.

45 "Testimony Shows Defendant Was at All Times Ready to Serve His Country," *Butte Bulletin*, June 27, 1919.

46 "Invitation to Banquet and Reception for the Honorable Eamon De Valera on November 7, 1919," Host Committee (October 1919), William F. Dunne Papers, *Butte Bulletin*, New York University, Tamiment Library, Robert F. Wagner Labor Archives.

47 "Meeting of County Council of Defense, Labor and Financial Interests," February 13, 1919, Military Intelligence Division Record Group 165, File 10110-903, National Archives and Records Administration.

48 "Lt. Germer to Department Intelligence Officer, San Francisco, California," Report (January 14, 1919), Military Intelligence Division Record Group 165, File 10110-903, National Archives and Records Administration.

49 Stewart, "Governor S. V. Stewart to Colonel Herman Hall, Commanding US Troops in Butte."

50 Herman Hall, "Colonel Herman Hall to Commanding General, North Pacific Coast Artillery District," Letter (May 24, 1920), Record Group 60: Records Relating to the Study of the Use of Force in Internal Disturbances by the Federal Government ("Glasser Files"), Box 3, National Archives and Records Administration.

51 A. B. Coxe, "Colonel A. B. Coxe, Acting Director of Military Intelligence to the Solicitor, Post Office Department," Letter (June 15, 1920), Record Group 60: Records Relating to the Study of the Use of Force in Internal Disturbances by the Federal Government ("Glasser Files"), Box 3, National Archives and Records Administration.

52 Harold Lord Varney, "Butte—A Soviet Strike," *The Revolutionary Age*, March 1, 1919.

53 Roger Williams, "Captain Roger Williams Jr. to Director of Military Intelligence," Letter (January 3, 1921), Record Group 60: Records Relating to the Study of the Use of Force in Internal Disturbances by the Federal Government ("Glasser Files"), Box 3, National Archives and Records Administration.

54 "Butte Irish Patriots Commend Bulletin," *Butte Bulletin*, June 14, 1919.

55 Dennis L. Swibold, *Copper Chorus: Mining, Politics, and the Montana Press, 1889–1959* (Montana Historical Society Press, 2006), xiv.

56 James E. Murray, "Present Status of Irish Question," *Anaconda Standard*, November 3, 1919.

57 David M. Emmons, *The Butte Irish: Class and Ethnicity in an American Mining Town, 1875–1925* (University of Illinois Press, 1989), 384–85.

58 Ibid., 348.

59 "Butte Teutons Have a Big Relief Fund," *Anaconda Standard*, April 26, 1915.

60 "President Wilson's Message to Congress," Speech (January 8, 1918), Records of the United States; Record Group 46, National Archives and Records Administration.

61 "Banker J. A. Murray to James E. Murray," *Anaconda Standard*, December 13, 1911.

62 "Deposition of Alexander Murray: James A. Murray Estate," December 5, 1922, Probate Case File #3274, County of Monterey Superior Court. Murray testified that he allowed his nephew, Alex, to take income from the property he held in his name for various business expenses.

63 "Irish Plea Is Up to Congress," *The Sun*, March 2, 1919.

64 Michael Hopkinson, "President Woodrow Wilson and the Irish Question," *Studia Hibernica*, no. 27 (1993): 96.

65 Francis M. Carroll, "The American Commission on Irish Independence and the Paris Peace Conference of 1919," *Irish Studies in International Affairs* 2, no. 1 (1985): 105.

66 Ibid.

67 "Irish Must Be Made Free," *Butte Bulletin*, March 17, 1919.

68 "Bishop Indorses [*sic*] Irish Bond Plan," *Anaconda Standard*, March 16, 1920.

69 "Investigation of Irish Question Starts Today," *Anaconda Standard*, November 18, 1920.

70 "Organize to Help Ireland," *Washington Times*, November 17, 1920.

71 "D.C. Members Fight to Join Irish Councils," *Washington Times*, May 5, 1922.

72 "The Parnell Meeting: A Large and Enthusiastic Gathering of Patriotic Irish Citizens," *Butte Daily Miner*, June 17, 1883.

73 "Tangled Up in the Law," *Anaconda Standard*, December 16, 1900.

74 "Miners' Memorial at Henderson Gulch. Formal Dedications in Honor of Pioneers Who Worked Famous Placer Diggings," *Anaconda Standard*, December 10, 1914; "Proud Shaft Guarding Dead," *Daily Missoulian*, December 10, 1914.

75 Frank Brown, "When Days Were Young In Emmetsburg," *Anaconda Standard*, May 13, 1906.

76 "Proud Shaft Guarding Dead." *Daily Missoulian*, December 10, 1914.

77 Amy Brown Spencer, "The Old Green House," ca 1955, Frank D. Brown Family Papers 1865–1950, Mansfield Library, University of Montana, Missoula.

78 "George Winter Dies after Brief Illness," *Ogden Standard*, December 10, 1914.

79 Leigh Gittens, *Pocatello Portrait: The Early Years, 1878 to 1928* (The University Press of Idaho, 1983), 121.

80 Ibid., 118.

81 Ibid., 123.

82 Ibid., 125–26.

83 "Water Is the Thing Everybody Needs It," *Anaconda Standard*, June 1, 1915.

84 Gittens, *Pocatello Portrait: The Early Years, 1878 to 1928*, 124.

85 "In the matter of the application of the city of Pocatello for certification that public convenience and necessity require the construction of a water works system," Case in *Report of the Public Utilities Commission of the State of Idaho*, Vol. 3–5 (Idaho Public Utilities Commission 1916).

86 Murray v. Public Utilities Commission, 150 The Pacific Reporter 47 (Supreme Court of Idaho 1915).

87 Alex Murray, "Alexander Murray to Ed Fletcher," Letter (September 21, 1915), Ed Fletcher Papers, Special Collections & Archives, UCSD.

88 Ed Fletcher, "Ed Fletcher to James A. Murray," Letter (November 12, 1915), Ed Fletcher Papers, Special Collections & Archives, UCSD.

89 "In the matter of the application of the City of Pocatello for a certificate that public convenience and necessity require the construction of a water works system," Case in *Report of the Public Utilities Commission of the State of Idaho* vol. 3–5 (Idaho Public Utilities Commission 1916).

90 Gittens, *Pocatello Portrait: The Early Years, 1878 to 1928*, 131.

91 Ibid., 131–32.

92 "Pocatello Chronicle Closed by Its Owner," *Idaho Statesman*, May 23, 1916.

93 Gittens, *Pocatello Portrait: The Early Years, 1878 to 1928*, 147.

94 Murray v. Ray, 251 Fed. 866 United States Circuit Court of Appeals Reports (US Circuit Court of Appeals, Ninth Circuit 1918).

95 James A. Murray v. H. E. Ray, as Trustee of the Estate of Alec Murray, Bankrupt (Transcripts), 60 (United States Circuit Court of Appeals, Ninth Circuit 1918).

96 Ibid., 34.

97 "Pocatello," *Idaho Statesman*, July 24, 1919.

98 "James A. Murray May Buy It," *Anaconda Standard*, September 24, 1904.

99 Donald C. Jackson, *Building the Ultimate Dam* (University of Oklahoma, 2005), 158; "Many Thousand Acres to Be Made Productive," *San Diego Union*, January 1, 1918.

100 "Measuring Worth," measuringworth.com (accessed April 24, 2016). Estimated using the Economic Cost measure (one of four measures for comparing project costs). This is the relative opportunity cost of a project as a percent of the output of the economy. The viewpoint is the importance of the item to society as a whole, and the measure is the most inclusive. This measure uses the share of GDP.

101 James A. Murray, "James A. Murray to Ed Fletcher," Letter (February 17, 1920), Ed Fletcher Papers, Special Collections & Archives, UCSD.

102 Ed Fletcher, "Ed Fletcher to James A. Murray," Letter, (November 23, 1915), Ed Fletcher Papers, Special Collections & Archives, UCSD.

103 "Those Were the Days of Real H.C. of L. in the Territory," *Anaconda Standard*, August 30, 1919.

104 "Jim Murray's Luck," *Oakland Tribune*, March 8, 1913.

105 "The Romance of Hackberry Mine Discovery," *Mohave County Miner*, June 8, 1974.

106 "Silver Nearing Dollar Mark Means Great Revival in Mining," *Mohave County Miner*, September 8, 1917.

107 "Those Were the Days of Real H.C. of L. in the Territory."

108 "Old Hackberry Mine Operators Organize," *Mohave County Miner*, February 24, 1917.

109 Gould Jr., "Report of Inheritance Tax Appraiser," 2.

110 "Hackberry: One of the Largest Silver Mines in Arizona," *Mohave County Miner: Mining Edition*, July 1919; "The New York Curb, Where E. S. Mendels Rules as the Boss," *Copper Curbs and Mines Market*, May 25, 1910.

111 "Preparing for Mill Installation," *Mohave County Miner*, April 20, 1918.

112 "The Deer Lodge Volunteers," *The New North-West*, August 24, 1877. Warren took the title of "General" after his brief service to a volunteer unit led by W. A. Clark in 1877 to protect Deer Lodge from a rumored raid by the Nez Perce Indians.

113 "Sheriff's Sale," *The New North-West*, September 5, 1874.

114 A Christmastime cocktail with eggnog, brandy, and rum.

115 "Fat Jack Takes the Cash A Tale of High Finance," *Anaconda Standard*, September 14, 1919.

116 "Fat Jack—Soldier," *Anaconda Standard*, January 27, 1920.

117 "Civil War Pension File for John C. Jones (1897 to 1920)," n.d. Union Pension Records, National Archives and Records Administration.

118 "Jehu 'Fat Jack' of Pioneer Fame Closes Career in Midst of Wealth," *Salt Lake Telegram*, December 20, 1920.

119 "Butte's Veteran Cab Driver 'Fat Jack' is Dead," *Anaconda Standard*, December 17, 1920.

120 In Chapter 4, the Blue Bird litigation is covered extensively. Murray sued the owners of the Blue Bird and won. His legal action contributed to the demise of the mine. The owner, Ferdinand Van Zandt, committed suicide immediately after Murray went to court and placed liens on the mine. Van Zandt's financial backers included the Rothschild family.

121 "Blue Bird Sold to New York Men," *Anaconda Standard*, June 15, 1919.

122 "Cummings Has Opinion of Mr. James A. Murray: Says He Is a Pretty Cute Fox," *Anaconda Standard*, May 10, 1906; "Cummings Loses Out In Murray Suit," *Anaconda Standard*, May 12, 1906.

123 Rufus Thayer, "Rufus Thayer to Bruce Kremer," Letter (August, 20, 1921), Probate Case File #3274, County of Monterey Superior Court.

124 "The San Francisco Woman and the Gown from Paris," *The San Francisco Call*, March 28, 1909.

125 "The Smart Set," *The San Francisco Call*, June 17, 1910, http://chroniclingamerica.loc.gov/lccn/sn85066387/1910-06-17/ed-1/seq-8/.

126 "Mummy's Here! It's a Live One, Back Seat for Hobble Skirt," *The San Francisco Call*, July 26, 1910.

127 "Society Chat," *San Francisco Chronicle*, October 27, 1913, Newspapers.com.

128 "Petition for Partial Distribution," February 24, 1923, Probate Case File #3274, County of Monterey Superior Court.

129 "Jacks Tells of Signing Will of Jas. A. Murray," *San Francisco Chronicle*, July 23, 1921.

130 "Death Certificate: James A. Murray," May 18, 1921, Monterey County.

131 "Two Monterey Men of Prominence Take Their Own Lives," *Santa Cruz Evening News*, June 21, 1921.

132 "Death Certificate: James A. Murray."

133 "Petition for Partial Distribution."

134 Gould Jr., "Report of Inheritance Tax Appraiser."

135 "Death Certificate: James A. Murray."

136 "Blood Heirs of Murray Are Claiming Will Is Forgery," *Border Call*, July 4, 1921.

137 Ibid.

138 "Prominent in Development of the Entire West," *Anaconda Standard*, May 12, 1921.

139 Gould Jr., "Report of Inheritance Tax Appraiser."

140 "Blood Relatives File Contest of J. A. Murray Will," *San Francisco Chronicle*, June 9, 1921; "Forgery Charge Hurled at James A. Murray Will," *San Francisco Chronicle*,

June 17, 1921; "Mrs. Murray Cited to Testify in $4,000,000 Fight," *San Francisco Chronicle*, July 30, 1921; "$15,000,000 Murray Will Fight Believed Settled," *San Francisco Chronicle*, October 9, 1921; "Fight over $15,000,000 Murray Will Is Settled," *San Francisco Chronicle*, October 11, 1921; Harry Donoho, "Futility of Attempts to Draw Contest-Proof Will Shown by Recurring Suits," *San Francisco Chronicle*, June 14, 1921.

141 James E. Murray, "James E. Murray to Ed Fletcher," Letter (May 20, 1921), Probate Case File #3274, County of Monterey Superior Court.

142 Mary H. Murray, "Mary H. Murray to Ed Fletcher," Letter (October 15, 1925), Ed Fletcher Papers, Special Collections & Archives, UCSD.

143 "Murray Will Is Forgery, Expert Witness Claim," *Seattle Daily Times*, June 21, 1921.

144 "Deposition of Alexander Murray: James A. Murray Estate."

145 Margaret Gleason, "Margaret Gleason to Jim Farley," Letter (January 30, 1993).

146 Supreme Court Transcript of Record with Support Pleadings: Murray v. Monidah Trust; Minnick's Estate (1929).

147 "Miss May Murray, Montana Girl, Heiress to a Fortune," *Powder River County Examiner*, November 17, 1922.

148 "Report of Executor Accompanying His First Account," June 12, 1930, Probate Case File #3274, County of Monterey Superior Court.

EPILOGUE

1 Bruce Brooks Pfieffer, *Frank Lloyd Wright Designs: The Sketches, Plans and Drawings* (Rizzoli, 2011).

2 Nathaniel Crosby and John Strege, *18 Holes with Bing: Golf, Life, and Lessons from Dad* (Dey Street Books, 2016).

3 "Popular Butte Man Wins Frisco Belle," *Anaconda Standard*, March 11, 1914.

4 "Prominent Society Leader Dies Suddenly," *Bakersfield Morning Echo*, February 10, 1915.

5 "Popular Butte Man Wins Frisco Belle."

6 "California Weeklies," *Oakland Tribune*, September 29, 1918.

7 "Banker Well Known Here, Drops Dead," *Woodland Daily Democrat*, January 8, 1923.

8 "Probate Records for Stuart Haldorn," October 16, 1973, File #MP03944, Monterey County Superior Court.

9 "D.C. Members Fight to Join Irish Councils," *Washington Times*, May 5, 1922.

10 "Treachery Is Cause of Irish Civil War," *Llano Colonist*, July 29, 1922.

11 Donald E. Spritzer, "New Dealer from Montana: The Senate Career of James E. Murray" (Thesis, University of Montana, 1980).

12 Stephen Kelly, "The Sinn Fein Millionaire: James O'Hara and the First American-Bond-Certificate Drive, 1919–1921," *New Hibernia Review* 15, no. 4 (Winter 2011): 75–94.

13 Spritzer, *Senator James E. Murray and the Limits of Post-War Liberalism* (Garland Publishing, 1985).

14 Stephen Kemp Bailey, *Congress Makes a Law: The Story Behind the Employment Act of 1946* (Columbia University Press, 1950), 41.

15 Edwin G. Nourse, *Economics in the Public Service* (Harcourt, Brace & Company, 1953), 340.

16 J. K. Galbraith, "Review: Economic Advice and Presidential Leadership: The Council of Economic Advisers," *The American Economic Review* 56, no. 5 (December 1966): 1249–50.

17 Harry S. Truman, "President Harry S. Truman to Honorable Philip Murray," Telegram (October 1951), AFL-CIO Community Service Activities Records, Box 17 Flat, Folder 1, University of Minnesota, Elmer L. Andersen Library Social Welfare History Archives.

18 Claude Pepper, "Claude Pepper to Honorable Leo Perlis," Letter (September 29, 1951), AFL-CIO Community Service Activities Records, Box 17 Flat, Folder 1, University of Minnesota, Elmer L. Andersen Library Social Welfare History Archives.

19 Hubert H. Humphrey, "Senator Hubert H. Humphrey to Leo Perlis," Telegram (October 2, 1951), AFL-CIO Community Service Activities Records, Box 17 Flat, Folder 1, University of Minnesota, Elmer L. Andersen Library Social Welfare History Archives.

20 Bill Farley, "Rocky Mountain Radicals," *Montana: The Magazine of Western History*, 66 no. 1 (2016).

21 Mary H. Murray, "Mary H. Murray to Ed Fletcher," Letter (October 15, 1925), Ed Fletcher Papers, Special Collections & Archives, UCSD.

22 W. S. K. Brown, "W. S. K. Brown to Ed Fletcher," Letter (October 25, 1922), Charles Frank Stern Papers, 1880–1960, UCLA Library Special Collections. The price would increase to $700,000 if the CWC was not purchased before an agreed-upon date.

23 Ed Fletcher, "Ed Fletcher to Charles Stern," Letter (April 3, 1923), Charles Frank Stern Papers, 1880–1960, UCLA Library Special Collections.

24 Charles F. Stern, "Charles F. Stern to Ed Fletcher," Letter (June 1, 1923), Charles Frank Stern Papers, 1880–1960, UCLA Library Special Collections.

25 Agreement between Mary H. Murray and Ed Fletcher and Charles F. Stern, February 1924, Charles Frank Stern Papers, 1880–1960, UCLA Library Special Collections

26 "Report of Executor Accompanying His First Account," June 12, 1930, Probate Case File #3274, County of Monterey Superior Court. The Executor of the Murray estate stated in 1930 that the value of the Cuyamaca Water Company was diminished by litigation. It was optioned to Ed Fletcher on October 25, 1922. There were only two payments prior to the ultimate sale: an initial deposit of $5,000 and a payment of $145,000 on May 28, 1924. The next payment of $150,000 was due two years later, on June 1, 1926, and a final payment of $400,000 was due on June 1, 1928. Fletcher and his new partner paid in full on January 4, 1926.

27 Fletcher sold the water plant to the irrigation district for $1.2 million, and the distribution system to the city of San Diego for $400,000.

28 "Ancient Note Is Basis for Action," *Evening Tribune*, January 13, 1925. Abraham Sauer raised the discrepancy of the sales price after the sale of the CWC to the irrigation district on January 4, 1926.

29 "Editor Sauer Makes Apology and Retraction; Proceedings in Criminal Court Dropped," *Evening Tribune*, February 3, 1928.

30 Ed Fletcher, *Memoirs of Ed Fletcher* (Ed Fletcher, Pioneer Printers, 1952), 177; "Sauer Defense, Prosecution Trade Shots in Last Round of Fierce Forensic Battle," *San Diego Union*, December 9, 1927.

31 James A. Murray, "James A. Murray to Ed Fletcher," Letter (June 10, 1910), Ed Fletcher Papers, Special Collections & Archives, UCSD.

32 "Defense Attorney Takes Heated Exception to Court Ruling on Sauer Testimony," *San Diego Union*, December 8, 1927. Sauer's defense team stated that they believed Fletcher's profit came from sale of the distribution system.

33 Fletcher, *Memoirs of Ed Fletcher*, 184.

34 Fletcher's version of the acquisition of the CWC states that it took only one day to convince Murray to purchase the system, and employs "we" in several references to financing and constructing improvements, when, in fact, correspondence between the two indicates Murray conducted extensive due diligence on his own, and Fletcher did not contribute financially to the project after borrowing money to purchase an initial one-sixth share in the CWC. Fletcher, *Memoirs of Ed Fletcher*, 163–77.

35 Heilbron et al., *History of San Diego County* (San Diego Press Club, 1936), 163. This is also used as the primary source for the biography of Fletcher posted on the San Diego History Center website in 2015.

36 "Twelve Who Shaped San Diego," broadcast on KPBS in 1978, San Diego State University, http://library.sdsu.edu/scua/raising-our-voices/san-diego-history/twelve-who-shaped-sd (accessed April 24, 2016).

37 Donald C. Jackson, *Building the Ultimate Dam: John S. Eastwood and the Control of Water in the West* (University of Oklahoma, Norman, 2005).

38 Leland Fetzer, *The Cuyamacas* (Sunbelt Publications, 2009), 161.

39 "Anthony Bourdain Says Livingston's Murray Hotel One of World's Best," *Bozeman Daily Chronicle*, December 26, 2015.

40 "Monterey Physician Kills Self with Gun," *San Jose Mercury News*, June 22, 1921.

APPENDIX

1 John Maguire, "James A. Murray's Home at Monterey," *Salt Lake Herald*, September 17, 1905.

2 "Tribute Paid by Senator Mantle," *Anaconda Standard*, May 21, 1921.

3 Editorial Staff, "James A. Murray," *Anaconda Standard*, May 12, 1921.

4 C. C. Goodwin, "John Maguire," *Goodwin's Weekly*, March 30, 1907.

5 "Fat Jack," *Anaconda Standard*, December 17, 1920.

6 Michael Klepper and Robert Gunther, *The Wealthy 100: From Benjamin Franklin to Bill Gates—A Ranking of the Richest Americans, Past and Present* (Carol Publishing Group, 1996).

7 Samuel H. Williamson, "Seven Ways to Compute the Relative Value of a US Dollar Amount, 1774 to Present," *Measuring Worth*, 2015, www.measuringworth.com.

8 Meryl Gordon, *The Phantom of Fifth Avenue: The Mysterious Life and Scandalous Death of Heiress Huguette Clark* (Grand Central Publishing, 2014), 128; Bill Dedman and Paul Clark Newell Jr., *Empty Mansions: The Mysterious Life of Huguette Clark and the Spending of a Great American Fortune* (Ballantine Books, 2013), xvii.

9 Dedman and Newell Jr. recognize this ranking in their book (page 114) despite estimating Clark's wealth at 3.4 billion in current dollars.

Bibliography

"A Deed Was Filed." *Seattle Daily Times*, June 26, 1903.

"A Gold-Region, Story. The Adventures and Romance of Mr. Ferdinand Van Zandt." *Elevator*, September 8, 1888.

"A Leading Irish Patriot." *Butte Semi-Weekly Miner*, October 20, 1886.

"A Truce Is Declared: The Troubles of J. A. Murray and the Blue Bird Company Settled." *Helena Independent*, March 6, 1891.

Aaron, Sam. "An American Pioneer: Memoirs of Sam Aaron." Edited by Jacob R. Marcus. *American Jewish Archives* 10, no. 2 (October 1958): 95–120.

"Accounting of Estate." 1923. Probate Case File 3274. County of Monterey Superior Court.

"Accused of Claim Jumping: Prospector Tries to Kill a Butte Banker." *Oregonian*, September 13, 1901.

Adams, James H. *Urban Reform and Sexual Vice in Progressive-Era Philadelphia, the Faithful and the Fallen*. Lanham: Lexington Books, 2015.

Aertsen, G. "Captain G. Aertsen, Jr. to File (I.W.W. Strike Conditions in Butte, Mont.)." Memorandum. October 10, 1918. Military Intelligence Division Record Group 165, File 10110-903. National Archives and Records Administration.

"Agreement between Mary H. Murray and Ed Fletcher & Charles F. Stern." February 1924. Charles Frank Stern Papers 1880–1960. UCLA Library Special Collections.

Albronda, Mildred. *Douglas Tilden: The Man and His Legacy*. Seattle, Washington: Emerald Point Press, 1994.

"American Bank Control Sought." *Seattle Daily Times*, August 20, 1914.

"American Millionaires, How Big Fortunes Are Made." *New York Tribune Monthly (Supplement)*, June 1892.

"American Savings Bank." *Seattle Daily Times*, May 24, 1908.

"An Interesting Relic." *Butte Semi-Weekly Miner*, September 12, 1888.

"An Old Fat Jack Story: But It's a Good One." *Anaconda Standard*, December 14, 1913.

"Ancient Note Is Basis for Action." *Evening Tribune*, January 13, 1925.

"Another Montana Millionaire: James A. Murray Planning to Give New York a Surprise." *St. Paul Globe*, June 10, 1900.

"Anthony Bourdain Says Livingston's Murray Hotel One of World's Best." *Bozeman Daily Chronicle*, December 26, 2015.

"Application for Patent." *The New North-West*, January 17, 1879.

"Ashes to Ashes: The Grave Receives Its Precious Prize. Thousands Pay Their Last Respects to W. J. Penrose." *Anaconda Standard*, June 13, 1891.

"Assassinated in the Street: W. J. Penrose, a Prominent Citizen of Butte, Mysteriously Murdered." *Chicago Herald*, June 11, 1891.

"Assassins Not Known." *Helena Independent*, June 25, 1891.

Astro, Richard. "John Steinbeck." In *A Literary History of the American West*. Western Literary Association. Fort Worth, Texas: Texas Christian University Press, 1987.

"At the Murray Home Down Near Monterey." *Anaconda Standard*, August 3, 1905.

"Attempt Being Made to Cause Strike of Miners." *Anaconda Standard*, June 13, 1917.

"Autographed Letter from Late General Custer Treasured by Maguire." *Anaconda Standard*, June 29, 1902.

"Banker J. A. Murray to James E. Murray." *Anaconda Standard*, December 13, 1911.

"Banker Well Known Here, Drops Dead." *Woodland Daily Democrat*, January 8, 1923.

Baumler, Ellen. "Devil's Perch: Prostitution from Suite to Cellar in Butte, Montana." *Montana: The Magazine of Western History*, Autumn 1988: 4–21.

"Big Bill Haywood Gets Twenty Years for Plot to Obstruct US War Work." *Denver Post*, August 31, 1918.

"Big Blaze at Butte: Complete Destruction of the Grand Opera House and the I.O.O.F. Building." *Philipsburg Mail*, July 26, 1888.

"Bishop Indorses [*sic*] Irish Bond Plan." *Anaconda Standard*, March 16, 1920.

"Blood Heirs of Murray Are Claiming Will Is Forgery." *The Border Call*, July 4, 1921.

"Blood Relatives File Contest of J. A. Murray Will." *San Francisco Chronicle*, June 9, 1921.

"Blue Bird." *Butte Daily Miner*, May 7, 1888.

"Blue Bird Mill." *Butte Semi-Weekly Miner*, December 1, 1886.

"Blue Bird Sale To-Day." *Helena Independent*, May 9, 1892.

"Blue Bird Sold to New York Men." *Anaconda Standard*, June 15, 1919.

"Bluebird Suit." *Helena Independent*, December 2, 1889.

"Both Want a Divorce." *Evening Star*, February 18, 1880.

"Bought by J. A. Murray." *Butte Daily Miner*, June 2, 1899.

Boulder Hot Springs. Photograph. 1920. Montana Historical Society.

Brown, Frank. "E. L. Chapman, Butte, Montana." April 5, 1905. Frank D. Brown Family Papers 1865–1950. Mansfield Library, University of Montana, Missoula.

———. "Frank Brown to D. M. Watt, Butte, Montana." Letter. December 19, 1908. Frank D. Brown Family Papers 1865–1950. Mansfield Library, University of Montana, Missoula.

———. "Frank Brown to James A. Murray, Butte, Montana." Letter. February 8, 1899. Frank D. Brown Family Papers 1865–1950. Mansfield Library, University of Montana, Missoula.

———. "When Days Were Young In Emmetsburg." *Anaconda Standard*, May 13, 1906.

Brown, W. S. K. "W. S. K. Brown to Ed Fletcher." Letter. October 25, 1922. Charles Frank Stern Papers 1880–1960. UCLA Library Special Collections.

Brown Spencer, Amy. "The Old Green House." ca 1955. Frank D. Brown Family Papers 1865–1950. Mansfield Library, University of Montana, Missoula.

Bryce, Derek. *Symbolism of the Celtic Cross*. York Beach, Maine: Red Wheel, 1995.

"Burial Probably in Rochester, NY: James Murray Had Expressed Wish to Lie beside His Mother." *Anaconda Standard*, May 13, 1921.

"Butte." *Intermountain Catholic*, August 14, 1900.

"Butte Current Notes." *Anaconda Standard*, May 30, 1897.

"Butte Department: Murray-Haldorn Case." *Anaconda Standard*, August 17, 1896.

"Butte Irish Patriots Commend Bulletin." *Butte Bulletin*, June 14, 1919. http://chroniclingamerica.loc.gov/lccn/sn83045085/1919-06-14/ed-1/seq-8/.

"Butte Millionaire Visits Friend Here." *Salt Lake Telegram*, March 29, 1918.

"Butte Pioneer, James McGovern Aged 79, Is Dead 'McGovern's Place,' North Main, Known for Atmosphere." *Anaconda Standard*, October 20, 1920.

"Butte Players Will Contest at Hunter's." *Anaconda Standard*, August 14, 1914.

"Butte Teutons Have a Big Relief Fund." *Anaconda Standard*, April 26, 1915.

"Butte's Pioneer Copper Miner." *Daily Inter Mountain*, November 21, 1900. http://chroniclingamerica.loc.gov/lccn/sn85053057/1900-11-21/ed-1/seq-3/.

"Butte's Veteran Cab Driver 'Fat Jack' is Dead." *Anaconda Standard*, December 17, 1920.

"Buys Boulder Hot Springs." *Anaconda Standard*, April 20, 1909.

"California Weeklies." *Oakland Tribune*, September 29, 1918.

Calvert, Jerry W. *The Gibraltar: Socialism and Labor in Butte, Montana, 1895–1920*. Helena: Montana Historical Society Press, 1988.

"Canneries Were Neighbors of the 'Queen of the Monterey Bay Waterfront.'" *Coasting*, March 27, 1985.

"Can't Attack Divorce Decree after 35 Years." *Anaconda Standard*, January 6, 1922.

Carroll, Francis M. "The American Commission on Irish Independence and the Paris Peace Conference of 1919." *Irish Studies in International Affairs* 2, no. 1 (1985): 103–18.

Cecil, Lamar. Personal communication, January 14, 2015.

———. *Wilhelm II, Prince and Emperor, 1859–1900*. Vol. 1. 2 vols. Chapel Hill: University of North Carolina Press, 1989.

Chapman, E. L. "E. L. Chapman to Frank D. Brown." Letter. January 17, 1905. Frank D. Brown Family Papers 1865–1950. Mansfield Library, University of Montana, Missoula.

———. "E. L. Chapman to Frank D. Brown." Letter. April 18, 1905. Frank D. Brown Family Papers 1865–1950. Mansfield Library, University of Montana, Missoula.

"Charged with Stealing Ore." *Garland Globe*, August 2, 1910.

"Charges of Fraud Made: A Sensational Suit Brought against James A. Murray." *Anaconda Standard*, May 22, 1898.

"City Streets as Private Property." *Anaconda Standard*, July 5, 1901.

"Civil War Pension File for John C. Jones (1897 to 1920)." n.d. Union Pension Records. National Archives and Records Administration.

Clark, Archie L. "John Maguire Butte's 'Belasco.'" *The Montana Magazine of History*, January 1952.

Cockran, W. Bourke, W. Bryan Jennings, G. Frisbie Hoar, and A. Jeremiah Beveridge. *Great Political Issues and Leaders of the Campaign of 1900*. Chicago, Illinois: W. B. Conkey Company, 1900. http://babel.hathitrust.org/cgi/pt?id=wu.89058674474;view=1up;seq=17.

"Collector Jessup Starts Winning First Time Out." *San Francisco Call*, March 17, 1905.

"Combines, Trusts and Monopolies." *Kansas City Daily Journal*, November 1, 1896.

"Concrete Work Complete." *Monterey New Era*, September 20, 1905.

"Contractors Sue, Balance Asked for Work Done on Boulder Hot Springs." *Anaconda Standard,* November 21, 1918.

"Convict Transportation Registers 1788–1868." 1868. The National Archives.

Cooney, Bryon. "Millionaire Jim Murray Was Fond of Cinch Bets; Used to Frame Them." *Montana News Association Inserts*, September 4, 1933.

———. "'Sandbar' Brown Got His Nickname When He Killed Two Piegan Indians in '72." *Cut Bank Pioneer Press,* August 20, 1928.

"Court." *Philipsburg Mail*, March 3, 1899.

"Cowardly Murderer." *Helena Independent*, June 11, 1891.

Coxe, A. B. Letter. "Colonel A.B. Coxe, Acting Director of Military Intelligence to the Solicitor, Post Office Department." Letter. June 15, 1920. Record Group 60: Records Relating to the Study of the Use of Force in Internal Disturbances by the Federal Government ("Glasser Files"), Box 3. National Archives and Records Administration.

Crosby, Nathaniel, and John Strege. *18 Holes with Bing: Golf, Life, and Lessons from Dad.* New York: Dey Street Books, 2016.

"Cummings Has Opinion of Mr. James A. Murray: Says He Is a Pretty Cute Fox." *Anaconda Standard*, May 10, 1906.

"Cummings Loses Out in Murray Suit." *Anaconda Standard*, May 12, 1906.

"Cuyamaca Water Company Financial Statement (1922)." Financial Statement. December 31, 1922. San Diego, California: Cuyamaca Water Company. Charles Frank Stern Papers 1880–1960. UCLA Library Special Collections.

"D.C. Members Fight to Join Irish Councils." *Washington Times*, May 5, 1922.

"Death Certificate: James A. Murray." May 18, 1921. Monterey County.

DeBourg, Roger. "A History of Theater in Butte, Montana." Thesis. University of Montana, 1963.

Dedman, Bill, and Paul Clark Newell Jr. *Empty Mansions: The Mysterious Life of Huguette Clark and the Spending of a Great American Fortune*. New York: Ballantine Books, 2013.

"Defense Attorney Takes Heated Exception to Court Ruling on Sauer Testimony." *San Diego Union*, December 8, 1927.

"Delegation Selected." *Daily Independent*, July 8, 1871.

Delgado, James P. *To California by Sea*. Columbia: University of South Carolina Press, 1990.

"Deposition of Alexander Murray: James A. Murray Estate." December 5, 1922. Probate Case File 3274. County of Monterey Superior Court.

"Diamond Is Sensation." *Oregonian*, April 2, 1911.

Donoho, Harry. "Futility of Attempts to Draw Contest-Proof Will Shown by Recurring Suits." *San Francisco Chronicle*, June 14, 1921.

"Dr. A. J. Hunter Developed Hot Springs in Park County; Old Historical Site Destroyed by Fire Three Years Ago." *Philipsburg Mail*, June 14, 1935.

Dubofsky, Melvyn. "The Origins of Western Working Class Radicalism, 1890–1905." *Labor History* 7, no. 1 (March 1, 1966): 131–55.

"Editor Sauer Makes Apology and Retraction; Proceedings in Criminal Court Dropped." *Evening Tribune*, February 3, 1928.

Editorial Staff. "James A. Murray." *Anaconda Standard*, May 12, 1921.

Emmons, David M. *The Butte Irish: Class and Ethnicity in an American Mining Town, 1875–1925*. Urbana: University of Illinois Press, 1989.

"Ending of Automobile Show Was Like the Big Night of a Very Gay Carnival." *Salt Lake Telegram*, February 28, 1910.

"Enlarged the Capital Stock." *Butte Semi-Weekly Miner*, August 24, 1887.

"Famous Old Building Shattered by Blasts Nine Charges of Dynamite Explode under Walls of Union Hall." *Anaconda Standard*, June 24, 1914.

Farley, Bill. "Rocky Mountain Radicals: Copper King James A. Murray, Senator James E. Murray, and Seventy-Eight Years of Montana Politics, 1883–1961." *Montana: The Magazine of Western History* 66, no. 1 (Spring 2016): 39–58.

Farmer, David John. "Dogs of War: Fighting Back." *Administrative Theory and Praxis* 37, no. 4 (2015): 252–67.

"Fat Jack." *Anaconda Standard*, December 17, 1920.

"Fat Jack—Soldier." *Anaconda Standard*, January 27, 1920.

"Fat Jack Takes the Cash A Tale of High Finance." *Anaconda Standard*. September 14, 1919.

Fetzer, Leland. *The Cuyamacas: The Story of San Diego's High Country, 1772–2003*. San Diego, California: Sunbelt Publications, 2009.

"$15,000,000 Murray Will Fight Believed Settled." *San Francisco Chronicle*, October 9, 1921.

"Fight over $15,000,000 Murray Will Is Settled." *San Francisco Chronicle*, October 11, 1921.

"Fine New Hotel for the City of Livingston." *Anaconda Standard*, January 4, 1920.

"First Avenue Lot Is Sold for $65,000." *Seattle Daily Times*, April 16, 1906.

"First Execution on Montana Soil." *Anaconda Standard*, January 7, 1906.

"First Mail Brought to Butte." *Anaconda Standard*, June 20, 1920.

Fletcher, Ed. "Ed Fletcher to Charles Stern." Letter. April 3, 1923. Charles Frank Stern Papers, 1880–1960. UCLA Library Special Collections.

———"Ed Fletcher to James A. Murray." Letter. November 12, 1915. Ed Fletcher Papers. University of California San Diego, Special Collections & Archives.

———."Ed Fletcher to James A. Murray Plea." Letter. November 23, 1915. Ed Fletcher Papers. University of California San Diego, Special Collections & Archives.

———. *Memoirs of Ed Fletcher*. San Diego, California: Ed Fletcher, Pioneer Printers, 1952.

Flynn, Elizabeth Gurley. *The Rebel Girl: My First Life (1906–1926)*. New York: International Publishers, 1979.

"Fo Old Ireland." *Butte Semi-Weekly Miner*, July 3, 1886.

"For Free Coinage." *Philipsburg Mail*, July 13, 1893.

"For Mrs. Thornton." *Butte Inter Mountain*, August 31, 1901.

"For Sale and Partition." *Anaconda Standard*, August 19, 1899.

"For Ways That Are Dark." *Butte Semi-Weekly Miner*, October 19, 1887.

"Forgery Charge Hurled at James A. Murray Will." *San Francisco Chronicle*, June 17, 1921.

"Former Mayor Is Dead in Stockton." *San Francisco Call*, October 15, 1909. http://chroniclingamerica.loc.gov/lccn/sn85066387/1909-10-15/ed-1/seq-5/.

"Fort Union Receipt for Purchase of Grubstake." Receipt. February 22, 1865. Frank D. Brown Family Papers 1865–1950, Box 3, Folder 21. Mansfield Library, University of Montana, Missoula.

"Fortune Is Left to Local Family by Copper King." *Wilkes-Barre Times-Leader*, June 30, 1921.

"Four Shacks Condemned by City: Unsanitary Frame Building Owned by Millionaire James A. Murray at Third and Union to Be Closed." *Seattle Daily Times*, September 21, 1909.

Fourteenth Census of the United States. Vol. 1. United States Bureau of the Census, 1921.

"Funeral of John Maguire." *Monterey Daily Cypress*, March 26, 1907.

"Genial John Maguire Laid to Final Rest: Venerable Actor Passes Away Surrounded by Material Comforts of Life." *Salt Lake Tribune*, March 28, 1907.

"George Winter Dies after Brief Illness." *Ogden Standard*, December 10, 1914.

"Gets Lake and 1400 Acres." *Monterey Daily Cypress*, June 5, 1910.

"Gift of Maguire to Historical Society." *Anaconda Standard*, October 1, 1903.

Gilot, Louie. "Border Painter's Life a Mystery." *El Paso Times*, January 11, 2006.

Gittens, Leigh. *Pocatello Portrait: The Early Years, 1878 to 1928*. Moscow: The University Press of Idaho, 1983.

Glasscock, C. B. *The War of the Copper Kings*. New York: Grosset & Dunlap, 1935.

Gleason, Margaret. "Margaret Gleason to Jim Farley." Letter. January 30, 1993.

Goodwin, C. C. "John Maguire." *Goodwin's Weekly*, March 30, 1907.

Gordon, Meryl. *The Phantom of Fifth Avenue: The Mysterious Life and Scandalous Death of Heiress Huguette Clark*. New York: Grand Central Publishing, 2014.

Gould Jr., George S. "Report of Inheritance Tax Appraiser." November 1, 1922. Probate Case File 3274. County of Monterey Superior Court.

"Grand Opera House Seats." *Butte Daily Miner*, June 10, 1885.

"Greatest Concert." *Inter-Mountain Republican*, April 23, 1906.

Gutfeld, Arnon. "The Speculator Disaster in 1917: Labor Resurgence at Butte, Montana." *Arizona and the West* 11, no. 1 (Spring 1969): 27–38.

"Hackberry: One of the Largest Silver Mines in Arizona." *Mohave County Miner: Mining Edition*, July 1919

Hall, Herman. "Colonel Herman Hall to Commanding General, North Pacific Coast Artillery District." Letter. May 24, 1920. Record Group 60: Records Relating to the Study of the Use of Force in Internal Disturbances by the Federal Government ("Glasser Files"), Box 3. National Archives and Records Administration.

Halverson, Guy, and William E. Ames. "The Butte Bulletin: Beginnings of a Labor Daily." *Journalism & Mass Communication Quarterly* 46, no. 2 (Summer 1969): 260–66.

"He Was a Character. Death of Poor Doc Larkin at Warm Springs Asylum." *Anaconda Standard*, August 6, 1898.

Heilbron, Carl H., A. H. Cawston, Robert F. Heilbron, and Barbara Biewner, eds. *History of San Diego County*. San Diego, California: San Diego Press Club, 1936.

Hemp, Michael. *Cannery Row*. Carmel, California: The History Company, 1984.

"He's John Maguire of Montana." *Anaconda Standard*, June 14, 1903.

"He's Supporting Deadwood 'Fat Jack' Is Wearing a Badge." *Anaconda Standard*, September 1, 1902.

"History Time Line." 2013. http://www.buttecvb.com/history/. Accessed November 20, 2013

Hoag, Betty Lochrie. "The Gifted Peters Family." Colton Hall Exhibition, 1968. Monterey Public Library, California History Room, 1986. Clippings File: Artists.

Hopkinson, Michael. "President Woodrow Wilson and the Irish Question." *Studia Hibernica*, no. 27 (1993): 89–111.

"Horse News." *Daily Independent*, April 6, 1884.

"Hot Springs Are Murray's Hobby." *Ronan Pioneer*, May 18, 1917.

Hotelling, Neal. *Pebble Beach: The Official Golf History*. Chicago: Triumph Books, 2009.

"How Trouble Began." *Anaconda Standard*, May 14, 1902.

"Huge Dam to Be Built on Cuyamaca System." *San Diego Union*, February 15, 1912.

Hunter's Hot Springs. Northern Pacific Railway, 1920.

"In Butte." *Anaconda Standard*, August 31, 1902.

"In Humorous Vein: Was the Testimony of J. A. Murray in Larkin Case." *Anaconda Standard*, May 7, 1899.

"In Maguire's Hands: The Opera House People Will Do Business with the Manager: Mr. Murray Is Out of It." *Anaconda Standard*, October 5, 1896.

"In Pre-Cannery Days, Giant Mansion Ruled Waterfront." *Monterey Peninsula Herald*, ca 1969. Landmarks Folder. California Room, Monterey Public Library.

"In the matter of the application of the City of Pocatello for a certificate that public convenience and necessity require the construction of a water works system." Case in *Report of the Public Utilities Commission of the State of Idaho*, vol. 3–5 (Idaho Public Utilities Commission 1916).

"Inventory and Appraisement." December 15, 1922. Probate Case File 3274. County of Monterey Superior Court.

"Investigation of Irish Question Starts Today." *Anaconda Standard*, November 18, 1920.

"Invitation to Banquet and Reception for the Honorable Eamon De Valera on November 7, 1919." Host Committee. October 1919. William F. Dunne Papers. *Butte Bulletin*. New York University, Tamiment Library, Robert F. Wagner Labor Archives.

"Irish Must Be Made Free." *Butte Bulletin*, March 17, 1919.

"Irish Plea Is Up to Congress." *The Sun*, March 2, 1919.

"Is It the Horse?" *The New North-West*, October 24, 1879.

"Is to Put Up a New Hotel." *Butte Inter Mountain*, September 12, 1903.

Issel, William. *Church and State in the City, Catholics and Politics in Twentieth-Century San Francisco*. Philadelphia: Temple University Press, 2013.

"J. A. Murray Turfman: Butte Capitalist Considering Plans of Entering Field." *Anaconda Standard*, May 25, 1902.

"Jacks Tells of Signing Will of Jas. A. Murray." *San Francisco Chronicle*, July 23, 1921.

Jackson, Donald C. *Building the Ultimate Dam: John S. Eastwood and the Control of Water in the West*. Norman: University of Oklahoma, 2005.

"James A. Murray Is Back: World Diminishing in Size." *Anaconda Standard*, March 27, 1903.

"James A. Murray Made One Million Eating a Two Bit Meal." *Butte Inter Mountain*, May 9, 1901.

"James A. Murray May Buy It." *Anaconda Standard*, September 24, 1904.

James A. Murray v H. E. Ray, as Trustee of the Estate of Alec Murray, Bankrupt (Transcripts). United States Circuit Court of Appeals for the Ninth Circuit 1918.

"James A. Murray's Suit Against Attorney George Haldorn: Counter Charges Made." *Anaconda Standard*, October 14, 1897.

"James Murray Pioneer Miner of Butte Dies." *Great Falls Tribune*, May 12, 1921.

Janis, Ely. *A Greater Ireland: The Land League and Transatlantic Nationalism in Gilded Age America*. History of Ireland and the Irish Diaspora. Madison: University of Wisconsin Press, 2015.

"Jehu 'Fat Jack' of Pioneer Fame Closes Career in Midst of Wealth." *Salt Lake Telegram*, December 20, 1920.

"Jim Murray Is Undecided." *Helena Independent*, April 28, 1900.

"Jim Murray Was Puzzled." *Anaconda Standard*, July 2, 1890.

"Jim Murray's Luck." *Oakland Tribune*, March 8, 1913.

"John Maguire." *Bozeman Avant Courier*, November 19, 1875.

"John Maguire." *Helena Weekly Herald*, September 9, 1875.

"John Maguire Appoints Jim Murray." *Helena Independent*, April 18, 1900.

"John Maguire in Harness Again." *Anaconda Standard*, September 22, 1901.

"John Maguire Recall Memories from the Stage." *Los Angeles Herald*, April 17, 1904.

"John Maguire's Benefit: It Will Be an Event of More than Usual Interest." *Anaconda Standard*, November 20, 1898.

Johns, Joshua Scott. "Empire Building, 1873–1885." *The Parks in Railroad Advertising*. August 1, 1996. http://xroads.virginia.edu/~MA96/RAILROAD/adverts1.html.

"Jumping Off Place: J. A. Murray Says He'll Begin to Tear Down the Opera House Today." *Anaconda Standard*, September 28, 1896.

Jungmeyer, Jack. "Millionaires Cowmen and Women of a Sort Jumbled in the Golden Cocktail." *Evening News*, February 9, 1917.

Kazin, Michael. *A Godly Hero: The Life of William Jennings Bryan*. New York: Alfred A. Knopf, 2006.

Kearns Goodwin, Doris. *Team of Rivals*. New York: Simon and Schuster, Inc., 2005.

Kelly, Stephen. "The Sinn Fein Millionaire: James O'Hara and the First American Bond-Certificate Drive, 1919–1921." *New Hibernia Review* 15, no. 4 (Winter 2011): 75–94.

Klepper, Michael, and Robert Gunther. *The Wealthy 100: From Benjamin Franklin to Bill Gates—A Ranking of the Richest Americans, Past and Present*. Toronto: Carol Publishing Group, 1996.

"Larkin Case Is Ended." *Anaconda Standard*, July 22, 1899.

"Late James A. Murray Was Second Richest Citizen of Montana; Dies in His 84th Year." *Redstone (Montana Newspaper Association Inserts)*, May 25, 1921.

Leavitt, M. B. *Fifty Years in Theatrical Management*. New York: Broadway Publishing Company, 1912.

Lichtman, Ethel Mintzer. "The Zest for Learning." *The Journal of San Diego History* 39, no. 3 (1993).

"Like Old Days." *Anaconda Standard*, April 2, 1913.

Lingenfelter, Richard E. *Bonanzas & Borrascas: Copper Kings and Stock Frenzies, 1885–1918*. Norman: University of Oklahoma Press, 2012.

"Local Brevities." *The New North-West*, October 3, 1874.

"Local Brevities." *The New North-West*, April 30, 1875.

"Local Brevities." *The New North-West*, October 15, 1875.

"Local Hits." *Butte Semi-Weekly Miner*, February 10, 1886.

"Lt. Germer to Department Intelligence Officer, San Francisco, California." Report. January 14, 1919. Military Intelligence Division Record Group 165, File 10110-903. National Archives and Records Administration.

"Made an Offer." *Anaconda Standard*, April 5, 1901.

Maguire, James G. *Ireland and the Pope: A Brief History of Papal Intrigues against Irish Liberty from Adrian IV. to Leo XIII*. San Francisco: James H. Barry, 1888.

Maguire, John. "Camping on the Trail: A Reminiscense of Pioche." *Daily Nevada State Journal*, October 4, 1905.

———. "How Heinze and His Parasite Bilked a Canadian Legislature: John Maguire Throws the White Light upon the Deals of These Two Friends of Labor—O'Farrell a Coward Who Needs Only Courage to Be an Assassin." *Anaconda Standard*, November 3, 1900.

———. "James A. Murray's Home at Monterey." *Salt Lake Herald*, September 17, 1905.

"Maguire in Bronze." *Evening World*, ca 1890. File Folders. Montana Historical Society.

"Maguire's Entertainment." *The New North-West*, October 8, 1875.

Makley, Michael J. *John Mackay: Silver King in the Gilded Age*. Reno: University of Nevada Press, 2009.

Malone, Michael P. *The Battle for Butte: Mining and Politics on the Northern Frontier, 1864–1906*. Seattle: University of Washington Press, 2006.

"Manager Maguire." *Salt Lake Tribune*, September 19, 1884.

"Manney Ridicules Cuyamaca Plant as Asset for City." *Evening Tribune*, November 24, 1913.

"Many Thousand Acres to Be Made Productive." *San Diego Union*, January 1, 1918.

"Marks Place of Serra's Landing." *San Francisco Call*, November 19, 1906.

"Married His Client." *Reading Times*, September 13, 1881.

"May Be Arbitrated: Early Settlement of the Opera House Trouble's Probable." *Anaconda Standard*, December 4, 1896.

McGlynn, Betty Hoag. "Casa De Las Olas Part II: The Murray Saga." *Noticas Del Puerto de Monterey* 26, no. 3 (September 1985): 1–11.

"Meeting of County Council of Defense, Labor and Financial Interests." February 13, 1919. Military Intelligence Division Record Group 165, File 10110-903. National Archives and Records Administration.

"Membership Records." 1883–1887. World Mining Museum, Ancient Order of Hibernians Collection. Butte–Silver Bow Public Archives.

"Memories of Murray Hospital." *Montana Standard*, January 23, 1977.

"Millionaire Moses." *Saturday Evening Post*, December 8, 1945.

"Millionaire Murray Dying at St. Francis." *San Francisco Call*, January 9, 1905.

"Millionaire Murray Said to Be Dying." *Monterey New Era*, January 11, 1905.

"Miners' Memorial at Henderson Gulch. Formal Dedications in Honor of Pioneers Who Worked Famous Placer Diggings." *Anaconda Standard*, December 10, 1914.

"Minute Details of the Robbery." *Anaconda Standard*, April 6, 1916.

"Miss May Murray, Montana Girl, Heiress to a Fortune." *Powder River County Examiner*, November 17, 1922.

Monidah Trust vs. Chas. Rollo Peters, Civil/Criminal Index: Defendants: 1890–1925 (Superior Court of Monterey County, State of California 1912).

Monidah Trust vs. Chas. Rollo Peters, Civil/Criminal Index: Defendants: 1890–1925 (Superior Court of Monterey County, State of California 1913).

"Montana Comment: Justice Has Been Done (Opera House)." *Anaconda Standard*, June 2, 1897.

"Montana Mentions (1)." *Daily Yellowstone Journal*, July 15, 1885.

"Montana Rancher Buys Valley Land." *San Diego Union*, February 1, 1910.

"Montana's Governor Selects a Delegation to the July Gold Convention." *Rocky Mountain News*, May 18, 1897.

"Montana's Latest Senatorial Suggestion." *Denver Post*, April 17, 1900.

"Montana's Mines." *Helena Weekly Herald*, December 9, 1886.

"Monument for Serra's Landing Place." *Monterey New Era*, August 30, 1905.

"Monument Has Arrived." *Monterey Daily Cypress*, March 24, 1908.

Morgado, Martin J. *Junípero Serra's Legacy*. Pacific Grove, California: Mount Carmel, 1987.

Morrison, John, and Catherine Morrison. *Mavericks: The Lives and Battles of Montana's Political Legends*. Helena: Montana Historical Society Press, 2003.

"Mrs. Murray Cited to Testify in $1,000,000 Fight." *San Francisco Chronicle*, July 30, 1921.

"Mrs. Murray Entertains." *Butte Inter Mountain*, September 4, 1902.

Mullan, Captain John. *Miner and Travelers' Guide to Oregon, Washington, Idaho, Montana, Wyoming, and Colorado*. New York: Wm. M. Frankling, 1865.

Murray, Alex. "Alexander Murray to Ed Fletcher." Letter. September 21, 1915. Ed Fletcher Papers. University of California San Diego, Special Collections & Archives.

Murray, James A. "James A. Murray to Ed Fletcher." Letters. March 1, 1909–June 6, 1914. Ed Fletcher Papers. University of California San Diego, Special Collections & Archives.

———. "James Murray to Frank Brown, Hot Springs, Arkansas." Letter. ca 1901. Frank D. Brown Family Papers 1865–1950. Mansfield Library, University of Montana, Missoula.

Murray, James A., and Ed Fletcher. "Option to Purchase." August 25, 1913. Ed Fletcher Papers. University of California San Diego, Special Collections & Archives.

Murray, James E. "James E. Murray to Ed Fletcher." Letter. May 20, 1921. Probate Case File 3274. County of Monterey Superior Court.

———. "Present Status of Irish Question." *Anaconda Standard*, November 3, 1919.

Murray, Mary H. "Mary H. Murray to Ed Fletcher." Letter. October 15, 1925. Ed Fletcher Papers. University of California San Diego, Special Collections & Archives.

"Murray Loses Claim for Mine—Set Precedent. Tried to Claim Mine Not Worked." *The New North-West*, May 21, 1880.

"Murray on Miner Wages." *Tombstone Daily Prospector*, December 9, 1896.

"Murray Purchases 25% Interest Smokehouse Lode." *The New North-West*, May 7, 1880.

"Murray Sued for Trespassing Underground." *The New North-West*, May 28, 1880.

Murray v. Public Utilities Commission, 150 The Pacific Reporter 47 (Supreme Court of Idaho 1915).

Murray v. Ray, 251 Fed. 866 United States Circuit Court of Appeals Reports (US Circuit Court of Appeals, Ninth Circuit 1918).

"Murray Visits Wrestler." *Anaconda Standard*, November 7, 1902.

"Murray Will Is Forgery, Expert Witness Claim." *Seattle Daily Times*, June 21, 1921.

"Murray's New Hotel." *Anaconda Standard*, March 3, 1897.

"Murray's Wardrobe: He Fails to Prove That Madame Wallace Mangled His Clothes." *Butte Daily Miner*, April 4, 1886.

Nelson Chesman & Co.'s Newspaper Rate Book. New York: Nelson Chesman & Company, 1921.

"New Building to Go On Third Avenue." Seattle Daily Times, January 17, 1909.

"New Mining Incorporation." *Helena Weekly Herald*, May 5, 1881.

"New Order Made in King Estate." *Anaconda Standard*, January 29, 1909.

"Newspaper Man Badly Beaten." *Sacramento Daily Record-Union*, October 24, 1881.

1908–16 Sinn Féin Propaganda Labels, 2015. Wolf Irish Stamps. Notre Dame University Special Collections. http://www.rarebooks.nd.edu/digital/stamps/irish/set4L/set4L.html.

"No Agreement Yet: The Destroyers of the Opera House Cease Work for Awhile." *Anaconda Standard*, October 2, 1895, morning edition.

"Notice of Dissolution." *The New North-West*, June 28, 1873.

"Notice of Dissolution." *The New North-West*, March 19, 1875.

Noyes, Alva Josiah. *The Story of Ajax : Life in the Big Hole Basin*. Helena, Montana: State Publishing Company, 1914.

O'Farrell, P. A. *Butte: Its Copper Mines and Copper Kings*. New York: Printing House of J. A. Rogers, 1899.

"Old Hackberry Mine Operators Organize." *Mohave County Miner*, February 24, 1917.

Oliver, J. K. *Views and Legends of Monterey and Surroundings*. San Francisco: The Murdock Press, , 1907.

Oliver, J. K. *Views and Legends of Monterey and Surroundings*. San Francisco: The Murdock Press, 1913.

"Organize to Help Ireland." *Washington Times*, November 17, 1920.

"Out of Court." *Anaconda Standard*, December 8, 1895.

"Overrun with Crooks: Butte Citizens Will Organize Vigilante Committees to Deal with Them." *Aberdeen Daily News*, June 27, 1892.

"Passing Throng." *Ogden Standard*, November 22, 1892.

Paxson, William Edgar. *E. S. Paxson: Frontier Artist*. Boulder, Colorado: Pruett Publishing Company, 1984.

Pearson, Drew. "Washington Merry-Go-Round." *Aberdeen Daily News*, May 8, 1960.

"Pennsylvania Divorces." *The Sun*, December 6, 1880.

Pentland, H. C. "The Development of a Capitalistic Labour Market in Canada." *The Canadian Journal of Economics and Political Science* 25, no. 5 (November 1959): 450–61.

"People Met in the Hotel Lobbies." *Washington Post*, April 30, 1906.

"Personal." *Butte Miner*, February 19, 1878.

"Personal." *Butte Semi-Weekly Miner*, December 27, 1884.

"Personal Mentions." *Morning Oregonian*, August 20, 1892.

Peters, Rollo. "My Father: Memoir of His Life and Times." *Monterey Peninsula Herald*, October 29, 1960.

Peterson, Richard H. *Bonanza Rich: Lifestyles of the Western Mining Entrepreneurs*. Moscow: University of Idaho Press, 1991.

———. *The Bonanza Kings: The Social Origins and Business Behavior of Western Mining Entrepreneurs, 1870–1900*. Lincoln: University of Nebraska Press, 1971.

"Petition for Partial Distribution." February 24, 1923. Probate Case File 3274. County of Monterey Superior Court.

Pfieffer, Bruce Brooks. *Frank Lloyd Wright Designs: The Sketches, Plans and Drawings*. New York: Rizzoli, 2011.

"Philadelphia Pickings." *Patriot*, February 17, 1880.

"Photo: Grave Marker of Daniel Murray." 1907. Box 1, Folder D. William Farley's Papers.

"Pilgrim Bar & Running Race." *The New North-West*, April 25, 1874.

"Pocatello." *Idaho Statesman*, July 24, 1919.

"Pocatello Chronicle Closed by Its Owner." *Idaho Statesman*, May 23, 1916.

"Popular Butte Man Wins Frisco Belle." *Anaconda Standard*, March 11, 1914.

"Premature Rumor, J. A. Murray Has Not Built That Hotel at Hunter's Springs." *Anaconda Standard*, April 11, 1897.

"Preparing for Mill Installation." *Mohave County Miner*, April 20, 1918.

"President Roosevelt Arrives To-Day. Distinguished Guests of the Great Mining Camp Will Be Greeted by Thousands." *Anaconda Standard*, May 27, 1903.

"President Wilson's Message to Congress." Speech. January 8, 1918. Records of the United States; Record Group 46. National Archives and Records Administraion.

"Probate Records for Mary Murray." December 15, 1952. File 6962. Monterey County Superior Court.

"Probate Records for Stuart Haldorn." October 16, 1973. File MP03944. Monterey County Superior Court.

"Prominent in Development of the Entire West." *Anaconda Standard*, May 12, 1921.

"Prominent Society Leader Dies Suddenly." *Bakersfield Morning Echo*, February 10, 1915.

"Property of Flume Company Deeded to New Owners." *San Diego Union*, June 2, 1910.

"Property Sale of Monterey Home from James A. Murray to Mary H. Murray." Legal document. March 6, 1905. Salinas, California.

"Proud Shaft Guarding Dead." *Daily Missoulian*, December 10, 1914.

Punke, Michael. *Fire and Brimstone: The North Butte Mining Disaster of 1917*. New York: Hyperion, 2006.

"Purchases Picturesque Tevis Villa." *Riverside Independent*, August 30, 1904.

Purple, Edwin. *Perilous Passage: A Narrative of the Montana Gold Rush, 1862–1863*. Helena: Montana Historical Society Press, 1995.

"Report of Executor Accompanying His First Account." June 12, 1930. Probate Case File 3274. County of Monterey Superior Court.

"Returned from Abroad: James A. Murray Saw Europe and Its Attractions." *Anaconda Standard*, October 27, 1900.

"Robbers of Bank Elude the Posse Officers on Trail of Bandits." *Anaconda Standard*, January 22, 1915.

"Robert J. Tobin Answers the Call of the Angel of Death." *San Francisco Call*, September 19, 1906.

Roosevelt, Theodore. "President Theodore Roosevelt to John Hay." Letter. August 9, 1903. Theodore Roosevelt Collection. MS Am 1785.2 (104). Houghton Library, Harvard University.

Rotundo, E. Anthony. *American Manhood*. New York: Basic Books, 1993.

"Rowdy Wins Race." *Daily Independent*, May 10, 1874.

"Salt Laker Gets Old Painting." *Salt Lake Herald*, September 16, 1906.

"Sauer Defense, Prosecution Trade Shots in Last Round of Fierce Forensic Battle." *San Diego Union*, December 9, 1927.

"Seattle Public Building Tied Up." *Seattle Post-Intelligencer*, July 26, 1899.

"Seized the Bluebird." *Helena Independent*, March 1, 1892.

"Senator Clark." *Semi-Weekly Tribune*, April 19, 1890.

"Serra Landing, (Sculpture)." Art Inventories Catalog. Smithsonian American Art Museum, 1994.

Sheridan, Gail, and Mary Pat McCormick. *Art from the Carmel Mission*. Carmel, California: Carmel Mission, 2011.

"Sheriff's Sale." *The New North-West*, September 5, 1874.

Shields, Scott. *Artists at Continent's End: The Monterey Peninsula Art Colony, 1875–1907*. Oakland: University of California Press and Crocker Art Museum, 2006.

Shoebotham, H. Minar. *Anaconda: Life of Marcus Daly, the Copper King*. Harrisburg, Pennsylvania: The Stackpole Company, 1956.

"Should Be Biggest Thing That Ever Happened." *Anaconda Standard*, May 14, 1906.

"Silas King Led a Useful Life." *Anaconda Standard*, February 10, 1908.

"Silver Convention in Iowa." *Philipsburg Mail*, March 15, 1894.

"Silver Nearing Dollar Mark Means Great Revival in Mining." *Mohave County Miner*, September 8, 1917.

Sklar, Martin J. *The Corporate Reconstruction of American Capitalism*. New York: Cambridge University Press, 1988.

"Smokehouse Executions." *Butte Semi-Weekly Miner*, June 8, 1887.

"Social and Personal." *Intermountain Catholic*, January 5, 1907.

"Some Inside History." *Seattle Daily Times*, February 18, 1902.

"Sons of St. George." *Anaconda Standard*, August 18, 1901.

"Splendid Monument to Maguire." *Salt Lake Herald*, July 18, 1909.

Spritzer, Donald E. "New Dealer from Montana: The Senate Career of James E. Murray." Thesis. University of Montana, 1980.

———. *Senator James E. Murray and the Limits of Post-War Liberalism*. New York: Garland Publishing, 1985.

Stern, Charles F. "Charles F. Stern to Ed Fletcher." Letter. June 1, 1923. Charles Frank Stern Papers 1880–1960. UCLA Library Special Collections.

Stewart, S. V. "Governor S. V. Stewart to Colonel Herman Hall, Commanding US Troops in Butte." Letter. April 25, 1920. Record Group 60: Records Relating to the Study of the Use of Force in Internal Disturbances by the Federal Government ("Glasser Files"), Box 3. National Archives and Records Administration.

"Still Maguire's: James A. Murray and Others Rescue the Opera House for Him." *Anaconda Standard*, November 19, 1890.

"Stockholder's Meeting." *Butte Daily Miner*, May 6, 1885.

Strathman, Theodore. "Land, Water, and Real Estate: Ed Fletcher and the Cuyamaca Water Company, 1910–1926." *Journal of San Diego History* 50, no. 3 & 4 (2004): 124–44.

Stuart, Granville. *Forty Years on the Frontier*. Edited by Paul C. Phillips. Lincoln: University of Nebraska, 1977.

"Sues for Division of Bank Stock." *Salt Lake Telegram*, May 6, 1913.

"Suicide of Ferdinand Van Zandt." *Salt Lake Herald*, March 6, 1892.

Sullivan Spence, Mary. *The Passing of an Oak*. San Francisco: Paul Elder and Company & Tomoye Press, 1909.

Supreme Court Transcript of Record with Support Pleadings: Murray v. Monidah Trust; Minnick's Estate, (1929).

Swibold, Dennis L. *Copper Chorus: Mining, Politics, and the Montana Press, 1889–1959*. Helena: Montana Historical Society Press, 2006.

Talbert, Roy. *Negative Intelligence*. Jackson: University Press of Mississippi, 1991.

"Tangled Up in the Law." *Anaconda Standard*, December 16, 1900.

"Tennis Champion Invited to Play in Montana Cup." *Anaconda Standard*, April 18, 1920.

"Tennis Players at Hunter's Hot Springs." *Anaconda Standard*, August 22, 1909.

"Territorial Exchange Items." *Benton Record*, February 23, 1882.

Territory v. Murray and Another, 15 The Pacific Reporter 145 (Supreme Court of Montana 1887).

"Testimony All in in Alex Scott Suit." *Anaconda Standard*, March 4, 1910.

"Testimony Shows Defendant Was at All Times Ready to Serve His Country." *Butte Bulletin*, June 27, 1919.

Thayer, Dorothy M. "New Faces in the Senate—Montana's Young Jim Murray." *Washington Post*, November 23, 1934.

Thayer, Rufus. "Rufus Thayer to Bruce Kremer." Letter. August 20, 1921. Probate Case File 3274. County of Monterey Superior Court.

"The Blue Bird Mine: Arrangements Making for Reopening of the Valuable Property." *Anaconda Standard*, November 11, 1892.

"The Bluebird Resumes." *Daily Independent*, March 9, 1891.

"The Bulletin Publishing Company (Investment Prospectus)." Investment Prospectus. Butte, Montana, 1921. William F. Dunne Papers. *Butte Bulletin*. New York University, Tamiment Library, Robert F. Wagner Labor Archives.

"The Butte Daily Bulletin." 1917. http://chroniclingamerica.loc.gov/lccn/sn83045085/.

"The Butte Elections. The Democratic Dollars Make a Clean Sweep." *Idaho Statesman*, April 17, 1890.

"The Butte Opera House." *Helena Weekly Herald*, July 30, 1885.

"The Deer Lodge Volunteers." *The New North-West*, August 24, 1877.

"The Federal Building Will Stand at the Southeast Corner of Third and Union." *Seattle Star*, August 20, 1901.

"The Kansans' Day." *Seattle Post-Intelligencer*, April 26, 1893.

"The Mining Metropolis in the Days of Its Infancy." *Anaconda Standard*, August 14, 1919.

"The New York Curb, Where E. S. Mendels Rules as the Boss." *Copper Curbs and Mines Market*, May 25, 1910.

"The Parnell Fund." *Butte Daily Miner*, June 23, 1883.

"The Parnell Meeting: A Large and Enthusiastic Gathering of Patriotic Irish Citizens." *Butte Daily Miner*, June 17, 1883.

"The People's Party." *Butte Daily Miner*, October 12, 1884.

"The Peoples Party of Silver Bow." *The New North-West*, October 17, 1884.

“The Pilgrim Bar Country.” *The New North-West*, May 31, 1873.

“The Romance of Hackberry Mine Discovery.” *Mohave County Miner*, June 8, 1974.

“The Rotten Borough.” *Helena Daily Herald*, October 15, 1889.

“The Sand Lot: Kearney Denounces the Irish Relief Subscription Fund.” *The New North-West*, February 27, 1880.

“The Smokehouse Lode Case Settled.” *Philipsburg Mail*, September 6, 1888.

“The Smokehouse Settlement.” *Butte Semi-Weekly Miner*, November 17, 1888.

“The Territorial Fair.” *Rocky Mountain Husbandman*, October 9, 1879.

“Then, Now, and Thereafter: Nuggets Found in a Pan of Butte Placer Gold.” *The New North-West*, August 19, 1881.

“Those Were the Days of Real H.C. of L. in the Territory.” *Anaconda Standard*, August 30, 1919.

“To Abolish the Smoke.” *Anaconda Standard*, November 16, 1890.

Tompkins, George R. *The Truth About Butte*. Second ed. Butte, Montana: Century Printing Company, 1917.

“Topics of the Town: A Firm Friend of Penrose.” *Anaconda Standard*, July 2, 1891.

“Topics of the Town: How John Maguire Proposes to Get Rid of That Mortgage.” *Anaconda Standard*, October 13, 1890.

“Treachery Is Cause of Irish Civil War.” *Llano Colonist*, July 29, 1922.

“Tribute Paid by Senator Mantle.” *Anaconda Standard*, May 21, 1921.

“Twelve Who Shaped San Diego.” KPBS, 1978. San Diego State University. http://library.sdsu.edu/scua/raising-our-voices/san-diego-history/twelve-who-shaped-sd.

“Two Marriages: J. A. Murray and Mrs. Haldorn—Mr. Haldorn and Mrs. Hubert-Jones.” *Anaconda Standard*, June 5, 1896.

“Two Monterey Men of Prominence Take Their Own Lives.” *Santa Cruz Evening News*, June 21, 1921.

“United States Federal Census, 1870, Montana Territory.” 1870.

“Valuable Picture by Trousette Found in Golconda, Nev. Hotel.” *Idaho Statesman*, August 29, 1906.

“Van Zandt to Be Buried Abroad.” *The Sun*, March 7, 1892.

Varney, Harold Lord. “Butte—A Soviet Strike.” *The Revolutionary Age*, March 1, 1919.

Warde, Frederick. *Fifty Years of Make-Believe*. New York: International Press Syndicate, 1920.

“Was Treated Like a Prince: Butte’s Hospitality Extended to Governor Roosevelt.” *Anaconda Standard*, September 19, 1900.

“Water Is the Thing, Everybody Needs It.” *Anaconda Standard*, June 1, 1915.

“Watson Made Guardian. He Will Sue the B. & M. in the Name of James Larkin.” *Anaconda Standard*, May 14, 1898.

Wetzel, Kurt. “The Making of an American Radical: Bill Dunne in Butte.” Thesis. University of Montana, 1970.

Wheeler, Olin D. *Wonderland 1902*. St. Paul, Minnesota: Northern Pacific Railway, 1902.

Whelehan, Niall. *The Dynamiters: Irish Nationalism and Political Violence in the Wider World, 1867–1900*. New York: Cambridge University Press, 2012.

"When Fat Jack Drove Teddy." *Anaconda Standard*, December 12, 1909.

"When the Saloon Door No Longer Swings To and Fro." *Anaconda Standard*, January 14, 1917.

"Where the Press Gang Met." *Yellowstone Monitor*, September 9, 1909.

Whyte, Kenneth. *The Uncrowned King: The Sensational Rise of William Randolph Hearst*. Berkeley, California: Random House of Canada, 2009.

Williams, Roger. "Captain Roger Williams Jr. to Director of Military Intelligence." Letter. January 3, 1921. Record Group 60: Records Relating to the Study of the Use of Force in Internal Disturbances by the Federal Government ("Glasser Files"), Box 3. National Archives and Records Administration.

Williamson, Samuel H. "Seven Ways to Compute the Relative Value of a US Dollar Amount, 1774 to Present." *Measuring Worth*, 2015. www.measuringworth.com.

Willis, Jack. *Roosevelt in the Rough*. Edited by Horace Smith. New York, New York: Ives Washington, 1931.

"Wine with a History: Twelve Precious Bottles That Once Came Across the Atlantic." *Evening News*, December 11, 1886.

"Woes of a Manager Mr. McFarland Has Troubles Enough for a Bonfire." *Anaconda Standard*, February 4, 1900.

Wolle, Muriel Sibell. *Montana Pay Dirt*. Athens, Ohio: Swallow Press, 1963.

Writers Project of Montana. *Copper Camp: The Lusty Story of Butte, Montana, the Richest Hill on Earth*. Helena, Montana: Riverbend Publishing, 2002.

"You'll Find It Here," *The Tacoma Times*, October 23, 1913.

Young, Otis E., Jr. *Western Mining*. Norman: University of Oklahoma Press, 1970.

Zimmerman, Ken, Jr. *William Muldoon: The Solid Man Conquers Wrestling and Physical Culture*. St. Louis, Missouri: Ken Zimmerman Jr. Enterprises, 2014.

Index

BILL FARLEY is a second great-grandnephew of James A. Murray. His interest in Murray's life was piqued when he found an obituary for Murray among the estate papers of his father in 2012. The obituary credited Murray with a significant role in pioneering the West, mentioned his obsession with practical jokes, and highlighted his generosity with pioneers who fell on hard times. Farley, whose career touched on mining, waterworks, and real estate, took the challenge to bring Murray's full story to life. Prior to this complete work, Farley treated excerpts of Murray's life in *Montana: The Magazine of Western History, The Journal of San Diego History*, and *Wild West Magazine*. A native of Sacramento, California, Farley is currently completing his PhD in public policy at Virginia Commonwealth University, with a concentration on urban and regional planning.

DAVID M. EMMONS, author of *The Butte Irish: Class and Ethnicity in an American Mining Town*, is a professor emeritus of history at the University of Montana.